BRITAIN'S
RESTORED CANALS

This book is dedicated to that ever-growing band of volunteer workers, the new navvies, who have individually worked so hard to revive the derelict waterways. The restored waterways are a lasting tribute to their efforts.

Landmark Pub

D1493951

CONTENTS

Acknowledgements

The original 'Canals Revived' started life in research work at London University in 1977, supervised by the late Professor E.M.J. Campbell, MA, FSA of Birkbeck College. My first thanks are due to her for the advice and encouragement so readily given throughout the years of research.

During research I have visited and discussed waterway restoration with hundreds of enthusiasts throughout the British Isles. To list them all would be a daunting task, yet they all have my sincere thanks for the help and hospitality they have given me. Without the access to their records, and more so their memories, such a book about the development of the restoration movement over the past sixty years would have been impossible. I owe to each of them a personal debt of gratitude.

Of the many people I have met some have offered particular inspiration to many others in the restoration movement. Of these I list but a few of the recognised leaders who have given me equally so much of their valuable time and provided access and permission to use items from their records: the late R. Aickman, the late C.D. Barwell, the late Mrs B. Bunker, the late L.A. Edwards, the late C. Hadfield, the late D. Hutchings, the late G. Palmer and the late L.T.C. Rolt. To them all I offer my sincere thanks.

The most consistent and valuable sources of published information have been the past issues of the Inland Waterways Association *Bulletin and Waterways* plus *Navvies* (formerly *Navvies Notebook)* and I am particularly grateful to the IWA and the Waterway Recovery Group for making complete sets of each available to me. Equally my thanks go to the editors of the numerous society journals and newsletters who made their archives available for research. Thanks too go to the various authors and publishers named in the text for permission to reproduce copyright material, and to the late R. Aickman, H. Arnold, C. Griffiths, Robin Higgs, Tim Lewis and R. Shopland for providing a selection of photographs to illustrate the book.

Also to Alan Cheal for updating the various maps used in this volume.

Finally, my sincere thanks are due to my wife, Amanda, for suffering so many hours of waterway restoration over the past forty years, as well as for all the proof-reading she has undertaken for me. But for her assistance this book would have never seen the light of day.

To everybody, named and unnamed, who has helped to make this book possible I offer my sincere thanks.

R. SQUIRES

THE GROWTH AND DECLINE
OF THE INLAND WATERWAYS

The saying, "the past provides the key to the present", rings very true in respect of the growth of the waterway restoration movement in post-war Britain. A short resume of the development and decline of the inland waterways network therefore provides a natural introduction to this book. In view of the subsequent significance of developments in the 1880s, and more especially those of the early 1900s, this period is given particular attention in the account that follows.

It can be claimed that the first canal navigations in Britain began in Roman times. The Fossdyke and Cardyke built in this era still remain today. The Fossdyke and the Witham navigation provided a through route from the Trent at Torksey by way of Lincoln to the North Sea near Boston. In AD 900 contemporary records confirm that the Witham was used by sea-going vessels to reach Lincoln, and in 1121 Henry I caused Fossdyke to be scoured out to revive the through route to the Trent.

The first truly commercial canal of the modern era developed much later. In 1539, Henry VIII sanctioned the "Amending of the River to Exeter"; after much delay, in 1563 John Trew of Glamorganshire was engaged by Exeter Corporation to make a canal alongside the River Exe. It was completed in 1566 and had three pound locks, the first on any British waterway. By this time the principal rivers of England, such as the Thames, Severn, Trent and Yorkshire Ouse, had all been improved and were carrying a good deal of traffic, including coal.

During the reign of Charles II (1649–1685) the official cartographer, Joseph Maxton, produced a map to prove that a navigable canal was practicable "for the unifying of the Rivers Thames and Severn from Letchlade to Bath", but the scheme did not immediately proceed. The seventeenth century saw rapid progress on other schemes. In 1628 Arnold Spenser made the Ouse navigable to within four miles of Bedford, and the Stour from Sudbury to Manningtree. By 1636 William Sandys had started work on making the River Avon navigable between Tewkesbury and Stratford. In 1651 the River Wey was declared navigable to Guildford.

The first construction of a commercial navigation in the Midlands was undertaken by Andrew Yarranton, who by 1665 had made the Stour navigable from Stourbridge to Kidderminster for the carriage of coal. By the early 1700s navigation projects became more and more prevalent, with improvements to the Rivers Lark and Dee, and more particularly to the Severn.

In 1712 work commenced on improving the Avon to Bath, and in 1715 the construction of the Kennet Navigation from Reading to Newbury was under way. The year 1720 witnessed the development of the River Douglas Navigation to Wigan and also the Mersey and Irwell as a route to Manchester. The construction of the Stroudwater Canal was authorised under an Act of 1730 but did not at first succeed.

By the middle of the eighteenth century many of the main rivers had been made navigable, and in all about 1,200 miles of river in England were passable for barges carrying goods which could otherwise only have been transported by pack-horse or on heavy waggons over the bad roads of the time. This period in England's history was the threshold of both the Agricultural and Industrial Revolutions. Demand was growing for quantities of limestone to be burnt into lime for land improvement; building materials were required for new farm buildings; and a means of carrying away the produce of the land was also sought. Similarly, inventors were waiting for better means of transport to enable supplies to be brought to the growing industrial towns, and the products of their machines to be carried away.

The first practical example of the means to attaining these ideals came with an Act of 1755 that authorised the Sankey Brook Navigation. The project was initially visualised as the canalisation of the Sankey Brook but it was ultimately constructed as a wholly artificial canal by the engineer John Eyes. It was, however, the publicity gained by the Duke of Bridgewater, who was authorised by Parliament in 1759 to build a canal from his coal-mines at Worsley to Manchester, which started the spate of canal building which reached its peak in the "Canal Mania" of the 1790s. Although the Duke of Bridgewater had previously seen the successful canals of the continent, including the Canal du Midi built by Riquet between 1666 and 1681, it was the ability of his engineer James Brindley, who developed his own techniques for canal building, which enabled the Bridgewater Canal and its aqueduct over the River Irwell to be opened with much acclaim in 1761.

The Bridgewater Canal was so successful that the Duke decided to continue it from Manchester to the Mersey at Runcorn, offering better communication than was possible by the old river navigations of the Mersey and Irwell. Brindley"s success caused him to be sought by businessmen, such as Wedgwood, when promoting other canals in the Midlands. Heartened by this tremendous support, Brindley put forward the idea

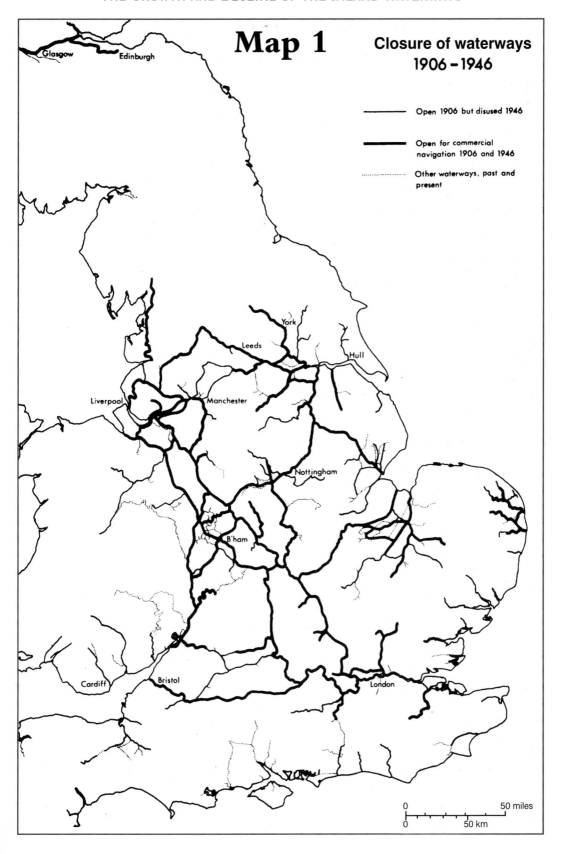

Map 1

Closure of waterways 1906–1946

——————— Open 1906 but disused 1946

━━━━━━━ Open for commercial navigation 1906 and 1946

·················· Other waterways, past and present

Glasgow Edinburgh

York
Leeds
Hull
Liverpool Manchester
Nottingham
B'ham
Cardiff Bristol London

0   50 miles
0   50 km

Lancaster Canal Trust Protest 1964

of a "Grand Cross", with canals linking the four great navigable rivers of England; the Mersey, Trent, Severn and Thames. The key feature of this scheme was the Trent and Mersey Canal or "Grand Trunk", with which further canals to the Severn and the Thames could ultimately be linked. In the eleven years between the completion of the Bridgewater Canal in 1761 and his death in 1772, Brindley was personally involved in the development of the canal system which joined the industrial Midlands to the Mersey, Severn and Trent.

The momentum of this development was delayed slightly by the American War of Independence which began in 1776. However, after the war ended in 1783, interest revived and by 1790 Brindley's vision of the "Grand Cross" was at last complete. By then a large number of other canals had been built and more rivers made navigable: the Forth and Clyde Canal had been built across Scotland; and the Thames had been joined to the Severn by way of Stroud and the Sapperton Tunnel.

The success of the early Brindley canals, the prosperity of the country and the demand for better transport, combined to make businessmen and speculators join in the scramble to promote canals all over the country. This led to the passing of a large number of Acts of Parliament and by 1793 "Canal Mania" was in full swing. Some of the canals proposed were purely speculative, but most had a solid, though perhaps optimistic, background of

local needs and sooner or later they were built. Progress was halted by the French Revolution and later by the declaration of war against France, which in turn led to steadily rising prices, shortages of man-power and rising wages. Although various canals were opened in these years, many were destined never to offer a dividend to those who had contributed towards their construction. As a result, by 1810 "Canal Mania" had died.

But by this time many of the British canals had been constructed and water routes linked the majority of sizeable towns in the land. Practical problems soon emerged because most of the canals had been built to serve a strictly local need and had been developed in isolation. This led to a variety of gauges being adopted, from narrow shallow routes only capable of passing boats with a pay-load of less than 30 tons, to the widebeam barge waterways capable of taking much heavier loads in craft which were also capable of negotiating coastal waters. An even greater difficulty was the general absence of national co-operation in the matter of quoting through-tolls over the lines of rival concerns. Similarly the majority of canal traders were more accustomed to short haul traffic and were less willing to quote for the longer cross country runs. This meant that canals like the Kennet and Avon, built mainly to join London and Bristol, never carried more than about 12 per cent of through traffic and most of the tolls were generated

Distribution of canal acts authorised - England						
	Per cent of District England	1751–70	1771–90	1791–1810	1811–30	Total
Northern, including Cheshire	28	7	11	52	14	84
North Midlands, including Derbyshire and Warwickshire	14.3	12	22	63	26	123
South Western, including Hereford and Monmouthshire	22.3	3	8	56	29	96
Northern Home Counties, including Oxfordshire	6.6	1	1	14	8	24
South Eastern Counties	11.2	-	3	17	24	44
Eastern Counties	17.6	1	1	13	7	22
Totals by period		24	46	215	108	393

(With acknowledgement to: Gladwin, D.D. and White, J.M. *English Canals:Part I: A Concise History*)

by short hauls. Even so, canals had revolutionised the transport system in Britain and provided a catalyst for both agricultural and industrial change.

After 1815 the improvement in road engineering, the increase in the output of goods to be carried, the reduction in the cost of horse fodder, and the relatively high cost of canal tolls made the roads a serious competitor for carrying merchandise. Land carriage also offered the virtue of door-to-door collection and delivery and, as a result, much of the profitable miscellaneous traffic left the canals, though the bulk traffic with lower tolls remained. In this way the waterways were financially weakened and lost ground which they were never again able to recover.

With the end of the war with France, commerce in Britain soon began to develop but few new navigations were built to meet the new demands except in the South-West. However, some other major schemes, such as the Leeds and Liverpool and Lancaster Canals, were completed. The Shropshire Union main line was built, and the Birmingham Canal Navigations improved. Much effort was devoted to increased efficiency and the course of many early contour canals, such as the Oxford, were shortened and improved.

Many books have been written about the canal era and they detail the growth of the network. For brevity the complete story is not recounted here, but the following analysis of the growth of the network is offered as a synthesis of the period to provide a picture of the way in which the network grew (see above table).

Three factors are apparent from this analysis: (a) the phenomenal increase in the number of projected navigations during the period 1791–1810; (b) the relatively late arrival of canals in the southern counties; (c) the uneven distribution of waterways throughout the different regions of England. Each of these factors was to have a bearing on the subsequent development of the canals.

Although the earliest railways or tram-roads originated during the reign of Elizabeth I in the 1570s, they were mostly used to transport coal from the mines to staiths on the banks of rivers such as the Tyne. Soon after the first canals were built, canal companies realised that it was cheaper to construct tram-roads than branch canals as feeder lines, and many tram-roads were constructed, from 1760 onwards by canal or colliery companies. Later still some longer railways were laid to connect with canals. The Cromford and High Peak line provided by far the best example. By the 1820s the merits of both systems were still in the balance. However, with the success of the steam locomotives on the Liverpool and Manchester Railway in 1830, the era of railway competition began. From 1830 to 1845 there was steady railway expansion and a great number of the main lines, such as the London and Southampton, the London and Bristol and the London and Birmingham, were built in direct competition to the canals. At first the canals benefited from the additional traffic created by transportation of railway construction materials, but by 1845 competition was clearly taking its toll.

By 1845 railways seemed to many people the means of untold prosperity, and "Railway Mania" began. It consisted of a rush to promote companies and to buy up competitors. The following statistics of railway Acts promoted convey the momentum of the boom:

1843   23 Acts
1844   48 Acts
1845   108 Acts

To protect the canals in some way three Acts of Parliament were promoted in 1845, 1846 and 1847, allowing canal companies to vary tolls; provide control over standards of maintenance for railway-owned canals; and, significantly, to allow canal companies to act as carriers in their own right. Although these provisions were helpful to canal traders the momentum of railway competition, with the desire of the railway companies to eliminate competitors, led to a rapid sale of canals. In 1845, five navigations totalling 78 miles came under railway control; in 1846, seventeen navigations with a total length of 774 miles changed hands; and in 1847 six navigations with a total length of 96 miles followed the same trend. In these three years about 80 per cent of the mileage of all railway-controlled canals was acquired, being 20 per cent of all the navigable waterways in Britain, including the 160 miles of the Birmingham Canal Navigations and the 204 miles of the Shropshire Union system. Only 15 more canals, with a total mileage of 300, subsequently came under railway ownership, although others came from time to time under railway direction.

For the following 20 years, the canals just managed to retain their existing traffic, but they failed to get a share of the vastly increased trade offered to the railways. With the growth of railway branch lines, many of which directly competed for remaining canal traffic, a quick decline set in, and from about 1865 onwards there were a series of canal company liquidations. During this era many of the small canal companies were lost and the rural canals closed. For each of the minor canal companies the story was the same: the receipts diminished until they went below the level of essential maintenance costs; without maintenance the pounds became unnavigable and the remaining traffic could not get through; and company meetings were not held and offices were shut for lack of means to pay wages. As each waterway decayed it became a nuisance to the towns and villages on its route and this forced the public authorities to take steps to end the life of the local canal and stop the nuisance.

Restored Canal Boats at Titford Pool 1978

Fortuitously the decline of canals introduced a new figure to the scene; the tourist. In 1867 a party took a boat through the Wey and Arun Canal, shortly before the canal was closed, and published a book, *The Thames to the Solent by Canal and Sea,* in 1868. The following year a similar book, *The Waterway to London,* appeared, describing a canoe trip by three men from Manchester to London by canal and river. Both stimulated an interest in the new vogue.

At much the same time the dangers of a railway bulk-transport monopoly began to be understood. A substantial lobby developed for the closer control of railway toll rates and this led to the 1873 Regulation of Railways Act, which compelled railway and canal companies to quote through-tolls or rates and to publish them. It also forbade railways to acquire a controlling interest in any canal unless the acquisition had the approval of Commissioners, appointed under the Act. It also stated that railways already controlling canals must adequately maintain them.

This change in emphasis stimulated a more open debate about the respective merits of waterway and railway traffic, with both parties seeking the modernisation and rationalisation of their own areas of interest. This awareness of the need for modernisation of the waterways prompted George Hicks to write a letter to the *Manchester Guardian* in 1876, proposing the idea of a ship canal to Manchester by means of an improved Mersey navigation. After various surveys and a period of local gestation the idea of a ship canal was publicly promoted in a pamphlet, *Facts and Figures in Favour of a Tidal Navigation to Manchester,* in 1882. After two abortive attempts to gain an Act of Parliament, a third was successful in 1885 and thereafter plans were developed to construct the new waterway.

As interest was developed in the Manchester Ship Canal another visionary, George Smith, started his campaign to improve the lot of the canal people. His two books, *Our Canal Population* (1875) and *Canal Adventures by Moonlight* (1881), with a concurrent press campaign, put before the people of England the harsh facts about the life of the bargees. The campaign raised a good deal of public interest, and almost entirely as the result of these efforts the Canal Boats Act was passed in 1877 to regulate living conditions on canal craft.

As public awareness of the waterways grew, so fears of railway monopoly were countered by a campaign for waterway revival. This culminated in a review of inland waterways by a Select Committee on Canals in 1883. The Royal Commission on the Depression of Trade in 1886, reiterated the theme of the Committee's report and recommended that the waterways should be developed and freed from railway control.

By 1888, interest in the revival of the waterways had become so intense that the Royal Society of Arts held a two-day conference on the subject. Various papers were presented and the theme of nationalisation was developed with the concept of a Water Commission to foster the redevelopment of the system being proposed. The conference concluded with a resolution that included the demand for "... local authorities to constitute Public Trusts, for the development of the existing system of canals." This provision was embodied in the *Railway and Canal Traffic Act 1888,* passed later that year. The Act also called for a review of the classification of traffic and schedules of rates, which were later embodied in a series of Acts passed in 1894.

Following the interest stimulated by the RSA conference of 1888, two books were published to increase public knowledge of the waterways. The first was *Waterways and Water Transport in Different Countries* (1890) by J.S. Jeans, and this was followed by a revised edition of *Rivers and Canals,* two vols., (1896) by L.F. Vernon-Harcourt.

With the prospect of a revival of trade, Henry Rodolph de Salis, a director of Fellows, Morton & Clayton the canal carriers, began an examination of the waterway system. He prepared a systematic survey of the network which was published in 1904 as *Bradshaw's Canals and Navigable Rivers of England and Wales.* Through this handbook he intended to inform commercial users of the possibilities of water transport.

This revival of interest in canals led the Associated Chambers of Commerce to pass a resolution in 1900 which asked the government to appoint a Royal Commission to consider the whole question of waterways. To develop this theme still further the same body initiated a Bill into Parliament in 1901, which favoured the creation of public canal trusts. Similar Bills were also introduced in 1904, 1905 and 1906, all seeking the consolidation of interests to improve facilities for water carriage and the establishment of an integrated system of intercommunication.

As the result of this growing pressure, the Government appointed a Royal Commission to review the inland waterways in 1906. The Commission compiled statistics during its review that showed that *2,556* miles of waterway were owned by independent companies carrying 28,168,813 tons; and 1,266 miles were owned or controlled by railways and these carried 14,191,073 tons. The twelve-volume report, presented in 1909, was the most comprehensive study of the waterways system that had ever been made. The Commission recommended the widening and deepening of the trunk waterway routes connecting the Thames, Severn, Humber and Mersey Rivers as well as suggesting that one of the trans-Pennine canals should be enlarged. It envisaged Birmingham as the central collecting point within the system and proposed a reconstructed route from the city to Sharpness using inclined planes. To facilitate this revival the report proposed the nationalisation of the trunk waterways and their branches and that the control of the system should be vested in a waterways board. The seventeen-million-pound cost of the programme to revitalise 1,040 miles of the canals was a great deterrent to the development of the scheme. This huge capital expenditure, together with a subtle campaign led by a railway supporter, E.A. Pratt, through his two books, *British Canals: Is their Resuscitation Practicable?* published in 1906, and *Canals and Traders,* published in 1910, led the proposals of the Commission to be stillborn.

Initially the struggle for Home Rule in Ireland distracted public attention, but finally the outbreak of war in 1914 sounded the death knell for the proposals of the report. The railway-owned canals became immediately under State control whilst the independent canals struggled on, but the tonnage they carried fell as men left to join the Forces.

On 1 March 1917 the effect of the decline was finally appreciated by the Board of Trade and in a belated attempt to restore some of the lost traffic many of the independent canals were united under a Canal Control Committee. By co-ordinating the system it was hoped that a revival would develop but much of the traffic had gone for good. In 1913 tonnage carried on British canals was 31,585,909, but by 1918 this had dropped to 21,599,850 tons.

On 31 August 1920 the canals reverted to private control, but with the rising costs of labour and materials and emerging road competition, their difficulties were greater than ever before. In order to review the post-war position the Government appointed a Departmental Committee under the chairmanship of Neville Chamberlain, MP, in 1920. The committee reported in 1921 and concluded that, owing to the further deterioration of the canals and the post-war increase in costs, the 1906 Royal Commission proposals were impractical. They suggested the establishment of public trusts, each responsible for a particular group of canals and subsidised by the state. They also recommended certain limited improvements, including one to the River Trent which was subsequently carried out. Apart from this no other action took place.

During the 1920s the impact of motor lorries was severely felt by the canals as they gradually absorbed most of the short haul traffic that remained. At the same time, mines and quarries adjacent to the canals became worked out, and the change in energy source, from coal to electricity from the grid, led to a further loss in trade.

By 1918 the canals carried about 21 million tons. This dropped to 17 million tons in 1924, and dropped further to 14 million tons by 1929.

Partly to combat this decline, the Grand Junction Canal Company linked with the Regent's Canal Company and the three other canals on the Birmingham route to form a new Grand Union Canal Company in 1929. In 1932 the amalgamated company absorbed three more concerns, the Leicester and Loughborough Navigations and the Erewash Canal, to create a combined unit of over 300 miles of canal linking London with the Nottinghamshire and Derbyshire coalfields and with Birmingham.

In 1930 another Royal Commission on Transport under the chairmanship of Sir Arthur Griffith-Boscawn was formed. The commission''s report concluded: "... that certain canals still possess considerable value as a means of transport, and ... they can be made to render much useful service to the community in the future." It recommended that the Ministry of Transport should set up public trusts to take over the waterways of the major inter-river "Cross".

In the spirit of this proposal the Government agreed to guarantee interest payments for a million-pound modernisation scheme, developed by the Grand Union Company, on the London to Birmingham route. This work was completed by 1934. The company also developed its own carrying company to stimulate trade. Unfortunately, over-expansion coupled with the dire shortage of boatmen, created crippling losses for the company and it was unable to pay any dividend.

The canal system elsewhere was even less fortunate and as carrying companies ceased to trade in the face of road competition, more waterways became semi-derelict. As the neglect became evident so local pressure for the abandonment of short lengths of canal grew and one by one the branch canals closed, particularly those only carrying agricultural produce. The 1930s saw several Acts of Abandonment including the Thames and Severn, the Grantham, the Nottingham and the Droitwich Canals, all of which left major areas of the country again unserved by a reliable water route.

The network of navigable rivers also declined as the demand for land drainage, clarified under the *Land Drainage Act* of 1930, took a higher priority for Government funds. The Act offered one benefit in that it created the Catchment Boards, which offered more uniform control. Often, where the Catchment Board became responsible for navigation this obligation was generally neglected, except where dredging work could be more easily undertaken if the navigation works were retained, as with the River Great Ouse.

However, as commercial traffic was declining on the rural waterways, the first pleasure craft were beginning to appear. George Westall, a leading advocate for waterways revival, published his unique and widely read book, *Inland Cruising on Rivers and Canals of England and Wales* in 1908 and this gave considerable impetus to the new development. He later led the National Inland Navigation League, founded in 1919, which did much to revive interest in canals during the 1920s. Several other books followed Westall's lead: among them were *A Caravan Afloat* (nd.) by C.J. Aubertin; *My Holidays on Inland Waterways* (1916) by P. Bonthron; *The Heart of England by Waterway* (1933) by W. Bliss; *Canal Cruises and Contentment* (n.d.) by Austin E. Neal; and *The "Flower of Gloster"* (1911) by E. Temple Thurston, all of which stimulated the more adventurous to explore the decaying water highways. Many others recorded their voyages in the motor-boat and yachting magazines of the time, stimulating others to follow their exploits. As demand for pleasure craft grew, G.F. Wain and others founded the Inland Cruising Association at Christleton, near Chester, in 1935 and started to hire motor-cruisers for canal use. This enterprise followed the longstanding example of the Broadland hire-craft industry that had developed in the 1880s, and became the forerunner of the multimillion pound hire-craft industry that we know today, providing many with the opportunity to cruise the inland waterways. One of the earliest recorded extended pleasure cruises on the canals, was a 1,000-mile

voyage from the Thames to Ripon and back by Peter Wilans in 1879. His son, Kyrle, recounted the journey to a young engineer, L.T.C. Rolt and, in 1930, provided Rolt with his first opportunity to undertake a trip on the canals in a new boat, *Cressy*. The impact of this encounter has played a vital role in the waterways revival which has developed since 1946. The memories of these early cruises and his later associations with *Cressy* and the canals, prompted Rolt to turn away from the motor engineering trade he knew and consider living on a boat and writing for a living. After an initial sortie in a hired boat on the Lower Avon in 1938, Rolt decided to take up his new vocation. In March 1939 he purchased *Cressy* from Willans and started to refit the narrow boat for his new life. He started with a voyage through the canals of England during the summer and winter of 1939–40. War intervened, and delayed the preparation of his book, *Narrow Boat,* that recorded the voyage; it was finally published in 1944. It came at just the right time for a new interest to be developed in the inland waterways.

With the outbreak of war in 1939, the railway-owned canals came immediately under the control of the Ministry of Transport. The independent canals at first remained on their own, backed by a government assumption that traffic would still devolve to them. However, the impact of war and the war effort caused a drastic shift in the channels of trade. It created a move

Huddersfield Narrow Canal restoration problems

of emphasis from the East Coast to the West Coast ports, which had a dramatic effect on canal traffic due to the inflexible nature of the deteriorating canal system. By June 1940 the canal companies had suffered a marked loss in revenue and this, coupled with the loss of vital maintenance staff and men to operate the boats, made the future of the inland waterways even more precarious. To give some help the government offered a 50 per cent toll subsidy to the carriers of traffic moved by canal, and tolls were raised to a level one-third above pre-war rates. Even with this help the waterways declined still further as insufficient revenue was raised to meet necessary maintenance costs.

In 1941 it was calculated that there were 58 separate canals in Great Britain, of which 35 were owned by the railways and 23 by some 22 independent undertakings. The length of these canals amounted to 2,566 miles, of which 2,118 were alleged to be open for navigation. These figures showed that 448 miles of canal, or 17 per cent of the total mileage, had fallen into disuse without officially being abandoned.

In view of the problems arising within the network, the Government appointed Frank Pick to review the optimal use of the canals in 1941. He was asked to make a confidential report on the best steps to take. His report, presented in 1942, recommended that the canals should be brought under unified direction, with the benefit of a guarantee of net revenue to the undertakers and financial assistance to the carriers. The Government heeded his advice and strengthened the Central and Regional Canals Advisory Committees with representatives from the canal industry and associated unions as well as from other government departments. The Parliamentary Secretary of the Ministry of War Transport also became chairman of the Central Canals Committee. The day-to-day organisation of the canals at the Ministry was placed in the hands of a new director of canals, Brigadier-General Sir Osborne Mance.

Under Mance's control some progress was made and between July and October 1942 three Orders were made by which 18 independent undertakings and a number of canal carriers were taken under State control. The agreements enabled those main waterway links that were essential for wartime transport to be maintained in reasonable order. Apart from these projects, subsidies were also continued to the remaining independent carriers and they were also offered representation on the Regional Canals Committees.

As the pressures of the war effort took their toll, attempts were made by the Ministry of War Transport to put as much traffic as possible on the waterways. To overcome the shortage of boatmen, an independent scheme to train women to run the boats was inaugurated. This scheme was later taken over by the Ministry who

Derelict Shropshire Union Canal

mainly used the crews to work pairs of boats on the Grand Union Canal. The story of this scheme was recorded in two books: *Idle Women* (1947) by Susan Woolfitt, and *Maiden"s Trip* (1948) by Emma Smith, which both recalled life on the canals at that time. A third book on the same theme, *The Amateur Boat women* by Eily Gayford, was published in 1973. Even with the efforts of the boatwomen, canal traffic declined still further during the war years. Thirteen-million tons were carried in 1938; by 1942 this had fallen to eleven million tons, and by 1946 a low of ten million tons had been reached, of which about half was coal traffic and much of this only short haul.

More critically the war years saw the passing of some major Abandonment Acts covering over 200 miles of canal, including the trans Pennine Huddersfield Canal, much of the Shropshire Union system and the Manchester, Bolton and Bury Canals. Many other canals were left in such poor repair that their future was equally uncertain. The full effect of the decline of the canals between 1906 and 1946 is shown in Map 1. This defines the extent to which the peripheral canals had been abandoned for commercial use. In that same period canal carrying had declined from forty million tons to ten million tons, and the ancillary equipment had equally deteriorated to the same degree.

Although a serious decline had taken place all was not lost. Perhaps the first realisation of this came when Rolt's book *Narrow Boat* was published in late 1944. H.J. Massingham, in the foreword, saw the true signficance of what Rolt had to say, noting:

Derelict Lower Avon Lock in 1950

"To regard Mr Rolt's book as nostalgic is, therefore, wholly to misinterpret it. He is pleading for something that is part of the soul of England."

The book was reviewed for *The Observer* by Sir Compton Mackenzie who commended readers to obtain a copy. Two such readers were Robert Aickman and Charles Hadfield, both authors and both also interested in the canals. Each separately wrote to Rolt, care of his publishers, congratulating him on his book and suggesting that they considered the canals still had a future. Aickman wrote first and was duly invited to visit Rolt on *Cressy* at Tardebigge. They discussed their ideas. A few weeks later, in mid-1945, Aickman was invited back to *Cressy* for a cruise on the canals to Banbury. It provided him with a lasting vision of what life on a converted canal craft could really be like.

When Hadfield wrote, he also suggested that after the war there was a need for some sort of canal association to promote the use of the waterways. Rolt wrote back saying that someone else (Aickman) had written making a similar proposal. Hadfield later visited Rolt to discuss this theme. At this time Hadfield's first book, *English Rivers and Canals* (1945) written jointly with Frank Eyre, appeared. It was published by Collins as part of their "Britain in Picture" series, and did much to supplement the small number of books readily available on the subject. At much the same time Ealing Studios produced the film *Painted Boats,* which highlighted and recorded the silent water roads of England and their way of life. Each in their turn invited many into a new and forgotten world.

With the war over, public attention turned to rebuilding the battered nation. At first little official attention was paid to the waterways; during 1945 and 1946 the railway-owned canals stayed within the control of the authorities who had run them during the war years. A small group of people, inspired by Rolt's book, had other ideas and started to promote the theme of waterway restoration. The development and progress of the waterway restoration movement provides the main theme for this book.

II 1946–50:

REVIVAL OF INTEREST

The year 1946 was one of both social and economic reconstruction after the ravages of war. It was the time for the demobilisation of servicemen and their reabsorption back into the economy, with industry converting itself back to peacetime production. It was equally a time of shortage – of capital, materials and resources. The legacy of the war effort continued to make its presence felt, with lack of fuel a major problem for all. Rationing continued and vital components of a new life were still in short supply.

The nation's infrastructure had been sorely stretched in the war years. The heavy burden of traffic, shortage of manpower and maintenance and lack of vital supplies, had left the whole transport network with considerable arrears of repairs and replacements to be made good after the war. The inland waterways suffered most because they were the least used (except for the coalfield links) and the overall network tonnage carried had significantly declined.

The advent of 1946 still saw the majority of inland waterways under the control of the Ministry of War Transport. This became the Ministry of Transport on 1 April 1946. Some of the minor waterways remained in independent control, particularly those that had no strategic use. The State-controlled waterways were operated by the Ministry of War Transport on the basis that all income devolved to the Ministry, which then met all outgoings and paid a 50 per cent subsidy of tolls to the independent carriers. The carriers had their own trade association which did little to fight the declining canal trade since it found the wartime support measures a satisfactory arrangement. Thus when Herbert Morrison made a statement in the House of Commons in November 1945 that:

"Government intends to nationalise the railways, canals and long distance haulage within the lifetime of the present Parliament."

the canal industry accepted the proposal without protest.

However, some members of the general public were not so complacent. For them Rolt's book, *Narrow Boat* by L.T.C. Rolt, published in 1944, had been a catalyst for the rebirth of new interest in the future of the waterways. As the result, early in 1946, Rolt was asked by the Association for Planning and Regional Reconstruction to prepare a discussion paper on the future of the inland waterways.

Clearing North Walsham & Dilham Canal

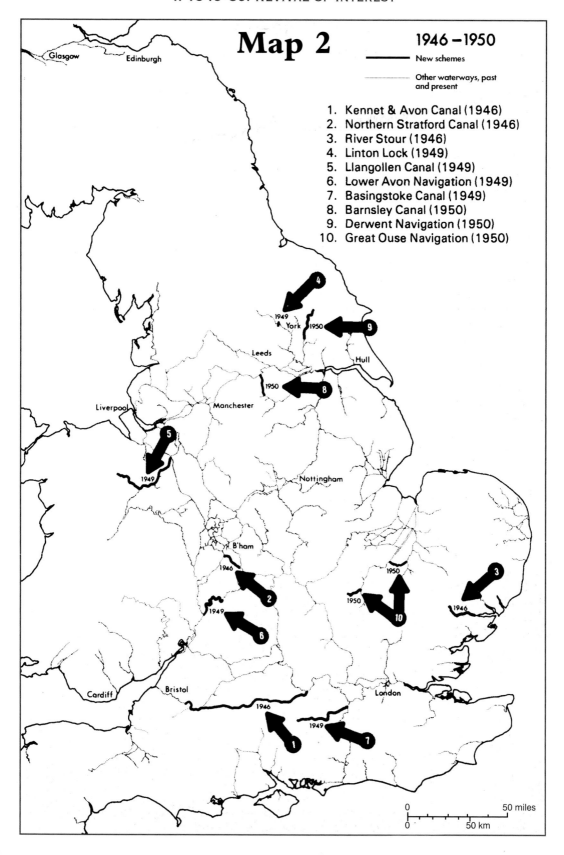

Map 2

1946–1950

——— New schemes

·········· Other waterways, past and present

1. Kennet & Avon Canal (1946)
2. Northern Stratford Canal (1946)
3. River Stour (1946)
4. Linton Lock (1949)
5. Llangollen Canal (1949)
6. Lower Avon Navigation (1949)
7. Basingstoke Canal (1949)
8. Barnsley Canal (1950)
9. Derwent Navigation (1950)
10. Great Ouse Navigation (1950)

The resulting report provided a vital component in the development of a campaign for a waterways revival. Amongst other things, it noted that even where waterways were still in regular use they were seldom maintained to former standards and all needed dredging. One feature given particular attention was the problem of the abandoned canals, and a particular plea was made for the retention of the then semi-derelict Kennet and Avon Canal for pleasure use. The report concluded with the view that the canals should be nationalised, but indicated that a revised toll structure should be introduced to offer access to the whole system for the payment of a single licence fee. It also expressed the real fear of a "ruthless policy of abandonment", and offered the advice that:

"... it is far easier and cheaper to maintain a waterway in navigable condition than it is to restore it to such a condition after it has been abandoned."

Robert Aickman

The report was widely circulated and subsequently proved to be a valuable means of generating a climate for reappraisal of the future role of inland waterways within the "corridors of power".

The boating press, principally the monthly periodical *Motor Boat and Yachting,* was also taking a renewed interest in the future of the canals and in March 1946 was able to announce that a minimal petrol allowance for pleasure craft had been agreed from 1 April 1946.

At about this time the author and theatre critic, Robert Aickman, started to propound his ideas for the future of the waterways. He was inspired by the book, *Narrow Boat,* and at a subsequent meeting with its author, L.T.C. Rolt, discussed the idea of an association for the revival of the waterways. Aickman's first contact with the waterways had been in his youth, with family towpath walks along the Grand Union Canal in Cassiobury Park, Watford. As his interest in the theatre grew, the regular pilgrimages to Stratford-upon-Avon in the late 1930s brought him into contact with the then decaying Stratford Canal. Although he did not immediately respond to the dereliction he saw, the theme of waterways inspired a continuing interest. As his ideas began to formulate, so the theme of a waterway restoration movement, organised by an Inland Waterways Association (IWA) became a reality in Aickman's mind.

To inaugurate the IWA, Aickman invited Rolt to his home at Gower Street in London in May 1946. They were joined at the meeting by F. Eyre, C. Hadfield, R. Kirkland, W. Luard and R. Smith. At the meeting they agreed to form the IWA and all but Luard, through pressure of other work, joined the governing council. Aickman was elected chairman; Hadfield, vice-chairman; Rolt, honorary secretary; and Eyre, honorary treasurer. Aickman offered to direct the organisation, on an honorary basis, for the first two years after which it was hoped to employ a full-time organiser. All contributed a subscription of one guinea and agreed to the appointment of a part-time paid employee to deal with enquiries and to dispatch literature.

Their first action was to mount a publicity campaign by the circulation of a letter announcing the aims of the Association and the production of a booklet, *The Future of the Waterways,* elaborating its ideals. The booklet, written by Rolt and published in June 1946, outlined the history of the waterways and highlighted the current problems. It stressed the potential for the multifunctional use of the canals and the way they could be developed for pleasure craft use.

The national press publicised the formation of the IWA and *Motor Boat and Yachting* offered to print an article outlining the Association's aims and objectives. This subsequently appeared in the October 1946 edition, and amongst other things suggested that various waterways, including the Thames and Severn Canal, the Suffolk Stour and the Yorkshire Derwent navigations should all be put back into use.

The IWA publicity prompted letters to the editors of various journals and in the national press on the subject of the waterways and provided a means of making many people, for the first time, aware of the problems that beset the waterways. The letters also gained many additional members for the IWA from those who would have otherwise been hard to attract. Such exchanges of published letters later became one of the most effective features in the development of public awareness of and participation in the waterways restoration movement.

By the close of 1946 the IWA had already made an impact on public imagination and some people were beginning to become "waterway minded". Various MPs had joined the Association and others supported its ideals. In the House of Lords, Lord Methuen, amongst others, took an interest in the campaign.

Robert Aickman recalls that:

"When the campaign began, most of the waterway 'enthusiasts', few in number at the best, were as gloomy about the prospects as any official, and often more so..."

This gloom was not, however, without foundation as numerous press reports highlighted the growing decay of both the Stratford and Kennet and Avon Canals, whilst the complicated legal background increased the plight of both the derelict Yorkshire Derwent and Suffolk Stour Navigations. It was, therefore, not unexpected that the first IWA council meeting designated the Kennet and Avon and Stratford Canals and the River Stour as the prime targets for restoration to good order and full navigability. To expedite action the council members each undertook a separate role. Aickman, as chairman, took personal responsibility for the major Kennet and Avon campaign, whilst R. Smith agreed to investigate the legal problems of the River Stour. Rolt, the secretary, started to investigate the prospects of reopening the Stratford Canal. To evaluate the legal position of the canal Lord

Methuen, at Rolt's instigation, tabled a question in the Lords concerning the damaged low-level bridge which effectively blocked the canal at King's Norton.

By 1947, the work of the IWA had been well publicised in the national press. In the same way the campaign for the restoration of the Stour received local coverage in a leading article in the *Essex County Standard*.

When the Government published its proposals for a new Transport Act in early 1947, the IWA decided to put forward the association's views on the future of the waterways in the form of a memorandum. Copies of the document, *The Case for Canal Revival Presented,* were circulated to all IWA members, the press, and to every member of the Parliamentary Standing Committee considering the Transport Bill. As the result of this the Transport Minister, Alfred Barnes, invited a deputation from the IWA to see him on 5 March 1947. Whilst he was unable to accept the IWA proposal that all navigable rivers and canals should be maintained as a public service, he took note of their views.

The wider circulation of the memorandum was timely, as a House of Lords Select Committee started to review a plan to extract water from the River Stour on 24 March 1947. The Dedham Vale Society was opposed to this plan and it became a corporate member of the IWA to assist with the campaign to protect and revive the river."

Thames & Severn Canal before restoration

The fears about the future of other waterways were also allayed when the Minister of Transport gave a Parliamentary reassurance that no immediate plans were afoot for the closure of the Kennet and Avon Canal and that the obstruction caused by underbridge support girders over the canal at Reading would also be removed. He also gave Lord Methuen an assurance that the obstruction at King's Norton, over the Stratford Canal, would also be removed to allow the passage of craft if 24 hours' notice were given. An outline of the IWA campaign to revive the Stratford Canal appeared in *Motor Boat and Yachting* for March 1947 in an article by its Midlands area organiser, J.H. Stables, which highlighted their efforts to restore the canal to full navigability.

To promote the case for the revival of the Kennet and Avon, Rolt and Aickman addressed a public meeting at Newbury on 8 March 1947. Local politicians and MPs spoke at the meeting and considerable support was offered towards the IWA ideas for the revival and restoration of the canal."

On a broader front, the IWA membership were kept informed of the Association"s progress by their journal, *Bulletin,* particularly in the March 1947 issue which highlighted the "outstanding commercial possibilities of operating boats for hire on inland waterways", and concluded:

"... every boat not only demonstrates the truth of our case, but actually, by its passage, improves the condition of the track itself. In the restricted modern world there seems here a remarkable investment opportunity, where profit combines with public service in the highest degree."

With the same journal the IWA circulated members with details of a ten-point plan that had been adopted as its development strategy. This included:

"That navigations no longer in use owing to deterioration by neglect should be restored."

"That no navigations should be abandoned until Bodies representing all the following have been consulted (a) commercial users, (b) users of the waterways for sport and pleasure, (c) defence services, and, in addition, Local Authorities and Catchment Boards affected and the Ministers of Health, Agriculture and Fisheries, and Town and Country Planning."

"That steps be taken vigorously to promote the use of the waterways for recreation and by tourists, including visitors bringing foreign exchange to this country."

These aims and an outline of the work of the IWA were the subject of an article by Aickman in *Country Life* of 11 April 1947, which gained considerable additional support for the IWA including several substantial donations towards the funds.

During 1947, as a means of developing the IWA's knowledge of the state of the various canals of the Midlands and the North-West, L.T.C. Rolt planned a voyage of exploration. At the same time J. Gould, a boat-owner from Newbury, gave notice that he planned to traverse the whole Kennet and Avon Canal during the summer of 1947. Both trips were part of the wider campaign to develop a greater public awareness of the potential of the waterways.

In much the same vein, the IWA arranged an outing to the Lancaster Canal in June 1947. The canal had come under the scope of an Abandonment Bill, in 1944, promoted by its owners, the London Midland and Scottish Railway, but had escaped abandonment due to the prompt action of the Kendal Council."

The first real opportunity for the IWA to "flex its muscles" came in May 1947. One of the campaigns it had been carefully developing was that for reopening the northern Stratford Canal. In the light of the assurance given to Lord Methuen, that an obstruction at Lifford Lane, King's Norton, would be removed at 24 hours' notice to allow the passage of craft, Rolt decided to test the commitment. He included the canal as part of his tour through the Midlands, which retraced much of the route of his 1939 voyage described in his book *Narrow Boat*. He gave notice of his intended passage through the canal and after a difficult voyage his boat *Cressy* cleared the obstruction on 20 May 1947. The trip provided a means of gaining substantial publicity for the IWA with accounts of the voyage appearing in the national press. Perhaps Aickman"s own recollections best sum up the significance of the event. He recalls:

"We rounded a few more corners, and there the crowd was: lining both banks several deep; on rooftops, up trees. A mild sarcastic cheer met our belated advent. The obstruction had been raised by a large gang. *Cressy* passed beneath it, though with a clearance of only an inch or two. The applause became a little warmer. We made statements. We posed for photographs. We accepted cups of tea. We proclaimed a great new future for the canals of Britain. The Association was only twelve months old, but our cause had arrived ... Here was evidence people cared. A public campaign, however right, good, and necessary, will not succeed unless it speaks to some need in the mass unconscious."

The idea of the campaign cruise later evolved as one of the stronger weapons used by the IWA for saving the canals. Apart from the value of the publicity that the Lifford Lane incident offered to the IWA, it also offered Aickman, the campaign director, new ideas of methods to develop public concern.

Although the first fruits of success were achieved on the Stratford Canal, events on the Kennet and Avon Canal went in the opposite direction. On 21 April 1947, as a boat was passing through Hale's Lock one of the lower gates collapsed. This effectively closed the navigation until it could be repaired. At the same time, it was heard that plans were afoot to demolish one of the canal's lock cottages at Bull's Lock, something that was to become even more frequent as the years went by. Both features made the IWA campaign to revive the Kennet and Avon more imperative. They also attracted a wide public interest in canals.

In mid-1947 the book *Idle Women* by Susan Woolfitt was published which recounted the experiences of the volunteer boatwomen who ran narrow boats on the canals in the war years. A second book, *Maiden's Trip* by Emma Smith, appeared in 1948. Both set the scene for the development of a new area of publishing, that of

Huddersfield Narrow Canal restoration

Huddersfield Narrow Canal with Robert Aickman, 1948

waterways books. At much the same time the Ealing Studios film *Painted Boats* came out on general release. The film and books did much to provide more up to date public knowledge of waterway life.

In the same vein Rolt produced a pamphlet *General Navigation Hints,* for issue to members and others wishing to navigate the inland waterways. The pamphlet was aimed at reducing any possible antagonism between pleasure craft and the remaining working boats."

This additional publicity for the waterways came at an opportune time as the parliamentary debate on the Transport Bill took place during May and June 1947. Although only the waterways aspects concerned the IWA, the major battles on the Bill were fought chiefly over the nationalisation of road transport and there were few mentions of canals in the debates. The actual nationalisation of the waterways, which had been seriously and regularly debated since 1888, thus came about almost without controversy."

Nationalisation in itself did not assure the future of the canals. Realising this, and as part of its publicity campaign to promote a revival of the waterways, the IWA decided to hold an exhibition of items of canal and river interest. They were assisted by a generous offer from Messrs Heal & Son Ltd of Tottenham Court Road, London, who provided the use of their Mansard Gallery free of charge. The exhibition, which opened on 14 October 1947 and was reported in *The Times* of the following day, was a great success, on most days attracting over a thousand visitors. As the result, the exhibition was taken on tour around the provinces after it completed its London season. At more than half the provincial galleries it visited it broke local attendance records. "Such was the growing public interest in the waterways at that time.

Unfortunately public attitudes were not so clearly focused on the waterways in Newbury, and in April 1947 the Newbury Town Council took the decision that they would not support the retention of the Kennet and Avon Canal in a navigable condition. Their attitude was influenced by the potential expense and inconvenience that seemed inevitable from a local bridge replacement scheme. To fight the decision, local IWA member, J. Gould, started to rouse local opposition to the plan.

As knowledge of the IWA exploits regarding the Stratford Canal became more widely known, so the plight of other canals was drawn to their attention. One such case was the Derby Canal, where abandonment was proposed. A local man, B.A. Mallender, called on the IWA to help organise a revival campaign. In similar circumstances, E.V. Waddington of Mexborough sought the help of the IWA in his fight to prevent the abandonment of the Barnsley Canal.

During the summer of 1947, Rolt took his boat *Cressy* as far as Ellesmere on the abandoned Welsh section of the Shropshire Union Canal. He found considerable local antagonism towards the unwarranted abandonment of the waterway. This highlighted another potential restoration scheme." As the first move in the promotion of this campaign Rolt prepared an article, "Waterway to Wales", that appeared in *Country Life* of 21 November 1947.

Similarly, to develop further support in the Midlands, the IWA, in association with the Solihull Society of Arts, organised a cruise along the Grand Union Canal. This was attended by over 130 people and gained substantial local publicity. With this growth of public interest it was significant that the IWA were advised by the Ministry of Transport that the obstruction on the northern Stratford Canal at King's Norton would be removed and replaced by a new swing-bridge.

During the summer of 1947, with more petrol available, interest in pleasure cruising on the canals developed. This was enhanced by a reprint of the standard work of reference, *Inland Waterways of Great Britain* by W.E. Wilson. One of the most significant cruises made during the summer was a passage, from end to end, of the Kennet and Avon Canal. The voyage was very difficult and an account of it appeared in the *Newbury Weekly News* of 11 September, which created considerable local interest. This was timely since the municipal elections in Newbury were in progress. Not surprisingly, the first item on one of the local manifestos was: ...."to press for the dredging and maintaining of the Kennet Canal in a decent state of repair for navigational purposes."

In the same way *Bulletin* No. 8 of August 1947, recounted a voyage through the Huddersfield Narrow Canal, which although abandoned was still open for pleasure craft, and IWA members were commended to navigate it. They were also asked to consider navigating some of Scotland's inland waterways.

Although the IWA did much to promote an interest in canal pleasure cruising at this time, they were unable to gain support from the British Tourist and Holidays Board. At first the organisation expressed an interest in IWA ideals, but in the light of official pressure, this support was quickly withdrawn. The news of the change of attitude was conveyed to the IWA in a letter which said:

"Regarding the development of rivers and canals, I have been in communication, through the Board of Trade, with the Ministry of Transport. The latter do not look very favourably upon any scheme for pleasure craft on the canals at the present time ... I am afraid that the canal projects are not possible at the moment."

Derby Canal Protest

This official rebuff did not augur well for the future of the canals under nationalisation and provoked greater efforts by the IWA to save them. *The Times* of 11 October 1947 recorded the nationalisation programme and reported that:"All canal carriers, whose undertakings were brought under Government control during the war, would cease to be controlled from 1 January 1948." On the same basis it noted that the subsidy on transit tolls, paid to the carriers by the canal owners, would be terminated on 31 December 1947. This, too, highlighted the changing economic scene with a further potential financial loss for the canals.

Formal details of the nationalised waterway system were reported in *The Times* of 23 December 1947 under the headline "Greater use of Canals", and the chairman of the newly created British Transport Commission, C. Hurcomb, outlined his strategy for development. He particularly noted .... "the Executive (Docks and Inland Waterways) would also advise the Commission on the desirability of exercising power ... to order abandonment of canals."

The powers of the 1947 Transport Act provided for the majority of the waterways controlled by the Ministry of Transport to be devolved to the British Transport Commission. The major exceptions were the Thames, the Manchester Ship Canal and the Bridgewater Canal, each of which were under separate control. Various other canals were omitted, some because they were

nearly derelict, and others because they were on the East Coast and had not been included in the wartime control scheme upon which the nationalisation schedules were based. Some 2,064 miles of canal were taken over by the BTC. This was less than half the original network, after allowing for the exceptions to nationalisation. Even so, at the time of nationalisation there were 6,000 working boats and barges on British waterways, and the industry had some 11,000 employees.

Under the BTC, responsibility for the canals was given to the new Docks and Inland Waterways Executive, whose chairman was R. Hill. The canals were first grouped into five areas, which later were reduced to four, and for an interim period some of the former railway-owned canals were run by the Railways Executive, until they could be transferred to DTWE and incorporated into the new organisation. On 1 January 1948 a new era for the waterways was about to begin. At this time also, a revised second edition of the book *Narrow Boat* was in preparation. In the preface, Rolt commented:

"... that soul is threatened today as it never has been threatened before, yet it will not perish ... an Inland Waterways Association has been formed for the purpose of safeguarding this particular part of our heritage. Already it has done much useful work ..."

As the new era dawned, so the IWA set out to adapt its own organisation to meet the ever-expanding campaign for waterway restoration. To do this a separate Midlands Branch was inaugurated at a meeting in Birmingham on 14 February 1948. In the same way, a meeting was held in Newbury, at which Aickman outlined the case for the retention of the Kennet and Avon Canal. This meeting provided the basis for a second local group led by J. Gould in the Newbury area.

To promote their national campaign the IWA leaders sought a meeting with the chairman of the BTC, so that they could outline the IWA case for waterway revival. This they did at a meeting on 1 March 1948. In particular, the delegation highlighted the need for a national canal policy, with safeguards to allow for a full review of future potential before any abandonment was authorised. Rolt laid particular stress on the dangers of allowing bridges to be lowered on the Welsh canal before such a survey was made. The delegation also stressed the need for publicising the value of canals, particularly for pleasure craft use, and concluded by offering IWA help in restoring the country's waterways.

On 4 March 1948 *The Times* added its weight to the idea of using the inland waterways for pleasure craft under a headline "Holidays Afloat". At the same time an editorial in *The Field* for 6 March developed the case for a revival of the waterways under the headline, "Hope for our Inland Waterways."

This hope was perhaps a little over-optimistic, for early in 1948 the River Boards Bill also came before Parliament for approval. The first draft of the Bill made no provision for the representation of navigation interests at the Board level. But after pressure by the IWA, an amendment was subsequently adopted enabling the Ministry of Transport to make nominations to represent navigation interests.

On 27 May 1948, IWA representatives had the opportunity to meet R. Hill, the chairman of DIWE, and other members of the executive. At the meeting Aickman and Rolt outlined the IWA case for the revival of the waterways and had a seemingly favourable hearing. They were told that DIWE was in the process of appointing officers to investigate the possibilities of increased pleasure traffic on the waterways, and that they were also considering the IWA proposals for a more uniform structure of tolls for pleasure craft.

Whilst the potential of making some progress seemed possible on the nationalised waterways, the plight of one of the independent waterways, the Derby Canal, became more critical. Rolt, who had been refused permission to navigate the canal, contacted the Ministry of Transport to seek their aid, under the provisions of the *Railway and Canal Traffic Act* of 1888. The Minister replied that he would not seek an immediate inspection of the canal as the canal company had indicated they were in the process of gathering estimates for the cost of restoring the waterway. IWA members were warned of the likely need for a stronger campaign to save the canal if an unsatisfactory reply was later received.

The inland waterways were the subject of a debate in the House of Commons on 5 May 1948. A plea was made for the revival of the Kennet and Avon Canal by J. Sparks, MP. He also stressed the general recreational value of the canals and indicated that he hoped this potential could be developed. To follow up this suggestion, IWA members were commended to use the two firms that specialised in canal cruising; the Inland Cruising Association Ltd of Christleton, founded in 1935, and the Canal Cruising Company Ltd of Stone, founded in 1947. To promote further interest in cruising and to evaluate the condition of certain canals, the IWA officers took one of the hire-craft on a cruise through the North-Western waterways between 7 August and 25 September 1948. Their route included the Peak Forest and Ashton Canals as well as the abandoned Huddersfield Narrow Canal.

In support of the cruising spirit E. de Mare, the author, took his own boat through the Northern Stratford Canal and again had the Lifford Lane bridge lifted. At much the same time, V. Bulkley-Johnson made a trip by canoe from Stratford to Evesham, down the derelict Avon Navigation. Both cruises were reported in *Bulletin* with a commendation that others followed the examples set. The journal also carried warning of a plan to close part of the Coventry Canal, including the town basin, and replace it with a new out-of-town basin; this proposal later caused considerable local controversy.

In the autumn of 1948 it was announced that the Basingstoke Canal was likely to be sold. At first the IWA decided to take a watching brief. Aickman wrote to the Editor of *Motor Boat and Yachting* for November 1948, commenting " .... the Association is neither constituted nor sufficiently rich to buy the canal ... but ... we think there is a good cause for its purchase", and offered "our full support for a policy of restoration and use". IWA members were told that a public meeting was being organised on 11 December at Woking, at which the future of the canal would be discussed and asked for their support. IWA member, L.A. Edwards, agreed to make the arrangements and Aickman offered to speak. As news of the pending sale became more widely known, the IWA received many letters asking what action they proposed to take to get the canal restored. Aickman recalls: "... it became obvious that the Association's entire prestige and position turned on our making a positive response."

In Surrey and Hampshire, local attitudes varied from those who supported full restoration of the canal to those who sought its complete obliteration. These opposing views became evident at the public meeting and were reported in *The Times* of 13 December 1948. As a result of the meeting, a Basingstoke Canal Committee was formed to examine the possibilities of purchase and restoration. *The Times* recorded this development as an event in which, "... one felt that the Inland Waterways Association had scored a notable triumph."

With the foundation of the Canal Committee, public interest rapidly developed in the future of the waterway. This was supported by a variety of local and national press reports. By early 1949 the prospect of a major restoration campaign for the canal was becoming evident, with donations being sent to the IWA to assist in its purchase.

Right: Kennet and Avon Canal, Devises, before restoration

Below: Kennet and Avon Canal Campaign Cruise 1956

This development was significant in three ways, as Aickman later indicated:

"One was the first full entering into public consciousness, of the Association"s general programme and campaign. The campaign had to be rendered down to the size of a particular well-known waterway in order that its unfamiliar ingredients be digestible. A second factor was that element of boom and bubble which commonly attends for a time a supposedly new phenomenon.... The third factor, and, in the context of the waterways far the most important, was that the Basingstoke Canal attracted interest because there seemed the possibility that we could own it, take possession of it, and operate it in our own way. People can hardly expect to feel much enthusiasm about waterways that have been nationalised ..."

As it appeared that one private canal was about to be restored, so the future for some other canals looked brighter as well. *Motor Boat and Yachting* of December 1948, recorded that the remainder of the railway-owned canals were to be transferred to the DIWE from 1 January 1949 and that, as part of its development programme, the executive was examining the pleasure traffic potential of both the Kennet and Avon Canal and the Welsh section of the Shropshire Union Canal. The magazine also printed an article by Aickman on the waterways of the North, in which he pleaded for the retention of another former railway canal, the Huddersfield Narrow.

More support for the restoration of the Kennet and Avon Canal was similarly generated by an article entitled *Bristol to the Thames* by Gould, which appeared in *Motor Boat and Yachting* of January 1949. This added weight to the growing waterways revival campaign and concluded: "Let us hope, and try to ensure ... that the Kennet and Avon shall in future be a useful amenity."

Hope for the revival of the Kennet and Avon was developed still further with the formal foundation of the IWA Kennet and Avon Branch at a meeting in Newbury on 29 January 1949. Aickman addressed the meeting and indicated that the canal should also carry heavy pleasure traffic. He concluded: "Newbury had nothing to lose by restoration." The local pressure made some impact and a note in *Bulletin* of February 1949 was able to reassure members that "... talk of abandoning it seems fortunately to have ceased."

A sign of hope in one area brought despair in another. The advent of 1949 brought news of the proposed abandonment of the Rochdale Canal and also portions of the Monmouthshire Canal. To make a case for the revival of the Rochdale Canal, Aickman decided to try to develop press support. Articles appeared in the *Daily*

Mirror of 31 December 1948 and the *Rochdale Observer* of 1 January 1949, both outlining the IWA case. In the same vein, D. Russell tried to gain local support for the ailing Union Canal in Scotland, which was also subject to abandonment proposals.

In much the same way local interest was beginning to develop to seek to have the Middle Level Navigation, which linked the Lower Ouse to the Fenland system, restored to full navigational standards. At the same time, another IWA member, Willans, was seeking boating access on the obstructed Bridgwater and Taunton Canal.

Prospects for the restoration of the Basingstoke Canal advanced when the canal was auctioned at Aldershot on 1 March 1949. The Basingstoke Canal Purchasing Committee, led by Mrs J. Marshall, managed to procure the canal for £6,000. After the auction Mrs Marshall announced that it was the committee"s intention to form a private company to develop the canal for pleasure and commercial use. These plans suddenly changed when, unexpectedly, the purchasing committee disassociated itself from the IWA and indicated that it had decided to restore the canal in its own way: a step which cast a doubt over the canal's longer-term revival.

A more hopeful note came from a meeting in York on 30 April 1949 when the IWA North-East Branch was formed. Two potential areas for revival were discussed at this meeting. One was Linton Lock and the other the River Derwent. It was agreed that the potential for restoring both should be explored. The greatest emphasis was placed on the revival of Linton Lock, as its closure prevented access from the Ouse to the Ure Navigation and the Ripon Canal, and the branch secretary, H. Comber, agreed to investigate how the lock could be restored.

At the same time the Midlands Branch of the IWA started to explore more fully the potential restoration of the southern Stratford Canal. Details of the poor state of the canal were outlined to IWA members in June 1949, and they were told of the need to evaluate the legal position of the canal, particularly the right to navigate it.

The *Evesham Journal* of 12 March 1949 carried a detailed article about "Shakespeare's Avon", which recorded the history and decline of the river. In response, Aickman wrote to the editor outlining the need for the waterway to be restored and indicating that this could be effected for a moderate sum. IWA members were told of the restoration potential of the Lower Avon by Aickman who indicated:

"... the restoration of the Avon, and perhaps to a lesser extent, the reconditioning of the Stratford Canal, should play a prominent part in any contemplated scheme ...

a start should be made with the easier sections ... the Stratford Canal and the Lower Avon."

He recalled K. Gill-Smith"s article on the Avon and recorded how valuable a public trust to restore the Avon could be.

By March 1949, the IWA membership was in excess of 800 and interest in inland waterways had substantially developed. On the basis of the continuing upsurge of interest, plans were made by L.A. Edwards to produce a new edition of the reference book *Inland Waterways of Great Britain*.

The future of the waterways was also the topic of a radio programme broadcast on 13 July 1949. Aickman contributed to the programme and was able to develop the theme of waterway holidays. In response to the broadcast, the IWA received nearly 500 requests for details of the boating holiday facilities that were available. This offered a clear indication of the growing interest in canals, but also highlighted that the supply of available boats was far short of the growing demand. The *Bulletin* of August 1949 records:

"the canal system could ... readily be restored to an economic and profitable condition ... and ... that pleasure traffic, properly exploited, could make an enormous contribution."

In the same edition the improved condition of the Welsh section of the Shropshire Union Canal was also a theme for discussion. An article put forward the idea that the whole of the Welsh canal should be designated a National Park. The fears about the lowering of bridges along the canal were particularly highlighted, and all IWA members were commended to take what action they could to fight these proposals which, if effected, could permanently close the canal.

By July 1949 some constructive action was beginning to develop over the restoration of Linton Lock. The Lock Commissioners had obtained estimates for the lock to be repaired and the local IWA branch members had indicated that they might be in a position to finance the work. Similar developments were also beginning to evolve on the Lower Avon, where members of the IWA Midlands Branch had started to investigate the state of the waterway and the extent of the repairs that were needed to bring it back to full working order.

Just as various restoration plans began to be published for the revival of the more derelict waterways, so the viable canals suffered a blow to their trade. The National Coal Board revised its pricing structure from 30 May 1949. This involved offering coal at pit-head prices in rail wagons. Where alternative loading operations were required, such as loading coal boats, an additional charge was to be made. The additional charge, of about 10p per ton, made a direct impact on the viability of coal-carrying by canal and as a result much of the remaining regular coal traffic, such as that on the Staffordshire and Worcestershire Canal, quickly ceased. This made the potential of the revival of the coal-carrying Barnsley Canal less likely, and as a response to IWA pressure the DTWE replied:

"The resuscitation of the canal involves major physical and financial considerations ... there is grave doubt as to whether it would be in the national interest to reinstate this waterway."

When the BTC published its report and accounts for 1948 in mid-1949, it was able to offer a more hopeful note:

"...attention is being given to the possibilities of encouraging the use for pleasure purposes of the less frequented waterways, on some, at least, of which it would be necessary to incur moderate expenditure if they are to be put into a condition in which they can be used."

The DIWE started to issue its own monthly paper in September 1949 entitled *Lock and Quay* and this further developed the theme of pleasure craft use on canals.

In October 1949, IWA members were advised of the plight of Linton Lock. They were told that to reopen the lock would cost some £2,000 and that the North-Eastern Branch were proposing to open a fund to raise the necessary finance. Contributions towards the restoration work were sought and in December 1949 it was announced that two IWA representatives were to be appointed as Lock Commissioners so that the restoration could proceed.

At a meeting in Huntingdon on 30 October 1949, the IWA Fenlands Branch was inaugurated and members started to actively review the potential for the revival of the lower reaches of the Ouse and Nene and other Fenland waterways. A speaker from the Ouse Catchment Board told them it was still the Board"s policy to ultimately restore the Ouse to Bedford. As a result it was initially agreed to devote branch resources to the revival of the Middle Level Navigation which had by then become badly silted and weeded.

The year 1949 closed, for the IWA, on a successful note. A letter was received from DIWE confirming that a new swing-bridge would be constructed at King's Norton on the Stratford Canal and that the bridge would be operational early in 1950. Other obstructions on the canal were also to be cleared by the close of the year, making unimpeded passage through the canal a possibility.

The *Bulletin* of December 1949, was similarly able to record the progress made in developing a scheme to restore the Lower Avon Navigation, with members of an IWA Midlands Branch committee led by C.D. Barwell seeking legal advice on the best method of proceeding with the revival of the navigation.

In another revival scheme J. Gould inaugurated commercial carrying along the Kennet & Avon Canal between Reading and Newbury with an aim of getting the canal restored to good order. His first voyage was reported locally and nationally, and did much to enhance the case for the full restoration of the canal.

However, on a less happy note, the campaign led by Rolt to stop the lowering of bridges along the Welsh section of the Shropshire Union Canal was not achieving the desired success. IWA members were again asked to press the County Councils to stop bridge destruction. This threat was partly removed in early 1950 when official negotiations started in relation to using the canal as a water-transfer link. This offered more hope for the longer-term restoration campaign.

At much the same time the IWA were advised that DIWE had nearly completed their review of the toll structure for pleasure craft. As a result the pleasure craft licence was introduced later in the year. The BTC Annual Report for 1950 recorded that 1,500 such licences had been issued, offering a good indication of the size of the pleasure craft fleet on the inland waterways in their charge at that time.

To meet the needs of this growing fleet the IWA decided to hold a festival and rally at Market Harborough during August 1950. They saw this as a means of both gaining publicity for their cause as well as unifying the ideals of the growing membership.

In much the same way, but to meet a far wider need, 1950 saw the beginnings of the post-war canals literature encouraging the general public to take an interest in the waterways.

Rolt produced a book, *The Inland Waterways of England;* Aickman produced *Know your Waterways;* E. de Mare introduced his superbly illustrated *The Canals of England;* and Hadfield wrote *Introducing Canals.* A second book by Hadfield, *British Canals,* was the forerunner of his subsequent comprehensive series, "Canals of the British Isles", that so greatly improved the amount of available knowledge of canal history. A new edition of *Inland Waterways of Great Britain,* completely revised by L. Edwards, also appeared to meet the growing demand for an up-to-date reference volume.

Perhaps the greatest event of 1950 was the inauguration of the Lower Avon Navigation Trust, through which the restoration of the Lower Avon was to materialise. News of this was given to IWA members in June 1950, and the BBC broadcast a feature on the river on 19 April 1950, making listeners aware of the developments that were taking place in the Avon valley.

The IWA North-Eastern Branch held its AGM in York on 6 May 1950. At the meeting it was recorded that the branch campaign to try to petition for the restoration of the navigation equipment on the River Derwent was not proceeding as planned. A public petition to promote the revival had only gathered some 200 signatures and the Catchment Board were not offering their co-operation. However, progress was by then being made on the restoration of Linton Lock and it seemed that sufficient funds would be forthcoming for all the repair work to be undertaken.

The same rate of progress was not being made on the Kennet and Avon Canal, where, after a successful rally of boats at Newbury at Whitsun, Heales and other locks had been closed because of their dangerous condition. The future of the canal was again in doubt.

Similarly the campaign for the restoration of the Barnsley Canal, which had been closed by an embankment breach some four years earlier, was also beginning to falter as the DIWE offers of compensation, in lieu of restoration and reopening the waterway, were gradually being accepted by the canal carriers who had an interest in the waterway.

The Bedford Boat Club was founded in the spring of 1950 to assist with and campaign for the restoration of the navigation on the River Ouse through to Bedford. Members started to develop a local publicity campaign for the revival of the navigation in Bedford whilst members of the IWA, Fenlands Branch, started to promote local support in the Huntingdon area with a view to stimulating the River Board to move ahead more rapidly with their own restoration plans.

The major waterway event of 1950 was the IWA Market Harborough festival and rally held in August. This was a great success with over 100 craft reaching the rally site. The whole event was widely covered by the national and local press with BBC radio and television also offering comprehensive reports, and even the *New York Herald Tribune* carried an article on it. During the rally over 50,000 people visited the festival site and Aickman recalls: "The 1950 festival changed the entire prospect for the waterways of Britain; in the main, by simply reminding people, other than specialists, of their existence, and especially by manifesting the enormous potential for pleasure boating. It would hardly be too much to say that an entire new form of public recreation entered history at Market Harborough."

For many the Market Harborough festival marked the end of the first era of the waterway restoration movement. The foundations for the revival of the waterways had by then been laid by the IWA. *The Transport Act* of 1947 had started a new era for Britain's inland waterways, with much of the system vested in the BTC from 1 January 1948. In the years that followed the DIWE began to feel its way.

In much the same way the IWA began to develop its campaign. The initial impact of these developments towards restoration are recorded in Map 2. At first, in 1946, the campaign was directed towards three waterways; the Kennet and Avon and the northern section of the Stratford Canal, with the legal problems of the River Stour also being investigated. As progress was made, particularly with the successful Lifford Lane campaign, so the range of developments was widened. By 1949 the Welsh section of the Shropshire Union Canal offered a chance of success, whilst the sale of the Basingstoke Canal, in the same year, forced that canal into the limelight as well. The critical problems of the Barnsley Canal also came to the fore through the interest of Waddington, an IWA member and canal carrier.

As the number of IWA branches grew, so the prospect of other restoration schemes developed. In the Midlands the potential of the Lower Avon was quickly exploited, whilst in the East the plight of the Great Ouse and Middle Level Navigations quickly attracted the interest of Fenlands Branch members. In the North-East the closure of Linton Lock forced the local branch to take action, whilst the longstanding decay of the Derwent Navigation also stirred some local interest.

The major feature of the period was the simple, yet very effective, revival of public interest in the waterways. The growth of pleasure craft use, and more particularly the spate of waterways' books issued in 1950s exemplify this trend. The conversion of a mass of separate toll charges into a single common licence fee together with the general growth of interest in water-based recreation during the period also assisted in this development.

The Central Government preoccupation in defining and legislating for the "Welfare State", and the volume of new and novel legislation during the period meant that central influence was at a relatively low level. The waterways revival campaign therefore rested mainly on ensuring that legal obligations towards the waterways were maintained. It was on this basis that the successful reopening of the northern section of the Stratford Canal, by the renewal of the swing-bridge at King"s Norton, was achieved. The same basic approach was adopted for the Kennet and Avon Canal but did not achieve the same success and by 1950 the canal, as a through route from London to Bristol, was again closed due to the failure of Heales Lock and other lock-gates.

The period 1946 to 1950 had its successes and its failures. The foundations laid during this time, however, greatly influenced the waterway restoration movement as it evolved in the years that followed.

Union Canal, Edinburgh, 1977

III 1951-60:
FIRST FRUITS OF SUCCESS

The national perspective of the year 1951 was very much influenced by the events of the preceding year. A general election in February 1950 registered a decline in Labour's popularity after nearly five years in power. The outbreak of the Korean war in July 1950 brought about another economic crisis in Britain and occasioned rearmament at a level which forced up both taxes and prices. Members of the Government became haunted by ill-health. First Bevan, then Cripps and finally Attlee became ill. Labour's prestige as a party dropped and the impetus behind the reorganisation of Britain's social infrastructure fell.

But by then the social revolution had taken place and Britain was firmly dedicated to the interests and welfare of every citizen. The Festival of Britain in 1951 was in some ways a symbol of this change, but the real revolution was a psychological one, with a spirit of national solidarity and a sense of community uppermost in many men's minds. This did not dispel conflict at Governmental or other levels and just as Bevan and Wilson resigned in April 1951, as a matter of principle over attitudes towards Health Service charges, in a similar way the IWA council was faced with a dispute of principle over the association's strategy towards economies that were being sought from within the waterway network. Soon after the Market Harborough festival, Rolt, Hadfield and others put their names to a memorandum calling for a policy of "priorities" within the waterways network. Aickman viewed this as "... keeping some waterways and letting others go", noting that the proposal "would make .... the association become more of a discussion group and less set upon a single aim."

The outcome of the dispute is perhaps best described by Hadfield, one of the founder members, who recalls:

"... a serious upset occurred in the Association: some original members were expelled and independent canal societies founded. The Association itself chose a protest role as a pressure group which had some success in preventing possible abandonments, but for a time kept it out of a constructive part in decision-making or co-operation with the Commission."

Although the IWA was suffering from internal conflict, other developments, to the benefit of the future of the waterways, were simultaneously being promoted. The Market Harborough festival saw the launching of the first of a range of holiday cruisers, specially designed for use on inland waterways. These were available for hire in 1951 by a new canal fleet operator, Canal Pleasurecraft Ltd of Stourport. Similarly the first pair of British canal "Hotel Boats", promoted by A. Smallwood of New Way Holidays, made their appearance and started their first season of operation in 1951. Both innovations laid the necessary additional foundations for the canal holiday industry that has since developed.

The Festival of Britain year also saw the introduction of *Jason* offering canal trips from Little Venice to London Zoo; a feature that became nationally known when a second more sophisticated craft of the same name was launched in 1953 and a photograph of it was published in the *Sunday Times*. Subsequently, many people have received their first introduction to canals on the *Jason*. The Festival's exhibition provided the site for two displays by the IWA. Two painted narrow boats were moored in the Thames, near Charing Cross, whilst a display of photographs and canalware was presented in the Lion and Unicorn Pavilion. Both attracted considerable interest and *The Times* of 28 April 1951 carried a photograph of the boats.

February 1951 saw the formal establishment of the second individual waterway restoration society (the first being the Lower Avon Navigation Trust (LANT) formed in 1950 to advocate and promote the restoration of the River Great Ouse from Temsford to Bedford. The group, which developed from the earlier Bedford Boat Club, was promoted by Scott and Aickman of the IWA among others, and, within the different legal constraints, planned to revive the Great Ouse following the LANT example. An appeal for support and funds was made to IWA members in April 1951. At the same time the possibility of LANT extending its work to the Upper Avon was also mooted. This highlighted the strengthening of support for the initial restoration scheme on the lower reaches of the Avon.

During March 1951 the inauguration of the North-Western Branch of the IWA, in Manchester, took place. The main priorities concerned the problems of the demise of the Rochdale Canal, the Huddersfield Narrow Canal, the Lancaster Canal, the Ashton Canal and the Welsh section of the Shropshire Union Canal, in that order.

As concern was developing in the North-West, so the plight of the Brecon and Abergavenny Canal was equally gaining attention in South Wales. The *South Wales Argus* of 19 June 1951 carried an account of the canal and

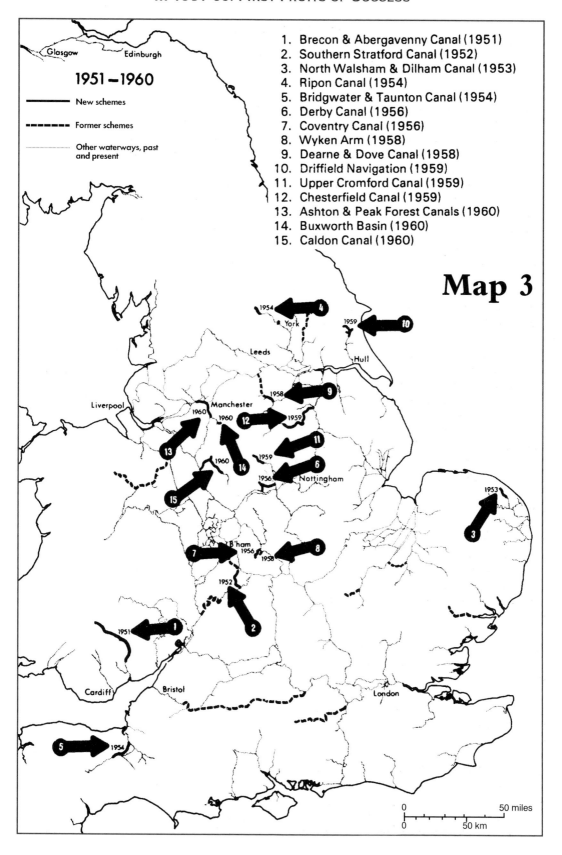

1. Brecon & Abergavenny Canal (1951)
2. Southern Stratford Canal (1952)
3. North Walsham & Dilham Canal (1953)
4. Ripon Canal (1954)
5. Bridgwater & Taunton Canal (1954)
6. Derby Canal (1956)
7. Coventry Canal (1956)
8. Wyken Arm (1958)
9. Dearne & Dove Canal (1958)
10. Driffield Navigation (1959)
11. Upper Cromford Canal (1959)
12. Chesterfield Canal (1959)
13. Ashton & Peak Forest Canals (1960)
14. Buxworth Basin (1960)
15. Caldon Canal (1960)

Map 3

1951 – 1960

New schemes
Former schemes
Other waterways, past and present

noted that DIWE wished to dispose of it to the County Councils. As much of the canal came within the area of a prospective National Park, envisaged by the *Countryside Act* 1949, the prospect of a public trust similar to either the Lower Avon or the Great Ouse proposals, was also mooted.

IWA members were told of these ideas in *Bulletin* No. 28, of July 1951, when it was explained that the provisions of the 1947 Transport Act limited the remit of the DIWE to the cargo-carrying possibilities of the waterways, and did not offer any authority or resources for a wider policy of renewal and development on the waterways it controlled. It was suggested that the only way to overcome this lack of legal authority was to develop public awareness of the problem so that criticism and public interest generated could be used as a means of gaining a generally more enlightened official attitude. In developing this theme, members were reminded:

"Our criticism may often provide them with a justification which might otherwise be lacking for adopting a certain policy or taking a certain action which they themselves know to be appropriate but would find difficult to adopt without external (and disinterested) stimulus."

Whilst this overall philosophy was being developed, a critical blow fell to the waterway system of the North-East with the announcement of the closure of Elvington Lock on the River Derwent on the grounds that it was no longer safe. This raised the problem of the loss of a navigable section of the river; local enthusiasts were advised that the navigation could only be revived through a private Bill in Parliament, which would enable tolls to be levied and repairs to be made. Plans to redevelop the navigation thus suffered a further setback. On a more constructive note, the Linton Lock Supporters Club was formed in June 1951 as a means of gaining continuing voluntary support for the maintenance and improvement of this lock for pleasure craft use.

Unlike the Derwent, the southern section of the Stratford-upon-Avon Canal did not have the same legal problems, and during 1951 IWA members tried to commit the DIWE to meet its legal obligations and refill the drained sections so that it could again be used as a through navigation. IWA members saw this as part of a longer-term plan to restore the whole link between Birmingham and the River Severn via Stratford and the River Avon.

During 1951 another link to the Severn, the Kennet and Avon Canal, was falling further into disrepair. When the IWA national organisation came under internal stress, members of the Kennet and Avon Branch decided to form an independent Kennet and Avon Canal

Association as a means of actively pursuing the canal's restoration on a local basis. The KACA thus became the third individual canal restoration body to be formed. Rolt and Hadfield, two of the IWA founding members who had parted company with the Association, gave it their personal support. An inaugural rally was held at Kintbury on 27 October 1951 where Hadfield gave a lecture on the history of the canal.

As the KACA developed, so national changes took place. Parliament was dissolved in September 1951 and in the following election the Conservatives gained control. Churchill again took office as Prime Minister in October 1951 with an election manifesto pledge to undo much of the nationalisation that had taken place. In effect, lack of political support together with the financial stringency of the time, meant that only road transport and the steel industry were seriously scheduled for denationalisation. The inclusion of the former meant that changes necessarily had to be made to the overall role of the BTC, under which the nationalised canals were controlled by the DIWE."

It was within this climate of stringency and change that the tangible success of LANT, in both raising over £4,000 and gaining 450 members to support the restoration efforts in reopening the Lower Avon, have to be viewed. A review of this progress appeared in *Motor Boat and Yachting* for December 1951, when it was also reported that R. Kerr was chairman of the Restoration Operating Committee which was dealing with the day-to-day affairs of the revival scheme.

Whilst LANT was making progress at local level, the IWA was also gaining national support. By the close of 1951 it had over 1,300 members, with a full-time paid general secretary to develop its campaign. This was fortuitous, as in response to a Parliamentary Question in the House of Lords on 12 March 1952 the Secretary of State for Transport indicated that:

"... a number of canals, however, (accounting for approximately one-third of the total mileage transferred to the Commission) were little or not at all used commercially or had already become derelict, and the Commission are satisfied that many are no longer required as a means of transport. It may be decided that some should be abandoned as no longer needed ..."

This clearly indicated that the case for retaining the canals for pleasure craft use was far from being officially accepted, even though the DIWE had published a booklet, *British Waterways,* that sought to encourage pleasure craft on the quieter stretches of the canals.

In May 1952 the Army, in the form of the Royal Engineers, first became involved in a waterway restoration project when they agreed to assist LANT in the restoration of Chadbury Lock on the Lower Avon as part of a training exercise. This not only saved LANT £1,000, but also set a precedent for similar future exercises. The publicity that this action received greatly assisted LANT when they launched an additional public appeal for funds later in that year. It also offered the IWA an added example to quote in publicising the broader potential of the restoration movement.

As work proceeded on the Lower Avon restoration so the IWA, Midlands Branch, began to intensify its campaign to get the southern section of the Stratford Canal reopened. They adopted a two-pronged approach through local publicity and direct overtures to the DIWE. In much the same way, the IWA decided to organise a rally of boats at Brecon to generate local interest in the revival of the Brecon and Abergavenny Canal. Similarly the North-Western Branch of the IWA organised a rally at Llangollen to continue their pressure for the retention and revival of the Welsh Canal for pleasure craft use.

As 1952 progressed, the IWA became aware of a proposal to abandon the Stroudwater Navigation. In view of the significance of the navigation to any possible hope of the revival of the Thames and Severn link, the IWA decided to take what action it could to keep the waterway open. IWA members were told of the plans in August 1952, when an outline of a campaign for the ultimate revival of the Thames and Severn Canal was proposed.

At the same time the IWA also produced a new publication, *Our Case,* that outlined the Association"s strategy for the revival of the inland waterways. Copies were distributed free to members and circulated to interested groups and, more particularly to all MPs, under cover of a personal letter seeking their support. This action was of considerable value to the waterways campaign as Parliament started to consider the draft of the proposed Transport Bill in the autumn of 1952 and the IWA considered the draft Bill had serious deficiencies. To overcome these problems, the IWA started to promote the alternative strategy of an Inland Waterways Commission, being an independent authority able to foster the redevelopment of the waterways. A letter outlining these ideals was published in *The Times* of 18 November 1952.

In the same vein, IWA members were entreated to widen their own vision for the future of the waterways to that of a whole system. To reinforce this ideal Aickman commented: "Parochialism and the short view are without doubt our biggest dangers", and he outlined his own view that Stratford-upon-Avon "... will again become the waterways centre of the Midlands", when he sought members" support for the restoration

of the Southern Stratford Canal in *Bulletin* No. 35, of Christmas 1952.

Parliament considered the draft Transport Bill during November 1952. At the same time the BTC started negotiations with Ripon Corporation to see if they wished to purchase the Ripon Canal. Although the offer was later declined by the corporation, it gave the Ripon Motor Boat Club and the IWA the opportunity to review the future of that waterway. In much the same way as the Ripon Canal was offered for sale, the DIWE started to negotiate with various county and local authorities for the possible transfer of some other canals that no longer served a commercial function. Details of this development appeared in an article in *The Times* of 29 January 1953 when an indication of the full extent of the proposals, covering some 600 miles of canals, was made known. The waterways involved included the Grantham, Ashton and Peak Forest, Cromford, and Lancaster Canals, amongst others, and many of those listed were viewed by the IWA as potential candidates for revival.

Sapperton Tunnel, Thames and Severn Canal

Morse Lock, Chesterfield Canal 1975

Steeled by this new urgency to retain the canals, Aickman presented a paper, *British Inland Waterways Today and Tomorrow,* to the Royal Society of Arts on 18 February 1953. At the meeting slides were shown of the restoration work at Linton Lock and on the Lower Avon together with others depicting the problems that had to be overcome to restore navigation on the Great Ouse. The paper and presentation were widely reported in the national press, including *The Times* of 19 February 1953, and this did much to develop a greater public awareness of the changes that might lie ahead for the waterways if action were not quickly taken.

Such problems were already beginning to loom on the Kennet and Avon Canal, where the DIWE had already been involved in a succession of major repairs and substantial expenditure. A letter from DIWE to the IWA in January 1953 spelt out the details of the problems involved in restoring the waterway, noting:

"The future of the central section of the waterway, including the Devizes Locks, must be reviewed in the light of the financial and physical circumstances. Indications are that the return of this section of the waterway to a good navigable condition would cost a large sum, without promising any prospect of a return on the expenditure involved, and this cannot be contemplated under present conditions."

A similar situation developed on the Chesterfield Canal, where only the lower reaches were available for commercial craft, with the upper reaches being full of weeds and little used because of a blockage in Norwood Tunnel. Here also local interest in the revival of the waterway for commercial use was insufficient to justify the additional heavy expenditure involved in completing the necessary repair work.

To direct IWA members" attention to the various waterways which were derelict, but still had not been officially abandoned by Act of Parliament, a list of those known to the Association was provided as an appendix to the *Bulletin* in February 1953. This did much to develop a further awareness of those canals that readily had restoration potential. In much the same vein, but on a local scale, LANT published a brochure with maps, entitled *Cruising on Shakespeare's Avon,* that showed the potential value of the upper reaches of the river if these too were restored."

This growing conflict of priorities was most effectively highlighted in an article by R. Hill (chairman of DIWE) entitled "The Inland Waterways Industry", which was reprinted in *Motor Boat and Yachting* of July 1953. It noted that over the past five years some seven million pounds had been spent on waterway maintenance. But, that out of the 2,000 miles of State-controlled waterways, some 1,200 miles carried 98 per cent of the commercial traffic.

On the remaining 800 miles commercial traffic had ceased and they "... no longer justified the heavy expenditure which would be involved in restoring them". The article also highlighted the growth in pleasure craft usage of canals, noting that 4,000 permits had been issued for 1953, and confirmed "... the recreational value of the canals is increasingly recognised and is to be encouraged." Although the article failed to offer a solution to the lack of funds, it made the public more aware of the problems involved.

These problems were beginning to gain some broader public debate. An example was a conference held by the Oxfordshire Branch of the Council for the Preservation of Rural England to discuss the future of the then little used Oxford Canal. This conference was reported in *The Times* of 15 June 1953 and the report identified the growing public concern.

It was within this climate of growing concern that the Transport Act of 1953 received Royal Assent. The Act returned part of the nationalised road transport industry to private enterprise and actively encouraged competition between various modes of transport, thus again moving away from a unified transport policy. The BTC was substantially weakened with the loss of control of road transport. Within the revised structure, the DIWE was replaced, in October 1953, by a Board of Management, with Hill continuing as its chairman.

In this changing political climate, with the aim of more effectively developing the presentation of its views to Parliament, the IWA started to develop the idea of a committee of Members of Parliament who could act in conjunction with the Association in matters connected with the waterways. IWA members were told of this proposal in August 1953. The development was timely as the 1953 Transport Act stipulated that the BTC should prepare, within 12 months, a scheme for the future administration of its undertakings. It also placed an obligation on the minister concerned to seek comments from interested parties on the resultant BTC proposals. The IWA council realised that they would require all the support they could muster if they were to effectively promote their campaign for the restoration of the waterways. With this in mind, public support was sought in various articles entitled, "Threat to Inland Waterways", one of which appeared in *The Daily Telegraph* of 6 August 1953. These articles, combined with the reports of the reopening of Chadbury Lock on the Lower Avon, such as that in *The Times* of 3 August 1953, created a greater public awareness of the leisure potential of the restored waterways.

At the same time a rally of boats at Macclesfield in August 1953 was organised by the IWA. This drew attention to the amenity potential of the waterways of the North-West, particularly the Ashton and Peak Forest Canals. In East Anglia, A. Walker, the secretary of the Dilham Canal Company, who was an IWA member, started to restore part of the North Walsham and Dilham Canal to show what could be achieved. Similarly in the Midlands the formation of an active Stratford Canal Club encouraged the fullest use of that canal. Whilst in North Wales the formation of a committee at Llangollen, to campaign for the retention and development of the Llangollen Canal, defined the further growth of local interest. In much the same way the KACA sent a deputation to meet the Transport Commission on 30 November 1953, seeking the restoration of the Reading to Newbury section of their canal.

At the national level, however, the same promise of a future role for all the waterways was not offered by the 1953 BTC *Annual Report*. It noted that although a few waterways were profitable, the maintenance of the remainder of the network created an overall deficit of £83,000. The report concluded:

"It becomes increasingly clear that the solution of this major problem requires more effective powers under new general legislation, specifically designed to deal with this highly complicated question."

Early in 1954 press reports of the potential closure of the Forth and Clyde Canal highlighted the extreme vulnerability of many of the country's remaining working waterways. It was this fear that prompted several of the canal pleasure-craft operators, who were by then offering some 75,000 people canal holidays each year, to join forces to form the Association of Pleasure Craft Operators on Inland Waterways (APCO), to protect their longer-term interests.

A degree of interest in the inland waterways was also developing in the House of Commons. This was shown on 23 February 1954, whilst the House was debating the ETC annual Bill, when speakers in the debate expressed their interest in the further development of the canals.

H. Molson, in summing up, noted:

"I am glad that so many honourable Members should have referred to the importance of the canals and I can give the House an assurance that the sense of the House will be strongly represented to the Transport Commission."

During a debate on transport freight charges in the House of Commons on 17 March 1954, the Minister of Transport announced that the BTC would be conducting a survey into the canal situation. The, terms of reference were, to inquire into the current use of the Commission's waterways, and in particular, whether steps were being taken to maximise all possible economic advantage from the canal system under the Commission's control.

On hearing that the BTC had agreed to conduct a survey of the canal network, the National Parks Commission offered its views on the possible amenity value of the canals, urging that they be kept open for their recreational potential. In particular they indicated that the Peak Forest, Basingstoke, Stratford and Stroudwater Canals were noted for their beauty and amenity value.

These views were timely, for as they were received the BTC Board of Survey, chaired by Lord Rusholme, set about its task. *Motor Boat and Yachting* of May 1954 gave details of the Board's work and noted that they had also been charged with making proposals for those sections of the waterways that had no commercial future. At this time Hadfield was in the process of writing his third book, *Introducing Canals*. Within the opening chapter he put forward his own thesis for the future of the waterways, after discussing it with the various interested parties. In essence he proposed that:

"(I) Certain commercial routes should be guaranteed for development and that they should be adequately maintained in the longer term; (2) Government should actively promote the use of the designated routes by subsidies or similar support and (3) those waterways not in the commercial category should be treated separately and either be taken over by private companies for pleasure development, or maintained by one trust, or a series of trusts like LANT. To finance this latter group he suggested that local authority subscriptions, central grants in aid, and contributions from volunteers would meet the deficit between minimal maintenance costs and pleasure craft and other revenue."

As these ideas were being propounded, the IWA was carrying its own lobby further, and was finally instrumental in the creation of an All-Party Parliamentary Inland Waterways Committee in the House of Commons on 17 June 1954 IWA members were told of this development in July 1954, when they were again warned of the proposed abandonment of the Stroudwater Navigation under a Bill being considered by Parliament at that time. In an effort to preserve the canal, the IWA created a local committee, in Stroud, to generate support for the waterway to be restored. At the same time some MPs who had expressed an interest in the waterways were offered honorary membership of the Association so that they could be kept in touch with all developments through the IWA publications and *Bulletin*.

With the same aim in mind, the IWA prepared a memorandum for the Somerset County Council, setting out its strategy for the restoration of the Bridgwater and Taunton Canal as an integral part of the Somerset Development Plan. This was circulated to all members of the County Council. To further activate local support to promote this scheme an IWA, West of England Committee, was formed in July 1954.

On 17 August 1954 a deputation from the IWA gave evidence to the Board of Survey, chaired by Rusholme, but the deputation left the meeting, ... "convinced ... that the Board is prevented from doing anything of fundamental use by its terms of reference." To provide the Board of Survey with some more factual information, members of the IWA agreed to prepare reports on some of the problem waterways. Surveys were conducted on the Erewash, Dearne and Dove, and Chesterfield Canals by one group, and on the Bridgwater and Taunton, and Oxford Canals by another. Copies of the reports were then sent to the review body.

By the close of 1954 some practical progress was being made towards the ultimate restoration of the Great Ouse. The River Board announced that it was going to restore Bedford Town Lock and also Cardington Lock as part of a flood control programme, and that the navigation equipment would be restored if the Great Ouse Restoration Society met one-fifth of the total overall costs.

In much the same way progress was being made on the Lower Avon with various charitable trusts making substantial contributions to LANT. Wyre Lock was reopened on 12 September 1954 and work had started on restoring Pershore Lock at the close of the year. A LANT, Upper Avon Committee, had also been founded when the Severn River Board had indicated that it proposed to clear some sections of the upper river over the next few years. All of these events were well publicised and set an example of the persistence of the voluntary organisations in achieving their aims.

By that time the Chelmsford Boat Club had also started its campaign to revive interest in the River Stour. A group of canoeists from the club traversed the lower reaches of the river on 17 October 1954 with the aim of stimulating support for a Stour Preservation Committee.

With the prospect of the BTC Board of Survey Report being published in 1955, the IWA decided to interest as many people as it could in the restoration of the waterways. It thus took a stand at the first National Boat Exhibition, held at Olympia in January 1955, to publicise its aims. At much the same time the BTC announced its own reorganisation under which the management of the docks were to be separated from that of the inland waterways. This proposal stemmed from the then confidential Board of Survey Report that had been submitted to the BTC in November 1954. The BTC immediately accepted all of its suggestions and put the report forward for ministerial agreement.

On 1 January 1955 a new Inland Waterways Board of Management was appointed and Kerr, former chairman of the LANT Operating committee, was appointed its chairman and general manager. The timing of this appointment was propitious for the Board of Survey had just published an interim report that had recommended the Kennet and Avon Canal should be abandoned. As Kerr understood the value of volunteer help he seemed a likely mediator between the Board of Survey proposals and the opposing view of the IWA and KACA, who had by then affiliated to resist any abandonment proposals.

The final version of the Board of Survey Report, *Canals and Inland Waterways,* was published in April 1955 and the BTC indicated it had decided to adopt the ideas put forward. The report suggested that the canals should be divided into three groups:

"Group I. (336 miles) To be developed. This comprised the principal navigable rivers, i.e., Severn, Trent, Lee and Weaver and the heavily used system based on the Aire and Calder, and also the southern portion of the Grand Union Canal. The report suggested these waterways should be improved.

Group II. (994 miles) To be retained. This comprised mainly the narrow canals that still retained some traffic and included some wide canals such as the Leeds and Liverpool Canal. The report suggested that further traffic on these canals should be encouraged, but if this did not occur then the canals should be downgraded to Group III.

Group III. (771 miles) For disposal. This comprised those canals that carried insufficient commercial traffic to justify their retention, but also included some 250 miles of canal already abandoned, mainly under the 1944 LM5 General Powers Act. Within this group were many canals popular for pleasure cruising including the Llangollen, the Kennet and Avon, the Southern Oxford, the Forth and Clyde, the Ashton and Peak Forest, Macclesfield and Lancaster Canals."

For the canals of Group III the report suggested they should be transferred to other bodies more appropriate than the BTC. It also suggested the Scottish Canals should be transferred to the Secretary of State for Scotland. The publication of the report created an immediate controversy, with the IWA taking the lead by opening a Fighting Fund Appeal for £25,000, "to campaign against the closure of the canals." The *Manchester Guardian* of 13 April 1955 commented that it was far from certain that the proposed disposals would lead to economies and went as far as to suggest that it would probably be better to spend the money on restoring rather than destroying the heritage. An editorial, in *Motor Boat and Yachting* for May 1955, suggested that readers:

"... use what influence they can to ensure that when the Bill comes before Parliament, there will be sufficient informed opinion ... to prevent the waterways system being virtually destroyed."

At the time this particular debate was developing, a general election was also being held. The IWA produced a *Circular to Parliamentary Candidates* detailing its aims for the restoration of the canals and the need for an independent inquiry to review the prospect of establishing a National Waterways Conservancy. This circular gained a substantial response, with much support for the proposals.

The Conservative Party gained an increased majority at the election and set forward with renewed vigour in the continued development of "the affluent society." This created a mood of growing prosperity in the country and provoked sympathetic remarks in the press about the canals, such as one by Cassandra in the *Daily Mirror* of 26 July 1955, that:

"... most of these waterways can, if enough imagination and capital is pumped into them, be revived again ... What we cannot afford is dreary accountants running England by selling a lovely heritage."

These set a formal lead for public reaction to follow. To further develop this public interest and to lodge local protests about the potential abandonment of some canals, the IWA organised a series of protest meetings in major centres, such as Manchester, Banbury, Lancaster and Newbury, during the summer of 1955. The meeting in Lancaster was particularly successful and, as the result of an associated rally of boats, the Lancaster Canal Boat Club was formed.

At a separate public inquiry in Wrexham to consider water abstraction from the River Dee, it was learnt that the Welsh section of the Shropshire Union Canal could well be restored as the result of the development of a water transfer scheme. This provided added weight to the IWA case for the multifunctional utilization of the canals.

Another similar development, that was later to have great significance to the waterway restoration movement, stemmed from an article by Michael Rix in the autumn 1955 edition of *The Amateur Historian.*

Llangollen Canal restoration

In it he detailed the need to preserve the heritage of the industrial revolution including "locks and canals". This set the lead for the development of support for a new theme, that of industrial archaeology, which rapidly gained a considerable following.

Perhaps the most significant strategic move was made when a petition was presented in the Chancery Division by Gould of Newbury for an injunction to restrain the BTC from causing any further deterioration of certain sections of the Kennet and Avon Canal. This, in conjunction with a protest meeting organised by the KACA at Devizes on 6 July 1955, did much to harden local opinion in support of retaining the canal.

As the result of growing public pressure to retain the waterways, the National Association of Parish Councils issued invitations, over the names of four MPs, to a meeting in the House of Commons to demand an independent public inquiry into the whole subject. Some 180 people, including 60 MPs and peers, attended the meeting on 23 November 1955, and heard C. Arnold-Baker and Aickman outline the case for an impartial inquiry into the best method of administering the national system of navigable waterways so as to retain, restore and develop them for both commercial and recreational purposes. The meeting concluded with a resolution supporting this proposal, which was carried without dissent.

With this growing pressure for an independent inquiry into the future of the waterways, the most critical gauge of official response rested on the publication of the draft of the annual BTC Bill, for it was within such a draft that any proposal to transfer or abandon the Group III waterways, as envisaged in the Survey Report, would have to be projected. The Bill was published on 28 November 1955 and only included proposals for the abandonment of two derelict canals, the Nottingham and Walsall, together with a request to restrict the Commission"s legal obligations to maintain the Kennet and Avon Canal as a navigation. The IWA saw this as a victory for their campaign and considered it as the turning point for the revival of the waterways.

Another important feature for this change in official approach was the attitude adopted by Kerr in managing the waterways. He personally completed an inspection cruise of 800 miles of the waterways during 1955 and actively campaigned within the BTC for funds to modernise the commercial waterways. This interest was rewarded in early 1956 when the BTC announced it hoped to spend five-and-a-half million pounds in the following five years on the development of Group I commercial waterways. At much the same time the Inland Waterways Board started its own publication, *Waterways*, in which the ideas of the new management arrangements were projected.

As the national outlook appeared brighter, so the problems of some individual waterways grew. In order of impact the first was the case of the southern Stratford Canal, where a bridge over the canal at Wilmcote needed renewal and local fears were expressed that the County Council might replace the bridge by an embankment. To prevent this taking place a Canal Protection Committee was established. The second was that of the Kennet and Avon Canal, where some sections had been drained to prevent leakage. In an effort to resolve this difficulty officers from LANT prepared a report on the state of the canal for KACA and offered suggestions as to the way in which it could be economically repaired. A third was the Dearne and Dove Canal where plans were afoot to culvert a bridge at Aldham and thus effectively block the canal. A fourth was the growing dereliction of the Derby Canal. To combat this a local committee was formed to seek the restoration of the waterway. A fifth was the Driffield Navigation, on which the upper three locks were inoperable. A sixth was the Coventry Arm of the Coventry Canal which had been designated as part of the route of the town's new inner ring road. The particular problems of all of these waterways were outlined to IWA members in the *Bulletin* of January 1956 and it was suggested that more active steps should be taken to promote their revival.

Perhaps the most spectacular of these steps was the campaign that evolved to fight for the retention of the Kennet and Avon Canal. A petition to the Queen was organised by the KACA, who secured more than 22,000 signatures. The petition, bound in two volumes, was then carried by boat and canoe from Bristol to London. Once in London the petition was carried in procession to the Ministry of Transport where it was presented on 26 January 1956. The press, film, radio and television coverage of the event was extensive and it made a considerable political impact.

On 1 February 1956 the Minister of Transport announced the setting up of an independent inquiry into the future of the inland waterways. The chairman was L. Bowes and the terms of reference were:

"to consider and report on the future of the country's system of inland waterways and to consider the present law relating to closing waterways to navigation."

Whilst the Bowes Committee were conducting their inquiries, the BTC Bill to abandon the Kennet and Avon Canal came before the House of Commons. After an extensive debate, on 13 March 1956, it was agreed that the proposal should be deleted from the Bill. As the result of this pressure the BTC agreed that the waterway should not be allowed to deteriorate any further whilst its future was reviewed. This action and subsequent rallies organised by the KACA developed further public support for the retention of that canal and other waterways.

Easter Monday 1956 saw the reopening of Bedford Town Lock on the Great Ouse. The work of the local restoration society gained a boost from this and a further appeal for funds to reopen Cardington Lock was launched. In much the same way publicity of the work of LANT, in opening the Lower Avon, was able to develop further support for other restoration schemes.

In the West Country, a commitment by the Somerset River Board and the Bridgwater RDC, that the Bridgwater and Taunton Canal should be kept navigable, enabled local IWA members to organise boat trips along parts of the canal. This added some further local support for the development of the waterways of the area. It was thus significant that when the four riparian parish councils covering the adjacent Grand Western Canal were asked for their views on the future of that waterway, three indicated their support for its retention and development.

Kerr too added his own encouragement for the greater use of the canals by inaugurating a small fleet of pleasure craft to be run by the Waterways Board for the 1956 cruising season. He also welcomed other private fleet operators who were introducing hire-craft to the canals. To further develop public interest he initiated a series of Inland Cruising Guides, the first of which was *The Llangollen Canal*.

By mid 1956 Aickman was able to report, at the IWA AGM:

"Public and official opinion is at last becoming convinced, on a big scale, of the importance of retaining and redeveloping the nation's rivers and canals."

To develop this theme the IWA and other waterway organisations prepared submissions for presentation to the Bowes Committee. These were completed during late 1956 and early 1957. At the same time as the IWA submission was prepared, its consulting engineer, C. Boucher, was preparing reports on the potential of restoring both the Stratford and Chesterfield Canals. These reports were passed to the local IWA branches so that they could actively promote local restoration campaigns.

The IWA officers made an oral submission to the Bowes Committee on 9 March 1957, after which the Association delegation held a press conference to make their views more widely known. In much the same vein, a conference was called to promote a public campaign of protest against the closure of the Dearne and Dove Canal. A meeting was held at Swinton on 13 March 1957 and the case for restoring the waterway was detailed. In both instances substantial press coverage was obtained detailing the case for restoration.

Later in 1957 two other events also did much to draw public attention to the development potential of the inland waterways. These were somewhat enhanced by the threat of fuel rationing due to the Suez crisis. The first was the IWA rally of boats held at Coventry in August 1957. This convinced many residents of Coventry, and more particularly the Mayor, Pearl Hyde, of the future potential of the Coventry Canal. It also provided the momentum to both inaugurate a local canal society and to fight the threat of the obliteration of the canal by a proposed ring road. In addition it gave D. Hutchings, a local IWA member, the chance to develop his organising skills in the promotion of the revival of the waterways. A second event was "Operation Flyboat" organised over 48 hours commencing on 4 October 1957. The aim was to prove that a boat could cover the journey from Birmingham to London within this timespan. The journey was finally completed in under 42 hours by L. Munk and gained much publicity for the IWA. To capitalise on this growing interest in the waterways, Kerr inaugurated the "Heart of England" boat trips for tourists on the Oxford Canal, getting further trade for the canals.

There were two other developments in 1957 that did not gain similar publicity, but later proved to be vital to the overall restoration campaign. The first was a canoe voyage through the southern section of the Stratford Canal, that took place during February 1957. The toll tickets for the voyage were later used as evidence to assure the future of the canal. In the autumn of 1957 the Stratford-upon-Avon Canal Society was formed to seek the restoration of the waterway.

The second was a reorganisation within the IWA caused by both the illness of the general secretary, the temporary incapacity of Aickman, as well as the desire to form the association into a limited liability company to protect the membership. The break in leadership from the central organisation ultimately led to the loss of the IWA Fenlands and North Eastern Branches. Some members of the former founded the East Anglian Waterways Association in April 1958, whilst some of the latter founded the Northern Waterways Association at much the same time. The strains within the IWA, and the debate over limited liability, did much to influence some members to develop the waterways restoration campaign in other ways. One group, led by Mrs B. Bunker, subsequently founded the Inland Waterways Protection Society. All of these changes were later to have a significant effect on the way in which the restoration movement developed and prospered.

The month of January 1958 saw the organisation of a scheme in Coventry, masterminded by Hutchings, for the restoration of the derelict Wyken Arm of the Oxford Canal. This ultimately gained the support of the City Council and provided Hutchings with his first practical experience of canal restoration work.

In early 1958 the Finance and General Purposes Committee of the National Trust, led by J. Smith, passed a resolution declaring the Trust's interest in the preservation of British inland waterways and its willingness to act as a holding body for them. This decision was announced at a public meeting in Stratford Town Hall on 26 April 1958 convened by the IWA and the Stratford Canal Society to make a public protest about the potential closure of the Stratford Canal. The meeting was reported in *The Times* of 28 April 1958 and gained considerable public support for the idea of restoring the waterway.

It was, however, the support of the National Trust that later proved to be the vital element of the restoration scheme that evolved.

By early 1958 the Bowes Committee had finished its work. *The Report of the Committee of Inquiry into Inland Waterways* (Cmnd 486) was published in July 1958. It developed the initial recommendations of the 1954 Board of Survey and grouped the waterways to be retained into two classes: Class A and Class B, that were similar to the Board of Survey's Group I and Group II with minor exceptions. The committee recommended these canals should be put into good working order and maintained to defined standards for not less than 25 years as a prescribed navigable system. It also recommended financial relief, in the form of Government support, for the Class B waterways to meet the cost of reinstatement. For the remaining canals of the country, independent as well as nationalised, the committee proposed a Waterways Redevelopment Board which should prepare, or secure the preparation of, schemes to redevelop them for purposes not primarily concerned with navigation, or to eliminate them.

The strategy adopted in the report in some way met the protestors' points that had originally generated the demand for the inquiry. The report, however, came at a time when the Government was fighting a growing balance-of-payments problem which ultimately led to the 1959 credit squeeze. It thus placed the Government with a dilemma to resolve: there was pressure for action on one hand, and constraint caused by lack of Government financial resources on the other. Because of the magnitude of the other national problems this dilemma was not resolved during 1958.

Concerned by growing fears about the destruction of the waterways system, the Inland Waterways Protection Society (IWPS) was formed by East Midlands canal enthusiasts on 21 April 1958. Its members were thus ready to take action when the Bowes Committee report was published in July 1958. As part of its strategy, IWPS members started the lengthy task of visiting and reviewing all those waterways that came within Group C of the report. They did this with the aim of making reports on the waterways should the need arise. Such surveys were undertaken on the Stratford, Dearne and Dove and Chesterfield Canals in 1958, and on the Pocklington, Macclesfield and Peak Forest Canals in early 1959–58 Surveys of the various other waterways were subsequently undertaken and reports prepared. With much the same aim, local enthusiasts formed the Staffordshire and Worcestershire Canal Society in February 1959 to protect their local canal, which was also subject to review.

Notwithstanding these other developments, at the close of 1958, by far the greatest public commitment was being gained by the campaign to have the southern section of the Stratford Canal reopened. A second public meeting on this subject was held in October 1958; a petition and protests over the state of the canal were subsequently sent to Warwickshire County Council.

In February 1959 the Government published a white paper (Cmnd 676), *Government Proposals following the Report of the Committee of Inquiry into Inland Waterways,* which indicated that many of the recommendations of the Bowes Committee would require complicated legislation. It put forward the suggestion that some of the report's proposals should be developed experimentally for an interim period of two years, during which time the BTC would be committed to maintain the waterways concerned in Class B, in their then present operational condition. To facilitate the redevelopment of the Class C waterways, the white paper also announced a commitment to create an Inland Waterways Redevelopment Advisory Committee (IWRAC), to assist in the promotion of schemes, and make recommendations, for the redevelopment of those waterways which could no longer be economically maintained for commercial transport.

IWRAC was appointed in April 1959 under the chairmanship of F. Parham, and the membership included Rolt and Munk, to represent user interests. The Government indicated to IWRAC that it would expect that the cost of any redevelopment proposals should be borne by those who would benefit from them, and gave a commitment that any future legislation would be developed with this in mind. It also drew attention to the possibility of grants under existing legislation which could assist such schemes and offered, in principle, to bridge a small gap in the funds required by a special *ad hoc* grant towards the capital cost of redevelopment. The white paper concluded:

"The report opens up a prospect of fresh action on the canals and it is the Government"s aim in initiating these proposals to make it possible for all those concerned to make a start in a new atmosphere ... Local authorities, amongst others, are asked to consider the part they can play. Canals can be redeveloped for amenity and recreation.... It is also important that voluntary organisations ... should take the opportunities for joint effort."

Stourbridge Arm

Restored Peak Forest Canal

The white paper also confirmed that the National Trust were already engaged in exploratory talks with the BTC with a view to taking over and preserving for the nation some lengths of waterways, and it commended this action. This was fortuitous, as in May 1959 an application for the abandonment of the southern section of the Stratford Canal, made by Warwickshire County Council, had been refused by the Ministry of Transport. The refusal was based on the grounds that the canal had been navigated within the past three years and the toll tickets issued to a canoe in 1957 provided the necessary proof. The refusal paved the way for the further development of plans made by the Stratford-upon-Avon Canal Society in conjunction with the National Trust to restore the canal by using volunteer labour.

The month of May 1959 also saw a further development in the campaign to retain the Chesterfield Canal with a protest cruise organised by the IWPS. In much the same way, in June 1959 the IWPS submitted a detailed case for the restoration of the Pocklington Canal to IWRAC, who were in the process of considering a request for the abandonment and in-filling of the canal. In August 1959 the iwis put forward similar schemes for the revival of various canals in the Birmingham area, including the Dudley and Stourbridge Canals and the Titford Branch Canal. IWPS members also started a campaign for the retention of the upper reaches of the Cromford Canal and the unique Leawood Pump.

At about the same time interest in reviving the Driffield Navigation began to develop with the announcement of a plan, by Hull Corporation, to use the canal for water supply purposes. The North-Eastern Branch of the IWA calculated that it would only cost an additional £17,000 to restore the waterway to navigation and began a local campaign to convince the corporation that the additional cost would be justified.

In the same way, on Munk's advice, the KACA began to prepare a detailed costing for the restoration of the Kennet and Avon Canal for submission to IWRAC to promote further local interest in the waterway, volunteers started to repair some of the locks at the eastern end, with the view to allowing a trip boat to use that section of the canal.

The general election of October 1959 cleared the political arena for a more formal debate on the Bowes Report. This took place in the House of Commons on 4 December 1959, and concluded with a motion welcoming the *Bowes Report* and the subsequent white paper (Cmnd 676) and calling for an urgent announcement of further decisions about the future of the inland waterways. By the close of 1959 some further action to assist in the redevelopment of the waterways seemed likely and the substantial progress made by LANT in restoring the Lower Avon, by the use of public subscription and volunteer labour, gave a firm pointer of a possible way to success.

The advent of 1960 was heralded by the growing fears of the waterways enthusiasts that some of the Bowes Class B waterways were continuing to fall into disrepair. In particular, the IWA turned its attention to the Stourbridge Canal, where the 16 locks at Wordsley had been closed whilst repairs were undertaken to an over-bridge. After an abortive voyage during November, two craft finally navigated the canal before the close of 1959.

The IWPS members continued their campaign for the restoration of the Chesterfield and Dearne and Dove Canals, with a further protest cruise on 30 April 1960 on the former, and the submission to IWRAC of a scheme for a new Leeds to London Direct Route Canal that involved sections of both canals on 7 April 1960. During the winter of 1959–60 members of the IWPS completed a tour of inspection of the Ashton Canal, and on 24 February 1960 commenced an inspection of the Peak Forest Canal and Buxworth Basin. These surveys, together with a review of the Caldon Canal, provided the basis for later reports to the IWRAC detailing the ways in which these waterways might be successfully and economically restored.

On 10 March 1960, the Prime Minister announced that he proposed to set up a committee to advise on the future administration of the national transport network, and in particular the railways. A further announcement on 6 April indicated that I. Stedeford would be the chairman of the advisory body.

At the same time the Stedeford Committee began its deliberations, the BTC was completing final negotiations to lease the southern section of the Stratford Canal to the National Trust. The BTC Act 1960 incorporated the provision for the lease to be transacted, and on 29 September 1960 the National Trust formally took over the canal on a five-year lease. The cost of restoring the canal was estimated at £37,500 and, under the provision for a small ad hoc grant, the Government agreed to provide £20,000 towards the work. The BTC, to commute its own commitments towards the canal, agreed to provide £7,500, over the five-year period of the lease, plus free water supplies, and the Pilgrim Trust offered a grant of £10,000 to finance the work. For its part, the IWA agreed to find the balance of the restoration costs through public subscription and to organise volunteer labour to complete the restoration work. Hutchings was appointed project manager on behalf of the Trust and the work on restoring the canal began. This was the first full-scale restoration of a derelict narrow canal and

provided a significant step forward for the restoration movement.

The BTC Act 1960 did not treat the future of the Kennet and Avon Canal so favourably and only provided for the continuance of the constraints on the canal. The KACA was thus forced to continue its campaign for the revival of the waterway.

The IWA held its annual rally of boats at Stoke-on-Trent in August 1960. One of the aims of the rally was to stimulate a revival of interest in the little-used Caldon Canal. To follow up this interest, a further voyage along the canal was organised in November 1960 by local IWA members and other boat-owners were also commended to use the waterway.

In December 1960 the government produced a white paper (Cmnd 1248) detailing the findings of the Stedeford Committee. The review, entitled *Reorganisation of Nationalised Transport Undertakings,* proposed that sweeping changes were needed to the control and structure of the undertakings administered by the BTC. It suggested that the size and difficulties of British Railways had preoccupied the Commission and had affected its outlook over the whole range of its activities. It stated, in relation to Inland Waterways:

"British Transport Waterways will be placed under an independent statutory board. This board will own and manage the nationalised inland waterway system. The composition, powers and duties of the new body will require further discussion. It will be necessary to take into account, on one hand, of the charge which the waterways system imposes on public funds, and, on the other, of the varied purposes which they can be made to serve."

Additionally, within the financial section of the white paper, it indicated:

"Special aid may, however, have to be given in the initial years to the Inland Waterways Authority."

The year 1960 thus closed with a renewed hope for the development of the waterway restoration movement. Over the period 1951 to 1960 quite radical changes in both public opinion and government approach to waterway revival had taken place. During the same period the number of pleasure craft licences for the waterways had similarly increased, from 1,500 in 1951 to 8,342 in 1960; and the hire-craft industry was beginning to offer a wide range of waterways holidays, which brought many more people in contact with the canals for the first time.

Map 3 shows the way in which the restoration movement had also begun to spread its net. Plans for

Stratford Canal sign and basin

Trent and Mersey Canal, Harecastle Tunnel

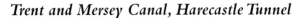

the revival of the Brecon and Abergavenny Canal were made in 1951 and in 1952 the plight of the derelict Southern Stratford Canal equally began to be noticed. The takeover of this canal by the National Trust in 1960 was perhaps the most significant step forward during the whole decade. 1953 saw the proprietors of the Dilham Canal starting their own restoration work, whilst the prospect of the transfer of the Ripon Canal to Ripon Corporation added another restoration scheme to those that had already been promoted.

In the same year the IWA West Country Branch was formed to promote the restoration of the Bridgwater and Taunton Canal; in the Midlands, the continuing decay of the Derby Canal prompted a local group of enthusiasts, with IWA support, to seek the restoration of that canal in 1956. Also in 1956 the threat of closure to the Coventry Canal Basin, by a projected ring-road plan, led to a local campaign to protect and revive that canal. The formation of the Coventry Canal Society in 1957, to fight the battle, led to a proposal to restore the derelict Wyken Arm of the Oxford Canal in early 1958.

In the same year the potential closure of the Dearne and Dove Canal led to an intensification of the local campaign to save and restore that canal. The practical approach adopted by the IWPS on the Dearne and Dove Canal equally spread to the Chesterfield and Cromford Canals in 1959 as similar schemes for their restoration were promoted. These were in contrast to Hull Corporation"s water-supply scheme which led the IWA to campaign for the restoration of the Driffield Navigation in 1959. In much the same way the

Ashton and Peak Forest Canals, and Buxworth Basin, were similarly singled out for restoration proposals. In this instance the IWPS started to prepare restoration proposals for submission to IWRAC. Whilst the Caldon Canal, and its Leek Branch, were the centre of IWA revival interests when a rally of boats was held at Stoke-on-Trent in August 1960.

During the decade, restructuring of the IWA in both 1951 and 1957–58 led to the development of various additional local and national restoration groups. Each in their own way added to the momentum of the restoration movement. Perhaps the greatest single impact was made by the KACA in their fight to have the Kennet and Avon Canal restored. This continued a battle started by the IWA in 1946, but even by 1960 little tangible progress had been made, except that the hardening of public attitudes in support of the revival of the Kennet and Avon Canal had done much to influence the political masters, as had the rapid escalation of the IWA national campaign. Even so by the end of 1960 the future of the inland waterways had still not been adequately resolved, but the foundations of the restoration movement had been firmly established and practical examples of progress were becoming clearly visible in various parts of the country. In this way the credibility of the volunteer worker was being firmly established as a force to be considered in future developments.

Stratford Canal,
Lock 55
under restoration

IV 1961-64:

FIRST MAJOR "REOPENINGS"

The closing months of 1960 and the advent of 1961 saw Britain, as a nation, undergoing further political and social change. The national debate over EEC membership was beginning to develop and the "pop" cult from America was already making its impact felt. Britain had become a nation of growing personal affluence with teenagers benefiting most from the new-found wealth. The image of the 1960s was that of a vigorous, growing nation, with a high proportion of young people. These young people were willing to respond to the novel stimulus that the idea of canal restoration offered.

The Stratford Canal restoration project led by Hutchings, a young architect and a man of considerable personal drive, offered the possibility of tangible rewards for part-time efforts which for many gave the opportunity they were seeking. Amid considerable publicity Hutchings was able to plan the restoration project over a sufficiently short period for the volunteer helpers to see quickly the cumulative results of their labours. This impetus at local level, coupled with the national possibility of a new independent statutory board, to be known as the Inland Waterways Authority, proposed in a Government white paper published at the close of 1960, offered a bright new prospect for waterways enthusiasts in 1961.

With this apparently bright future ahead, the IWA were still much concerned that the initial impetus might be lost by the potential disputes that were likely to arise over the future of those waterways that were no longer needed for transport use. A letter by Aickman in *The Times* of 2 January 1961 outlined these fears, and they were more critically detailed to IWA members in the *Bulletin* for January 1961.

Concern about the future of the redundant waterways was best exemplified in a debate that had developed during 1960 over the potential closure of the Dudley Tunnel. This particular dispute was brought to a head on 23 October 1960 when the IWA, Midlands Branch, organised a protest cruise through the tunnel after a road convoy of trailed boats had toured the Black Country. This provided a local show of strength, with members of the Coventry Canal Society and the Staffordshire and Worcestershire Canal Society adding their weight to the fight to retain the canal. The event was covered by television news and reports of the protest cruise appeared in the press throughout the country, including *The Times*. This did much to draw public attention to the value of the potentially redundant canals, as part of the heritage, and added support to the case being projected by the IWA for their revival.

As one battle to retain and revive a canal achieved success so another loomed on the horizon. *The Daily Telegraph* of 18 January 1961 reported that a conference of representatives of five local authorities in the Manchester area had decided to recommend closure of the Ashton Canal between Ashton-under-Lyne and Manchester. The reason stated to support the closure indicated that the canal was no longer commercially used and that since 1943 some 15 children had been drowned in the canal. IWA members were warned of this proposal in January 1961, when it was suggested that local members should take a boat through the threatened waterway to prove that it was still used. Aickman realised:

"It is emotion, as already observed, that rules the day; and that people are willing to go to so much trouble, generates sympathetic emotion – quite rightly."

He noted that "every boat will surely tell, and that nothing else tells as surely", concluding:

"The case of the Ashton Canal is the very essence and epitome of our case for all the waterways. On the Ashton Canal, everything is at stake."

This statement positively defined the stance then being adopted by those who supported the idea of waterway restoration.

The use of the gambit of a campaign cruise, which expressed the legal public right of navigation, was particularly developed to strengthen local public support for the retention of the lesser-used waterways. It was with this aim in mind that the IWA organised a rally of boats at Aylesbury, on a little-used arm of the Grand Union Canal, in August 1961. As the result a local boat club was formed to protect the canal.

The IWA also tried to develop similar interest in the amenity potential of the adjacent Buckingham Arm of the Grand Union Canal, but lack of local members, plus the fact that the canal wandered through the rural Upper Ouse valley, did not help the project. The case for revival was equally not assisted by the attitudes of the local authorities of the area who supported its closure. This attitude was in contrast to the stance adopted by the local authorities of the Tiverton area, where the

Map 4

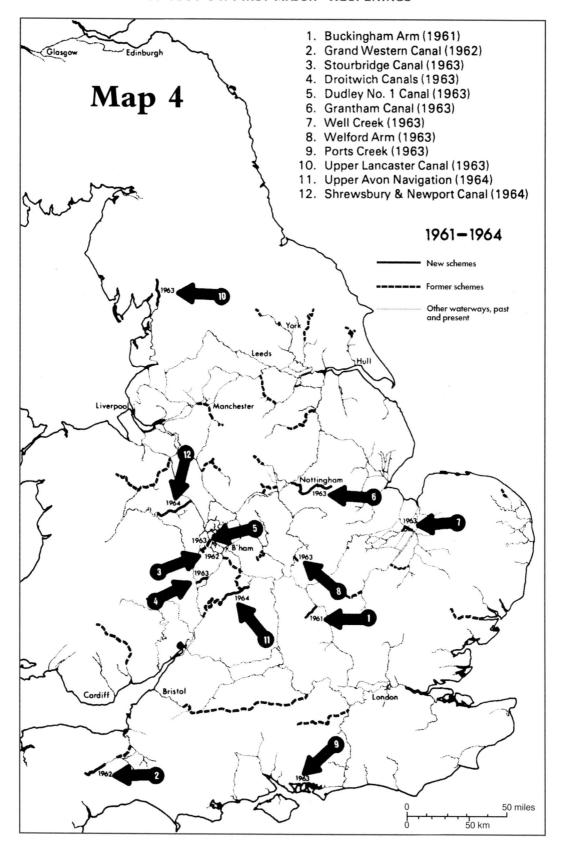

1. Buckingham Arm (1961)
2. Grand Western Canal (1962)
3. Stourbridge Canal (1963)
4. Droitwich Canals (1963)
5. Dudley No. 1 Canal (1963)
6. Grantham Canal (1963)
7. Well Creek (1963)
8. Welford Arm (1963)
9. Ports Creek (1963)
10. Upper Lancaster Canal (1963)
11. Upper Avon Navigation (1964)
12. Shrewsbury & Newport Canal (1964)

1961–1964

—— New schemes

----- Former schemes

········ Other waterways, past and present

case for redeveloping the Grand Western Canal for agricultural purposes was firmly rejected by Tiverton Council, who indicated they wished it to be retained as a local amenity.

On the brighter side, the future of the Brecon and Abergavenny Canal, which had been in doubt during the early 1950s, seemed more assured in 1961 with the development of a restoration programme by British Waterways in support of the Brecon Beacons National Park. Growing local interest had also stimulated the growth of a canal-cruiser hire base near Abergavenny to service the land-locked waterway. An article in the *Western Mail* of 17 January 1961 outlined the value of the canal, whilst the growing public interest in its amenity value prompted Pontypool Urban District Council to consider the possibility of restoring that part of the interconnected Monmouthshire Canal within the town boundaries for public pleasure use.

The same support for its local canal was not similarly forthcoming from Derby Council, who were quite prepared to see the local canal closed and infilled. Prompted by the growing dereliction of the canal, members of the IWA, Midlands Branch, added their support to the local Derby Canal Restoration Committee"s campaign. The *Derby Evening Telegraph* of 1 February 1961 published a letter from the group calling for the restoration of the waterway. This achieved little impact as the Derby Council declined to offer comment on the proposals that were made. This attitude, however, prompted a series of other letters to the editor debating the future of the canal. To capitalise on this growing interest the IWA organised a protest cruise, along the adjacent Erewash Canal to the entrance lock of the Derby Canal. This was aimed at drawing public attention to the restoration potential of the waterway. This achieved considerable publicity and *The Times* of 1 May 1961 recorded the event. Subsequently a protest meeting was held in Derby on 27 May 1961 at which a call was made for a public inquiry into the best means of rehabilitating the canal for amenity and transport use.

The theme of a protest cruise was also developed to draw local attention to the Ashton Canal, which had been withdrawn from the scope of the national pleasure craft licence during the spring of 1961. On 20 May 1961 a flotilla of boats passed along the Peak Forest Canal and started to traverse the Ashton Canal. The cruise came to an abrupt halt when it was found that one of the lock-gates had been demolished and thrown into the lock chamber. This action by vandals further jeopardised the future of the canal.

In much the same way fears began to grow for the future of the Forth and Clyde Canal. On 6 June 1961 it was announced that, because of the growing problems created in the replacement of canal crossings, "... the Government have decided that the balance of advantage lies in its closure for navigation." IWA members were told of this proposal and it was suggested that a local campaign, similar to that adopted to save the Stratford Canal, should be developed to prevent the closure of the waterway. Unfortunately there were few IWA members in Scotland and the plea did not make much impact. It did, however, give rise to more general public debate over the cost of retaining canals in relation to the larger costs involved in closing them and filling them in. This was outlined in *The Daily Telegraph* of 12 April 1961 and more fully considered in *The Surveyor* of 15 April 1961. The conclusions reached were supported in an article about the IWA in *The Times* of 3 June 1961, which commented:

"Money will have to be spent on canals. Paradoxically, the most expensive course would be to close them down indiscriminately."

The debate over the comparative costs of dealing with canals was particularly relevant to a scheme, prepared by Munk and Glaister of the KACA, for the restoration of the Kennet and Avon Canal. Details of these proposals were published in *The Times* of 18 February 1961. In the preamble to their scheme it was suggested that the cost of the work would bear no relation to the value of the longer-term amenity that the restored waterway could offer. At the instigation of Munk, and to provide a more acceptable body to promote these restoration proposals, the KACA held a meeting in Newbury on 19 June 1961 at which it was agreed that the Association should reform itself into the Kennet and Avon Canal Trust Ltd, a non-profit distributing charitable company.

A similar theme of potential amenity development was projected in respect of the derelict Buckingham Arm of the Grand Union Canal when the *Northampton Chronicle and Echo* of 24 March 1961 published an article calling for the rehabilitation of the first section of the canal to Old Stratford. As the result of this suggestion R. Faulkner, a local IWA member, offered to try to form an action committee to formulate a restoration plan. IWA members were asked for their support for the project in June 1961, but few came forward to assist.

Much the same idea was developed in relation to the Caldon Canal, which had also come under further threat of closure during 1961. In this instance, to rally local support, the Stoke-on-Trent Boat Club organised a cruise along the entire length of the canal, from Stoke-on-Trent to Froghall, in September 1961. It also promoted a public protest meeting in the Victoria Hall, Hanley, on the same day. Both were reported in the

Staffordshire Evening Sentinel, of 8 September 1961, and as the result of the meeting a local petition was organised seeking to retain the canal.

This gained the support of the local authorities and prompted the North Staffordshire Area Youth Organiser, W.G. Myatt, to offer the services of youth club members to prevent the closure of the canal and participate in its revival. It was also proposed that either the National Trust or some specially constituted society should take over the canal to develop it as a local amenity feature.

At much the same time, on the other side of the Pennines, support was being given to the proposal to retain the Cromford Canal by Ripley UDC. They decided to rescind an earlier proposal to close the canal. Instead they supported a suggestion by the Derbyshire County Council, that the future of the canal needed to be further reviewed in relation to its amenity potential." Such attitudes were much enhanced by growing publicity about the work on the Lower Avon and Stratford Canal recovery schemes. These were detailed in an article in *Light Craft,* for September 1961, which stated the schemes:

"... helped to restore a shaken faith in the ability of the British to feel real concern about something and to express that concern in direct action."

The progress was also detailed in an article in *Architectural Review* of August 1961, which related the course of events leading to the developments and offered a progress statement of the work already completed on the projects.

The growing spirit of hope for the revival of the waterways engendered by these schemes was somewhat depressed after the contents of a paper, *The Future of our Inland Waterways,* read on 3 November 1961 to the western section of the Institute of Transport by W. L. Ives, a senior official of British Waterways, became more widely known. The paper highlighted the diverse functions of the waterways and noted the substantial financial deficit that they incurred. In particular it examined the problems of those waterways that had outlived their commercial usefulness and noted, "... the biggest obstacle is the existence of vested rights." It also commented on the support given by the Minister of Transport in the passage of the recent BTC Bill, even "to the extent of putting the Whips on." The paper highlighted the fact that, "no waterway can be closed except under statutory authority", and continued, ".... there is a very strong case for the modification of this procedure... to abandon a canal or close it to traffic." The paper concluded: "At the moment it is not possible to make significant progress because the persons entitled to these rights are reluctant to give them up ... it is essential this position should be altered."

The first official movement in this direction came with the presentation of the annual BTC Bill in November 1961. This proposed, amongst other features, the closure of four waterways which IWRAC had earlier recommended should be kept open. To placate local interests the Minister of Transport offered an assurance that for three of the four sections, the Chesterfield Canal from Stockwith to Worksop, the upper reaches of the Erewash Canal, and the first section of the Buckingham Branch, no changes adverse to navigation would immediately be made. For the fourth, the Dudley Tunnel and Canal, no such assurance was offered, and this canal together with nine other waterways were scheduled for immediate closure action." The IWA and IWPS made formal protests against these proposals, but to no avail.

To reiterate the official attitude, Ernest Marples introduced the draft of the 1962 *Transport Act* in Parliament on 20 November 1961 with the statement: "The canals are not viable in their present form." In a later statement, about the proposed Inland Waterways Authority, he indicated that its duties "may well involve the closure of canals and their conversion or disposal if, thereby, the burden on the tax-payer can be relieved."

Even as the gloom created by these statements began to develop, so a brighter hope appeared on the horizon when it was announced, in early 1962, that the Lower Avon Navigation would be reopened through to Evesham at Whitsun of that year. LANT had, by then, raised some £50,000 from the public to finance the work and plans were already beginning to materialise for the restoration of Evesham Town Lock and, in the longer term, for the upper reaches of the river.

At that time plans were also being made for the reopening of the Stratford Canal as part of the Shakespeare"s Quartercentenary Celebrations planned in 1964. Details of the project and the progress made were publicised at a National Trust demonstration on 29 March 1962 at the Royal Festival Hall. An appeal for more volunteers to assist with the restoration work was made in the *Bulletin* of April 1962, when readers were told: "Not only the Stratford Canal is at stake; but all our waterways: and a whole way of life."

This statement rang true when, as the result of the publication of further BTC abandonment proposals, local fears for the longer-term future of the Chesterfield Canal grew. These led to the establishment of the Retford and Worksop Boat Club in February 1962. The club was launched as the result of support gained from a local protest cruise that the IWA had organised along the canal in November 1961. At a subsequent protest meeting, held in Worksop at the end of February 1962, the local campaign-leader, C. Clarke, was able to announce that he had received an assurance from British Waterways, confirming that:

"Irrespective of the outcome of the Parliamentary Debate, the British Transport Commission would keep the canal open for pleasure craft for two years." He told those present that the future of the canal thereafter rested on the use that was made of it during this interim period, and called for their support in keeping it open.

In much the same way, further support was gathered for the revival of the Kennet and Avon Canal at two meetings organised early in 1962. The first was held at Reading on 8 February, when more than 800 were present, and the second was in Bath on 16 March 1962. Both meetings concluded with resolutions calling on the Minister to use his maximum endeavours to ensure that the waterway was quickly put back into navigable order."

In much the same way local residents at Marple, in Cheshire, were prompted to take action in supporting the restoration of the Peak Forest Canal when part of the spandrel wall of Marple Aqueduct collapsed and it was feared that the canal would remain closed. To ensure this did not happen the Marple Residents Association formulated a local campaign to have the aqueduct repaired and the canal reopened.

Similarly, enthusiasts in the West Midlands were stirred into action when news of a proposed IWA national rally of boats at Stourbridge in 1962, prompted British Waterways to erect notices indicating the "16 locks are unsuitable for the passage of vessels", and also to seek IWRAC approval for the abandonment of the Stourbridge Canal. This action prompted IWA, Midlands Branch members to make an even more determined effort to keep the canal open, especially the Stourbridge Arm that had recently become blocked by a shoal." The final outcome of this local commitment to reopen the arm did much to forward the case for waterway restoration in the West Midlands area.

After making initial overtures to the authorities, requesting the clearance of the arm, volunteers led by Hutchings decided to take the action into their own hands. This campaign of action provoked a series of letters to the editor of *The Daily Telegraph* from IWA members, St Davids, Morton and Horsfall and in turn replies from Ives and Knight, of British Waterways, arguing the merits of the case. This offered considerable advance publicity for the rally and gained much support for the volunteers who cleared the Stourbridge Arm using an imported dragline. The outcome was that some 118 boats visited the rally site and the event gained

First boat along Stratford Canal, 22 February 1964

substantial local and national publicity, including reports in *The Daily Telegraph* of 14 August, and *The Times* of 15 August 1962, both of which showed an appreciation of the rally"s underlying object. The rally equally provoked considerable local authority support for the revival of the canal and, above all, local recognition for the Staffordshire and Worcestershire Canal Society who had jointly organised the event.

As events progressed on the local level, so the national debate over the 1962 Transport Bill evolved. One of the technical issues that developed was the legal argument as to whether the waterways were public rights-of-way, similar to roads, or whether they were private rights-of-way, similar to railways, where the maintenance obligation rested only with the company in relation to public safety. As the result of extensive debate in the House of Lords, during May, June and July 1962, the view that the waterways were public rights-of-way prevailed and this tenet was ultimately reaffirmed and incorporated in the 1962 Transport Act, which received Royal Assent on 1 August 1962.

A paper presented by Ives to the Sussex Group of the Institute of Transport, on 15 October 1962, entitled, "The Future of the Inland Waterways." perhaps offered the best review of the Act and noted its shortcomings from an official's viewpoint. The paper highlighted the fact that the initial duties of the new British Waterways Board were to be directed to a further review of the manner in which inland waterways could be redeveloped and how they should be run. At the same time it recorded the abolition of the former review body IWRAC. It also noted that some of the cases considered by IWRAC, including the Kennet and Avon Canal, were still under review and suggested that the decision taken on the future of that canal could be a pointer to future Government policy. The paper concluded by suggesting that the new management would be powerless to act until the fundamental Government decision was taken either to run the waterways simply as a commercial undertaking or as a social amenity.

The comment about the Kennet and Avon Canal was significant in so far as IWRAC had recommended, in June 1962, that a joint committee consisting of representatives of British Waterways and the KACA should redevelop the canal. IWRAC proposed that the basic funds to carry this out should come from the current maintenance allowance for the canal. which it suggested could be divided to provide funds to both maintain the canal in its present state and to finance restoration work. It also envisaged that the money available would be substantially augmented by massive voluntary efforts on the scale of the Stratford Canal restoration scheme, both in fund-raising and the provision of labour. Whilst no decision

was taken to implement these proposals before the new British Waterways Board (BWB) became operational on 1 January 1963, the statement of options did give an indication of the way in which future policy might evolve in relation to other non-commercial waterways.

Four other events of 1962 had a considerable later significance in the development of the restoration movement. The first occurred at Easter 1962 when the London and Home Counties Branch of the IWA organised a small boat rally at Woking on the Basingstoke Canal. When plans were made for the rally it was realised that a considerable amount of clearance work would be needed to allow the boats to reach the rally site. As a result members of the IWA branch, led by D. Horsfall and T. Dodwell, started pre-rally volunteer working parties to clear the canal. Groups of 20 to 30 people met once a month to undertake the work, travelling mainly from London and the surrounding area. Although the group ceased activity after the rally they later provided the nucleus of the IWA, London Working Party Group which later became the forerunner of the mobile "Navvies" units which developed in the late 1960s.

The second was the inauguration of the Tiverton Canal Preservation Committee at a public meeting organised by the Mayor of Tiverton in April 1962. As the result of decisions taken at the meeting, boys from Blundells School started to restore sections of the Grand Western Canal and negotiations evolved that ultimately led to the retention of the canal as a Linear Country Park by the Devon County Council.

The third was the issue of *A Guide to the River Stour,* by the River Stour Action Committee, as a means of promoting public interest in the legal problems that prevented the reopening of the river as a navigation. This was complemented by a protest cruise by canoes, owned by members of Chelmsford Boat Club, along the river from Langham to Brantham in September 1962 to add further publicity to the revival campaign.

The fourth was the closure of the Linton Lock on the Yorkshire River Ouse due to the dangerous state of the upper gates and the inability of the Linton Lock Commissioners to raise sufficient funds for the lock's repair. This highlighted the continuing problems of maintenance that the waterways incur even though subject to earlier restoration, as was the case with Linton Lock, which had been restored as the result of IWA pressure and activity in 1949.

Against this climate of activity the hopes of waterways enthusiasts rose when the names of the members of the British Waterways Board were announced in late 1962. They included Parham, the former chairman of IWRAC, J. Dower, of the National Parks Commission, and Hadfield, the author of various canal books and a founder member of the IWA, all of whom seemed to offer a new perspective to a review of the problems of the canals which they commenced in January 1963.

The Board was appointed at a time of considerable political change. The reverberations of the 1962 Conservative defeat in Orpington were perhaps symptomatic of the path ahead. They also started their review at a time when unemployment was rising. Yet many were experiencing a higher standard of living, with longer holidays and shorter working hours, and providing a growing demand for increased facilities for leisure and recreation. Each of these features provided a new stimulus for change.

The first dramatic change came quickly for the narrow boat industry, which had been unable to withstand the impact of the severe winter of 1962–63 when the canals froze for several weeks. As the result the BWB, who had acquired the BTC narrow boat fleet, decided to cease most canal carrying as part of its national policy and began to dispose of the craft as circumstances permitted.

On the brighter side a member of the IWA, who wished to remain anonymous, offered £80,000 towards the restoration of the Upper Avon Navigation. This paved the way for the revival of the link between the restored Lower Avon and the National Trust restoration scheme for the Stratford Canal which was due to be completed in 1964. Discussions were opened between the IWA and LANT to consider the most effective way to proceed. The prospect of this revival was, to a degree, enhanced by the 1963 Water Resources Bill, which proposed the creation of River Authorities incorporating the provision for representation of navigation interests. However, a proposal in clause 75 of the Bill, which empowered a River Authority to apply "at any time" for an order to take over a navigation authority, presented some potential problems in the longer term. This did not deter LANT from accepting a £5,000 donation towards the restoration of Evesham Lock, which was quickly put in hand. The Bill, however, did offer some potential problems for a proposal by the River Stour Action Committee, that the lower reaches of the River Stour be taken over by the National Trust and restored for navigational purposes.

Events in relation to the nationalised waterways continued to progress. Although BWB did not halt the immediate closure of the Forth and Clyde and St Helens Canals it started its own review of the prospects of other waterways. Whilst this task was under way, various features developed on the narrow canals that later proved to be significant for their individual future revival. One such instance was the interest shown in the Welford Arm of the Old Union Canal by G. Baker. He hoped to restore the arm and use the terminal wharf area as a base from which to run a canal hire-fleet.

A second was the action of the Bredbury and Romiley UDC in convening a conference to consider the future of the damaged Marple Aqueduct on the Peak Forest Canal. As a result of the meeting, steps were taken to have the aqueduct scheduled as an Ancient Monument which enabled the Cheshire County Council to contribute towards its restoration and maintenance costs. In this way it was hoped that the Peak Forest Canal route between Marple and Dukinfield could be reopened.

A third was a plan to transfer the Caldon Canal to the National Trust. This scheme was promoted by a consortium of a dozen local voluntary organisations led by the area youth officer, W.G. Myatt. Although the planned National Trust takeover did not finally succeed, the local organisation, the Caldon Canal Committee, became the forerunner of the Caldon Canal Society and was later instrumental, with BWB co-operation and the use of "Operation Eyesore" funds, in gaining the canal's restoration and reopening.

The early months of 1963 also saw the development of one of the most unique of the restoration schemes, that of Ports Creek which had formerly been part of the inland Portsmouth and Arundel water route. The creek became blocked during the Second World War with a temporary causeway, and subsequent redevelopment plans envisaged a new bypass route obliterating part of the creek. The IWA gave its support to the campaign led by W. Evans, a local councillor, and the case for the restoration of the waterway was promoted by Aickman and others at a public meeting in Portsmouth on 29 March 1963. As the result of this meeting, support for the scheme gradually developed and the waterway was later reopened.

National developments were also evolving, as an answer to a Parliamentary Question on 31 July 1963 to the Minister of Transport confirmed. This indicated that the BWB were in the process of examining the future use of the waterways and that they hoped to give the Minister a preliminary report of their general views by the end of the year. This provided an outline timetable within which developments might take place, but equally constrained progress in the development of any new schemes. It did not deter members of the Staffordshire and Worcestershire Canal Society from exploring the Dudley Canal Tunnel, which had been officially closed by the BTC in 1962. As the result of these explorations a Dudley Tunnel Committee was formed to co-ordinate local interest in the canal. Members started to organise last chance" boat trips through the tunnel, and found them so popular that they formed an autonomous Dudley Canal Tunnel Preservation Society on 1 January 1964.

In a similar way local interest began to develop in the future of the Grantham Canal. This was initially stimulated by a proposal to infill a section of the canal in Nottingham to make way for road improvements. This led to various letters about the canal appearing in the Nottingham press, which stimulated I. Cane, a student at Kesteven Teacher Training College, to make a study of the condition of the whole canal. A copy of the resultant report was presented to the Grantham Civic Society who were later instrumental in the promotion of a scheme for its restoration for amenity use.

During 1963 Salter's Lode Lock on the Lower Ouse was reconstructed and the operating mechanism electrified. Whilst this reopened access to some of the Middle Level cruising waters, one of the routes through to the River Nene, called Well Creek, remained closed due to silting. Members of the East Anglian Waterways Association and the Middle Level Watermens Club started a local campaign to have the waterway dredged. IWA members were told in March 1964, that this campaign was likely to be successful. In much the same way, the problems of the derelict Droitwich Canal developed as a regular topic of debate for Droitwich Borough Council during 1963. As the result various proposals were made about the canal's long-term future. An IWA member, M. Sinclair, started to promote a local campaign in the press and elsewhere, to interest the council in its restoration, suggesting, "the work could be completed within 18 to 24 months, as the lock chambers are in a very good condition."

In November 1963 the National Trust announced that it was willing to accept as a gift a second major inland waterway, the River Wey Navigation from Guildford to the Thames. The waterway was then still used commercially by its owner, H.W. Stevens, and his interest continued after its official transfer in January 1964. On a less happy note Lancaster Boat Club members saw the draining and infilling of a further section of the upper reaches of the Lancaster Canal near Kendal. This loss, with the infilling of the Preston terminus of the canal, stimulated them to seek support for their campaign to keep the upper reaches of the canal open.

The much awaited BWB interim report, *The Future of the Waterways,* was submitted to the Minister of Transport on 12 December 1963 and published in January 1964. Of greatest significance to the restorationists was the way in which the "multi-user" role of the waterways was projected rather than the traditional idea of viewing the waterways as simply a part of the national transport system. The report suggested that a "multi-user" role which embraced commercial transport, water storage and supply, pleasure cruising, recreation and amenity, should be developed as fully as possible on as many of the waterways as could justify all or any of the uses

sufficiently. It also proposed that this approach could be best achieved by treating each of the waterways as a separate undertaking, capable of a variety of combined functional roles, but so organised and so fortified by contributions of one form or another as to minimise financial loss. For this purpose it suggested that new general legislation must ultimately be developed. The report concluded that a more detailed evaluation was necessary for each individual waterway and indicated that this would be the basis on which the Board's final views would be presented.

The report mentioned particularly the Kennet and Avon Canal, which it indicated "merits sympathetic, careful and urgent consideration", and confirmed that the Board proposed to start discussions with the Kennet and Avon Canal Trust and other potential helpers to establish what might be a practical scheme with an ultimate objective of complete restoration. It also commented on the Stourbridge Canal noting it was a borderline case, the future of which depended on the extent to which practical support might be forthcoming from interested parties.

The proposals were in general favourably received, as is shown by the following comment that appeared in the Staffordshire and Worcestershire Canal Society *Broadsheet* for February 1964:

"This interim report seems to confirm the attitude previously felt, that the new Board were prepared to lean over backwards where there is any possibility of keeping alive any waterway."

Many journals, including *Motor Boat and Yachting* of 21 February 1964, and *New Society* of 6 February 1964, saw the report as a vindication of the IWA campaign for the revival of the waterways.

Of even greater significance to the restorationists was an answer to a question in the House of Commons on 12 February 1964, when Ernest Marples said: "The British Waterways Board has said that it would like consultations with any amenity group interested in particular canals." This invitation gave the Staffordshire and Worcestershire Canal Society, in particular, the chance to offer their own proposals for the restoration of the Stourbridge Canal. Various discussions took place between the Board and the society which culminated, in July 1964, with a meeting between the chairman and members of the Board and the full society committee. At that meeting the restoration of the Wordsley 16 locks was agreed on the basis that the Board would provide the capital items and skilled labour, whilst the society would provide an unskilled labour force to complete much of the work. The Board saw the project as a pilot scheme for their

Reopening of the canal to Stratford-upon-Avon by Queen Elizabeth the Queen Mother on 11 July 1964

ideas and, after obtaining the approval of the trades unions to which its employees belonged, inaugurated the joint restoration project in October 1964.

Although the Wordsley project was significant, perhaps the greatest event for the restoration movement came on 22 February 1964, when the first boat for some 30 years navigated the restored southern section of the Stratford Canal. The voyage was well reported in the press, including a leading article in the *Daily Mail* of 24 February 1964, which offered advance publicity for the formal reopening planned for 11 July l964.

The event gave added impetus to the IWA Upper Avon Committee, who were already considering the restoration of the river between Evesham and Stratford. This project was further enhanced when the civil engineers, A.E. Farr Ltd, offered to conduct a survey of part of the river to provide a more definitive financial and engineering statement of the problems likely to be encountered. They offered to undertake the survey without charge as a contribution to the waterways campaign.

As 1964 progressed so the public interest in the waterways rapidly developed. This was enhanced first by the press reports about the BWB interim report, and subsequently by various other events that took place during the year. The Dudley Tunnel Preservation Society held one such event on 23 April 1964 when it organised a series of trips through the tunnel to launch a £5,000 appeal to safeguard the waterway. A second was the formal reopening of Evesham Town Lock, on the Lower Avon, on 7 June 1964. This ceremony offered considerable publicity for the proposal to reopen the Upper Avon Navigation to Stratford, a theme that was the major topic of conversation on that day.

The third, and perhaps the event that most captured the public imagination, was the reopening of the canal to Stratford-upon-Avon by Queen Elizabeth the Queen Mother on 11 July 1964. The rebirth of the Stratford Canal was commemorated by a Festival of Boats and Arts which extended over the week during which the opening took place. The tremendous amount of publicity that was gained for the waterway restoration movement did much to enhance the prospects of the various other projects that were to follow. It was perhaps best exemplified by an article in *The Times* of 16 July, under the headline, "Towpath Message for a Nation".

One of the most comprehensive restoration schemes that followed was that of the "Cheshire Ring", which included the Ashton, Peak Forest and Rochdale Canals amongst others. The idea of the "Ring" was promoted as part of the prospectus of the Peak Forest Canal Society, inaugurated in 1964. The first plans made by the Society were based on the restoration and reopening of the Marple locks and were linked with a scheme proposed by Marple Civic Trust to make the canal-side more attractive in the region of Posset Bridge. Another advance made in 1964 was the fruition of a scheme to restore the Welford Arm which was promoted by the Market Harboroughbased Old Union Canal Society, inaugurated in August 1964, to both promote the project and protect the Old Union Canal.

A third was the foundation of the Shrewsbury and Newport Canal Association (S&NCA) in December 1964 to campaign for the complete restoration of that particular section of the Shropshire Union Canal system. This project was inaugurated in September 1964 after a report appeared in the local press that BWB proposed to empty part of the Newport Branch of the canal. The Shrewsbury and Newport Canal Association was formed at the suggestion of the North-Western Branch of the IWA to provide a local organisation to develop the restoration campaign. Although the S&NCA was unsuccessful in its initial campaign, it later formed the nucleus of the more successful Shropshire Union Canal Society.

The month of October 1964 saw two significant changes that were later to affect the restoration movement. The first was the retirement of Aickman as director of the IWA national campaign. This enabled the IWA to develop a new policy of trying to co-operate with ewe on the lines suggested in their interim report. Munk, the IWA chairman, assumed control of IWA policy development and provided the central co-ordination point for the waterways revival movement from that time. The second, at national level, was the defeat of the Conservative Government and the election of a Labour Government, with Harold Wilson as Prime Minister. The change of government offered a further prospect of national support for the revival of the waterways as a recreational amenity. The creation of the post of "Minister for Sport", within the Department of Education, added weight to this ideal.

By the close of 1964 a new prospect for the future of the waterway restoration movement was becoming apparent. Reinforced by the successful reopening of both the Lower Avon and the Stratford Canal the new

Lower Avon Reopening

Lower Avon reopening 1962

"navvies" were able to present tangible evidence of the strength of their actions. Map 4 indicates the extent of the growth and spread of the restoration movement over the period 1961 to 1964. A chronological review of projects is provided by the list below:

1961	Buckingham Arm, Grand Union Canal.
1962	Grand Western Canal.
	Stourbridge Canal and Arm.
1963	Dudley Canal and Tunnel.
	Droitwich Canal.
	Lancaster Canal.
	Ports Creek.
	Welford Arm, Old Union Canal.
	Well Creek, Middle Level.
1964	Shrewsbury and Newport Canal.
	Upper Avon Navigation.

During the period 1961 to 1964 the Transport Act of 1962 provided the way forward for the restoration movement overall and the formation of the BWB on 1 January 1963 gave the movement the boost that it needed. The BWB interim report, published in January 1964, provided the first public statement of an official commitment to the development of a "multi-user" role as the prime feature by which the future of the waterways could be reviewed. Above all else, it established a means through which the financial constraints, that had until then inhibited the custodians of the canals from reaching a compromise with those who saw the waterways as an amenity resource, might be overcome. The inauguration of the Stourbridge Canal restoration scheme formally marked this change of official approach and offered a new climate within which the restoration movement could both prosper and flourish, capitalising on the ever-growing public interest and support.

Yorkshire River Derwent

V 1965-70:

THE LEISURE REVOLUTION

One significant impression of the changing attitudes in Britain during 1965 was graphically portrayed by M. Dower in his book, produced for the Civic Trust, *The Challenge of Leisure*. The following quotation effectively sets the scene:

"Three great waves have broken across the face of Britain since 1800. First, the sudden growth of dark industrial towns. Second, the thrusting movement along far-flung railways. Third, the sprawl of car-based suburbs. Now we see, under the guise of a modest word, the surge of a fourth wave which could be more powerful than all the others. The modest word is leisure."

By 1965 the challenge of leisure had become of major concern to the layman and planner alike. For the layman the increase in leisure time, with more income at his/her disposal and greater personal mobility, presented the opportunity to seek more outdoor interests. The canals and rivers, for many, provided a means of access to the peace and isolation valued so highly, yet rapidly becoming more elusive. For the planner the need to conserve and develop the scarce resources of land and amenity, to provide for their fuller use and enjoyment, presented an urgent and varied challenge that could not be ignored.

It was within this climate of challenge that the new Labour Government, elected in October 1964, started to review the allocation of priorities and resources within the leisure area in relation to national financial demands. To enable the Government to assess the various factors involved, the Sports Council was established in January 1965, to advise the Government on matters relating to the development of amateur sport and physical recreation services".

The IWA, under Munk's chairmanship, also adopted a policy of realism and flexibility. Members were told in the *Bulletin* of January 1965:

"If the authorities do what we want them to do then our relationship with them will be cordial. Until they make up their minds what they are going to do. our relationship should at least be amicable providing that the delay is not unreasonable and that there is no marked deterioration of the waterways in the meantime."

It was within this improved atmosphere of realism and revival that the Upper Avon Navigation Trust, led by F. Flower, launched its first appeal for funds to assist in the preliminary work needed in its plan to ultimately restore the 17 miles of river between Stratford and Evesham. The scheme envisaged the construction of nine new locks to replace those that had fallen into decay after the navigation was abandoned in 1873, and offered the prospect of a new circular cruising route for canal craft in the Midlands. This was propitious, as the public awareness of the holiday potential offered by the waterways was substantially enhanced by a series of six BBC television programmes, under the title "Voyage Into England", broadcast in the summer of 1964. An estimated twenty-seven million people watched the series and it did much to broaden the public knowledge of the waterways, and greatly enhanced both the demand for canal hire-craft and the public commitment towards the waterways revival.

While popular support for the waterways grew, so did the march of progress towards further motorway development. One of the first conflicts between the two transport systems developed when plans for the M6 motorway north of Preston were published. The new route crossed the upper reaches of the Lancaster Canal at a number of points and fears grew that if bridges were not provided then the restoration plans for the upper 11 miles of the canal might be prejudiced. The IWA and the local interested organisations pooled their resources to monitor developments so that a united front could be offered to save the canal. Unfortunately, for all concerned, the extra cost of providing bridges instead of culverts was a burden the Ministry of Transport were unwilling to bear and the first round of the battle was lost when abandonment proposals for the upper reaches were published in mid 1965 to allow the canal to be blocked.

At this time the IWA started to investigate ways to overcome a threat to the Cheshire "Canal Ring" from a proposed Rochdale Canal Company private Bill which sought authority to close the canal. The potential loss of the short navigable length in Manchester, between the Ashton and Bridgewater Canals, had a much wider implication because it offered an irreplaceable link in the circular cruising route provided by the Macclesfield, Peak Forest, Ashton, Bridgewater, Trent and Mersey Canals and its loss was likely to be prejudicial to the future of each of the other interlinked canals. This fear

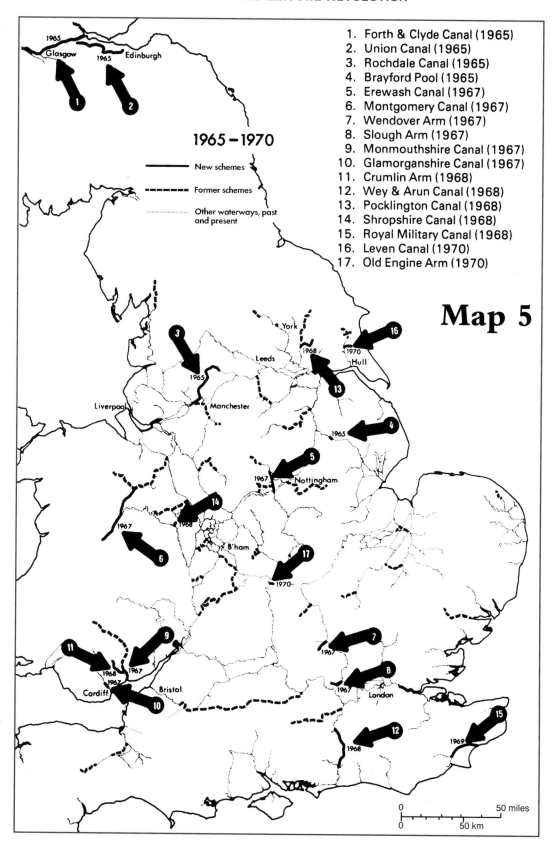

1965 – 1970

—————— New schemes

– – – – – – Former schemes

·············· Other waterways, past and present

1. Forth & Clyde Canal (1965)
2. Union Canal (1965)
3. Rochdale Canal (1965)
4. Brayford Pool (1965)
5. Erewash Canal (1967)
6. Montgomery Canal (1967)
7. Wendover Arm (1967)
8. Slough Arm (1967)
9. Monmouthshire Canal (1967)
10. Glamorganshire Canal (1967)
11. Crumlin Arm (1968)
12. Wey & Arun Canal (1968)
13. Pocklington Canal (1968)
14. Shropshire Canal (1968)
15. Royal Military Canal (1968)
16. Leven Canal (1970)
17. Old Engine Arm (1970)

Map 5

led members of the Peak Forest Canal Society to add their weight to the IWA campaign.

The IWA decided that, with the help of local interests, it would petition against the Abandonment Bill when it came before Parliament. D. Owen of the Manchester Section of the IWA organised a public meeting in Manchester, during February 1965, which was attended by over 300 people. The meeting closed with the acceptance of a resolution urging Parliament to reject any closure proposal.

One other event of importance in the battle to retain the Rochdale Canal occurred in 1964. By then the Store Street Aqueduct at the lower end of the Ashton Canal had developed a leak and had been emptied; this meant that although the adjacent Ashton Canal was legally open it had become impassable.

The Rochdale Canal Bill went before the House of Lords in March 1965 and an IWA petition was lodged against it. Rather than pursue the dispute, the Rochdale Canal Company indicated that they were willing to reach a compromise. The company solicitors indicated that they were willing to incorporate a clause in the Bill, agreeing to maintain the navigation until such time as the Ashton Canal should be abandoned. This was accepted and the Bill, with the revised clause, received Royal Assent in the summer of 1965. The future of the Cheshire Ring thus rested on the retention and restoration of the Ashton Canal, to which the IWA and the Peak Forest Canal Society turned their attentions.

As the campaign to retain the Manchester section of the Rochdale Canal developed, so IWA members in South Wales prepared to oppose a plan proposed by the Cwmbran Council to convert a four-mile section of the abandoned Monmouthshire Canal, within the town boundaries, into a series of water gardens and play parks. In order to provide an effective local group the IWA, South-West Branch, formed a South Wales section at a meeting in Newport on 20 February 1965. Members of the new section immediately started a local campaign to protect both the Monmouthshire and Brecon Canals from further decay and erosion.

By April 1965, in another part of the country more favourable progress was being made when the Kennet and Avon Canal Trust joint project with BWB for the restoration of Sulhampstead Lock finally got under way. Prisoners from Oxford Gaol assisted with preparatory site work and a unit of Royal Engineers, on a training exercise, moved onto the site at the end of April for the construction work to begin. The K&ACT envisaged that the rebuilding of Sulhampstead Lock would act as a model and pilot scheme for their comprehensive restoration project which was awaiting Government approval.

Concern for the visual amenity offered by the waterways became evident in three developments during 1965. Perhaps the foremost was the achievement of the Paddington Waterways Society in gaining local authority acceptance of their campaign to improve the surroundings of the Regent's Canal, between Maida Vale and Little Venice. The group, established in 1958

Lancaster Canal Trust

to fight a scheme to build flats over the canal in Little Venice, became the forerunner of the Regent's Canal Group, formed in 1965, to improve and develop the amenity of the whole of the Regent''s Canal through London. The activities of members of the group also led to the formation of the London Canals Consultative Committee by the Greater London Council in late 1965, which subsequently became a coordinating group to enhance the future of London's waterways.

The second development was at the derelict Brayford Mere in the centre of Lincoln, which had become a rubbish-strewn eyesore with a collection of sunken wrecks, due to the decline in the commercial traffic that formerly frequented the wharf areas. In an effort to restore the water area as a local amenity the Lincoln Chamber of Commerce formed the Brayford Improvement Committee. The IWA were invited to send representatives to offer advice as to the best method of restoring the mere which linked the River Witham and the Fossdyke. The committee later became the forerunner of the Brayford Mere Trust, which subsequently cleared the Mere of wrecks and actively rebuilt the facilities required for its revival as a base for visiting pleasure craft.

The third development was the inauguration of the New Glasgow Society, which started to promote a local campaign to retain and develop the Forth and Clyde Canal as a recreational facility and public amenity within the Glasgow area.

The year 1965 also saw rapid progress being made on the repair of the Wordsley 16 locks on the Stourbridge Canal, with volunteers from the Staffordshire and Worcestershire Canal Society, assisted by members of the Coventry Canal Society and Dudley Tunnel Society, holding regular weekend working parties to tackle the considerable amount of canal-clearance work involved. IWA members were told of the progress achieved towards reopening the locks in April 1965, when an appeal for more volunteers was made.

This appeal for volunteers later bore fruit in a constructive way and in September 1965, T. Dodwell mooted the idea of forming a Working Party Group within the London and Home Counties branch of the IWA. Following his experience of organising volunteers to clear the Basingstoke Canal at Woking for the 1962 rally of boats, he decided to organise a mobile group of volunteers to assist with various restoration schemes throughout the country. The idea proved a great success, with visits to the Kennet and Avon and Stourbridge Canals, and the River Wey, being organised during the first few months. It later led to the foundation of the *Navvies Notebook* in October 1966 to keep members informed of sites where work was being undertaken

to which the could enroll. This growth of co-ordinated working party operations subsequently became a vital part of the development of a national restoration movement.

As the idea of volunteer "navvies" evolved to undertake the practical restoration work, so the IWA promoted the idea of a Waterways Trust, to act as an organisation similar to the National Trust, to safeguard the future of the potential amenity waterways, many of which needed active restoration work undertaken on them. The IWA plans envisaged that well over 1,000 miles of the nationalised waterways should be transferred to the Trust, which would be a charitable body, capable of harnessing the services of volunteers, prisoners and the Armed Forces on training exercises, to restore the canals. The proposal was submitted to the Minister of Transport on 26 April 1965 with the support of the Parliamentary Waterways Group. Although it was not accepted, it did provide a base for some of the ideas later developed in Government proposals.

A greater public understanding of the history and potential of the waterways was also being generated in other ways. One of the most remarkable developments in this respect was the rapid growth of the number of books on canals. The most absorbing of these appeared in 1965 when P.A.L. Vine produced a history of the waterways of southern England under the title, *London's Lost Route to the Sea*. The book was received with acclaim in press reviews, including one in *The Daily Telegraph: Weekend Magazine,* of 21 May 1965, which devoted five pages to the story of the Wey and Arun Canal. The book was a forerunner for the publication of many other individual canal histories. At much the same time the first edition of the annual *Canals Book* was also being prepared, of which 36,000 copies were produced and sold, giving some indication of the growing public interest in the waterways.

The use of specialised publications to assist with the promotion of ideas for the revival of the waterways has since become a prime feature of the waterways restoration campaign. The first of these booklets was *The Lancaster Canal: Proposed Linear Park and Nature Reserve* prepared by T.S.H. Wordsworth for the Association for the Restoration of the Lancaster Canal, and published in 1965. Booklets were subsequently developed for various other amenity development schemes. The Lancaster Canal booklet set out in pictorial terms the way in which the whole canal could be redeveloped as an asset to the area through which it passed. Although lacking the same professional style, the Peak Forest Canal Society similarly produced their own scheme for the rehabilitation of the canals of the North-West in a booklet entitled, *The Cheshire Canal Ring*. This was later to prove to be one of the significant documents in support of the reopening of the Ashton and Peak Forest Canals.

Perhaps the most awaited publication of 1965 appeared on 16 December, when the BWB issued its final survey report, *The Facts about the Waterways*. The report was issued at the time that Mrs Barbara Castle was appointed Minister of Transport, and provided her with a detailed analysis of the then current state of the various nationalised waterways, suggesting possible alternative proposals for dealing with their future and the comparative costs involved. The report was of vital significance to the restorationists as it made the point that whichever course was finally adopted there was a continuing inescapable bill of some £600,000 per year, even if all of the canals were closed. It also recorded that for an additional £300,000 per year the whole of the then current system could continue to be available for pleasure craft use. The report concluded:

"Clearly, therefore, the question of the future is not one that can be solved simply on commercial grounds; it brings in broad social questions as well. As far as these broader questions are concerned we realise that we form only part – we think a unique part – of a bigger subject, the subject of general future policy towards recreation."

The IWA received the report with interest, noting that the Government now needed to take the appropriate long-term policy decisions. An appreciation of the report was circulated to IWA members as a *Supplement* to *Bulletin* in January 1966. In this Munk highlighted that the five year stay of action, offered by the 1962 Transport Act, expired in November 1966 and that after this time BWB would be required to fully restore all the waterway system, unless formal relief from the obligation had been obtained in the interim. As such the Government would be required to make a final decision, supported by appropriate legislation, for the role of the waterway system in the near future. The IWA, although differing from BWB in general attitude and regarding certain of the figures quoted, indicated that they considered the report offered a basis for future negotiation.

Ashton Canal restoration

The IWA immediately started its own negotiations to clarify the report's comments in respect of the Kennet and Avon Canal. A memorandum was sent to the Minister of Transport in February 1966 urging the Government to put into immediate effect a Joint Scheme of Restoration for the whole of the canal between Reading and Bath.

The Government separately responded by producing a broader statement on its policy in a white paper, *Leisure in the Countryside* (Cmd 2928), in February 1966. This promoted the idea of Country Parks, and also noted the "considerable potential for all kinds of recreation in the extensive network of inland waterways." The white paper referred to the BWB report on the waterways and significantly noted:

"There are many people in this country who are knowledgeable about, and care greatly about, the use of rivers and canals for recreation. There must clearly be opportunities for these talents and energies to play their part in the future of the waterways."

The waterways restoration enthusiasts took heart from this statement, and an editorial in the *Bulletin* of May 1966, noted:

"Now, in 1966, we appear to be on the very threshold of seeing all that we have fought for becoming a reality ... Who among our earlier members can fail to forget how we were savagely ridiculed for our belief that pleasure boating on the waterways would soon develop into a national pastime and ... that the day would dawn when our 3,000 mile canal network would be regarded in Government circles as a priceless amenity – a vast linear park?"

To capitalise on this change in official attitude the IWA decided to terminate its national policy of co-operation with the authorities and to take an independent line, reserving the right to criticise the authorities strongly, when justified. In an effort to press for an early decision on the future of the waterways, the IWA decided to hold a number of open public meetings, in May and June 1966, as a means of seeking more public support."

The IWA commitment to a policy of public protest was fully justified when the Government white paper on *Transport Policy* (Cmd 3057) appeared in July 1966. It proposed that only part of the network should be maintained for pleasure craft, and that even this reduced network would be subject to a further review after five years. The Government also indicated that, apart from these regular reviews, it reserved the right to close waterways it deemed unnecessary, during the inter-review period.

The IWA chairman, Munk, immediately reacted to the proposal of regular reviews and commented:

"Such wicked nonsense must effectively stifle the development of all transport and pleasure boat trade on the canals and even the purchase of boats by private individuals."

To fight the white paper proposals he launched an urgent drive to increase IWA membership, which then stood at 4,250, and planned a National Waterways Conference, to be held in April 1967. Each of the IWA Branches were asked to organise local protest meetings to advocate waterway restoration."

Whilst the broader debate over the white paper began to evolve, the restoration movement was itself moving forward into new areas. The most remarkable of these was the Upper Avon project. To both stir further public support and to get the scheme under way Hutchings, the project manager, gained approval for the construction of the first new lock at Stratford-upon-Avon in early 1966. A limited appeal for £6,000 was launched, and work started on the site of the new lock on 19 July 1966, after the first £3,000 had been received. A report of the event appeared in the *Bulletin* of October 1966, when IWA members were told that work had commenced "... upon the assumption that enough people care enough to help."

In much the same way plans were also being made by Droitwich Council to develop the derelict Droitwich Canal as an amenity feature for the New Town. An illustrated article about the development appeared in the *Worcester Evening News* of 14 June 1966 to test public reaction to the scheme. In a similar fashion Newport Town Council debated a proposal that the council should take over three miles of the Monmouthshire Canal within the town boundary and restore it for amenity use. This scheme, which was reported in *The South Wales Argus* and *The South Wales Echo* of 19 July 1966, did not immediately gain council support and a decision was deferred for two years. IWA members were told of this in October 1966, when it was suggested that there was "a chance for local pressure to achieve something." Local residents in Newport also felt strongly about the waterway and by mid 1967, the Newport (Monmouthshire) Canal Society had been founded to seek to promote the retention and revival of the canal.

Perhaps the centrepiece of the restoration campaign for 1966 was the IWA rally of boats held at Marple in August. Over 200 boats assembled at the top of the Marple flight of locks. The aim of the rally was to publicise the importance of restoring the "Cheshire Canal Ring" and in particular to add weight to the work

Basingstoke Canal, Lock 24 restoration

of the Peak Forest Canal Society in rejuvenating the local canal. A subsidiary rally was organised in central Manchester to highlight the connecting links of the Rochdale and Ashton Canals. This was the first of a series of annual rallies held at Marple to advance the local restoration project. It was fully reported in the *Bulletin* of October 1966, to ensure all IWA members were aware of the significance of the Cheshire campaign to the overall restoration movement. In the light of the BWB's continuing silence on the question of restoration and the revival of the waterways of the area, the Peak Forest Canal Society brought out a new and revised edition of their booklet, *The Cheshire Canal Ring*, for sale at the event.

Another new publication, entitled *Navvies Notebook*, was first published in October 1966 by G. Palmer, the then secretary of the IWA, London and Home Counties Branch. He had noted the growing number of working parties restoring the waterways throughout the country and realised the need to co-ordinate and advertise where such activities were taking place. He also wished to offer a record of what had been achieved by the events. Whilst *Navvies Notebook* was primarily the responsibility of the London Volunteer Working Group and detailed their work programme, IWA members were told that it was

ultimately intended to reflect the national scene and was therefore available to all members of the Association. The first edition recorded planned working parties on the River Stour, at Brantham Lock, as well as others on the River Wey and the Kennet and Avon Canal. It also provided a review of the progress already achieved in the restoration of the Stourbridge 16 locks. Later editions of the publication, renamed *Navvies* in April 1971, provided considerable stimulus to the spread of the waterways restoration campaign and the development of a network of local working party organisers.

A formal debate on the future of the waterways was held in the House of Commons on 18 November 1966. The Government indicated that they accepted the analysis in *The Facts about the Waterways* as the basis for future policy development and they would consult with interested parties and amenity organisations to define the best way forward. During the debate R.G. Grant-Ferris, MP, indicated that there were three unsatisfactory features in the existing proposals: (1) The failure to recognise the inviolability of through routes; (2) the five year reviews; and (3) the closure of canals by statutory order.

J. Morris wound up the debate for the Government and agreed the necessity for a revised financial basis for waterways control and agreed that all the points mentioned in debate would be duly considered.

Three other events during 1966 assisted the development of other restoration schemes. Two were in the West Country, and the first was the foundation of the Somerset Inland Waterways Society, as a local pressure group, to seek the full restoration of the Bridgwater and Taunton Canal.

The second was the revival of the Tiverton Canal Preservation Committee to advocate the restoration of the Grand Western Canal, the future of which had been pronounced "in the balance" in the 1965 BWB report. The committee quickly gained local council support and in 1967 were instrumental in the development of an amenity survey, to consider the recreational potential of the canal, which was conducted by the Dartington Amenity Research Trust (DART). The ideas promoted in the DART report later provided the basis for the Devon County Council to take over and restore the canal as a Linear Country Park.

The third was the formation of the Surrey and Hampshire Canal Society, in November 1966, to promote the full restoration of the Basingstoke Canal.

This group was later successful in gaining the support of the two County Councils to take over and restore the waterway.

In the same month, on a less successful note, the Shrewsbury and Newport Canal Association heard that their plan to restore the local canals had failed. The group, slightly disheartened by its initial lack of success, reformed itself into the Shropshire Union Canal Society to protect the remainder of the canals in the former railway company system.

The year 1966 closed with the prospect of a better climate ahead for the restorationists" ideals. Perhaps these ideals were best defined at a meeting held at County Hall, London on 9 December 1966, when the GLC Canals Consultative Committee heard various views for the revival and redevelopment of London's waterways, which were later reproduced in a booklet, *Regent's Canal: Policy for the Future* (1967).

By adopting much the same theme, the IWA organised a public meeting at Watford Town Hall on 19 January 1967 at which the future of the Grand Union Canal was the main topic of debate. At this meeting the formation of the Grand Union Canal Society was proposed and 61 people indicated their interest. The society was officially formed at a second meeting, in February 1967, and later

Basingstoke Canal restoration

led campaigns for the revival of both the Slough and Wendover Arms of the Grand Union Canal. The fight to revive the Slough Arm ultimately achieved success but that for the Wendover Arm failed through both lack of local support and, more particularly, from an inadequate legal base from which a successful campaign could develop.

Perhaps the first advance of 1967 was the commitment of Staffordshire County Council to support in principle the restoration work being undertaken on the Caldon Canal by the Caldon Canal Committee. This commitment paved the way for a scheme of joint co-operation between the volunteers, the BwB, and the County Council, for the complete restoration of the whole canal. The project was ultimately financed by grants from the "Operation Eyesore" derelict area reclamation scheme.

A second advance was made with the official reopening of the Stourbridge 16 locks by the Joint Parliamentary Secretary to the Ministry of Transport, on 27 May 1967. This marked the successful completion of the BWB pilot scheme, involving co-operation between volunteers and Board staff, and laid firm foundations for other similar schemes to develop.

A third advance was provided by the granting of Royal Assent to the *Civic Amenities Act* 1967. The Act offered the facility to designate whole groups of structures as a conservation area. This was particularly relevant to the inland waterways as it both provided for whole units to be preserved and also offered the potential of grants to assist with the conservation work.

The year 1967 proved to be an equally vital year for the development of the national waterways restoration campaign. The IWA submitted a memorandum, *The Way Ahead for Amenity Waterways,* to the Minister of Transport in January 1967 to present its own thesis to the Government. This was followed by a National Waterways Conference, held at Christ Church College, Oxford, between 20–22 March 1967. Presentations at the conference included papers on: *Restoration by Voluntary Efforts,* by D. Hutchings; *The Recreational Potential of Waterways,* by M. Dower; *The Plans of Local Authorities,* by I. Harrington and B.R. Cowles; and *Waterways in the Urban and Rural Landscape,* by S. Crowe, all of which made considerable impact on those present and generated ideas for future developments."

Similarly the IWA laid plans for a National Waterways Week to coincide with the presentation of the Government's plans to be outlined in the Transport Bill, that was due to be laid before Parliament in the late autumn of 1967. Details of these plans were outlined to IWA members in September 1967.

As the IWA plans developed so the "leader" writers of the national press appeared to realise that the inland waterways were worthy of their attention. More than 30 leaders on waterways appeared between March and July 1967, all of which supported the IWA cause."

The IWA held its 1967 rally of boats at Leicester. One of the most useful contributions was the transformation of the area surrounding Lime Kiln Lock into a local amenity space. The Leicester City Council provided assistance to volunteer working-parties, led by A. Davies, who converted the lock-side area into a small park, with seats for the public to watch boats passing through. This, together with a similar development at Little Venice in London, provided a clear example of what could be achieved by developing the canal side as a public amenity. These two early schemes provided a lead for the many similar developments that followed."

On 7 September 1967 the Government published its second white paper on the future of the canals, *British Waterways: Recreation and Amenity* (Cmnd 3401). The statements made offered the IWA a firm ray of hope for the inland waterways, for not only did they seemingly agree that all of the waterways then open for pleasure cruising should be retained, but also suggested that some waterways which were then unnavigable should be restored. The white paper divided the waterways into three major groups: Commercial, Cruising and the Remainder. In respect of the latter, it suggested that each waterway required further individual study before plans for the longer-term future could evolve. To undertake this task the Government proposed the creation of an Inland Waterways Advisory Council, composed of qualified members from a variety of waterways interests. The white paper envisaged the council being both a statutory consultative body as well as being able to examine the merits of all proposed restoration schemes.

More importantly the white paper commended the efforts of volunteers and stated that the Government was keen to encourage further volunteer efforts to develop the amenity waterways network. It equally suggested that local authorities could do much to foster restoration and that they could perhaps partly finance the various schemes. The white paper concluded with the phrase "A New Charter for the Waterways", noting: "In the waterways this country possesses a priceless asset, an asset whose value will grow as the demand for leisure facilities intensifies."

In the light of this broad acceptance of the IWA views it was decided to cancel plans for the National Waterways Week and instead to continue its work, to save the waterways, firmly but diplomatically. Perhaps *Yachting and Boating Weekly,* of 21 September 1967, best summed up the situation with its comment:

"The Inland Waterways Association therefore while having good reason to celebrate victory, should keep its powder dry. This would not be the first time that a Promised Land, as seen through Whitehall, has turned out to be an ideal spot for ambush."

When the IWA council had had more time to study the white paper the full implications of the threat to the long list of waterways that were in the "Remainder" category became apparent. These were listed in the *Bulletin* of December 1967, when members were told that, "appropriate action was being taken in all of these cases."

A survey team from the IWA toured some of the "threatened waterways" and public meetings were held to establish the local reactions to the white paper proposals. The first of these visits was made to the Slough Arm of the Grand Union Canal on 21 October 1967, which was followed by a meeting at Iver on 25 October, organised by the Grand Union Canal Society. As a consequence a specialist Slough Canal Group was later inaugurated to carry forward the local restoration campaign. The IWA team's second visit on 28 October was to the Liverpool Arm of the Leeds and Liverpool Canal, and this culminated with plans being made for a rally of boats on the arm during 1968. A third visit was made to the Erewash Canal on 29 October 1967. Subsequent to the visit, members from the IWA Midlands Branch and local residents, formed the Erewash Canal Preservation and Development Association to carry forward a local restoration campaign to revive and preserve the Erewash Canal.

As part of the same series of visits the IWA Midlands Branch and the Staffordshire and Worcestershire Canal Society combined to organise two weekend cruises, at the end of October 1967, over those parts of the Birmingham Canal Navigations that were also placed in the Remainder Group. To further develop the interest

Restored section of the Driffield Navigation

Slough Arm

that these cruises created, members later formed the Birmingham Canal Navigations Society to promote the restoration and revival of the BCN system. In the same vein a West Midlands Waterways Study Group was promoted by a local architect and IWA member, P. White, who was also responsible for the City of Birmingham Farmers Bridge canal-side redevelopment plans, which were a further refinement of the ideas of canal-side revival originally formulated by the Regent's Canal Group in London.

In a quite different way, new interest also developed in part of the Glamorganshire Canal, near Cardiff, during 1967. This originated from a proposal by the Cardiff Naturalists" Society, led by M. Giliham, that part of the canal should be preserved as a nature reserve. The canal, which had been purchased by the City of Cardiff in 1943, provided an ideal site for such a novel development and the scheme was later converted into a reality by the City of Cardiff Parks Department.

Two other developments that took place in 1967 were also worthy of note because of their significance to the growth of the restoration movement. One was a conference for County, Local and Parish Council representatives to consider the future of the Basingstoke Canal promoted by the Surrey and Hampshire Canal Society. At the conference a plea was made for the

canal to be taken over by the local authorities and redeveloped by a trust representing their interests. The second development was the inauguration of a trust by the River Stour Action Committee. This was backed by the Essex Rural Community Council and was formed to provide a body to redevelop the navigation and to care for the locks. Each of these schemes later evolved to enable parts of the waterways concerned to be restored.

By the close of 1967 the journal, *Navvies Notebook,* had successfully completed its first year of distribution and its circulation had risen to over 350 copies per issue. A wide variety of working parties had been publicised during the first year, from Marple locks in the North, to the River Wey in the South; the River Stour in the East, and the Kennet and Avon Canal in the West. During this time some 45 people had attended one weekend working party on the Stourbridge Canal; and a grand total of 97 people met on 22 October 1967 to clear a section of the Kennet and Avon Canal at Reading, giving the organisers an idea of the potential resources the "Navvies" movement could tap into to undertake volunteer restoration work.

The advent of 1968 saw the Government developing a comprehensive expenditure review in the aftermath of the devaluation of the pound. Against the backcloth of financial stringency, outlined by Harold Wilson to the House of Commons on 16 January 1968, real fears were expressed by the IWA that the proposals of the 1967 white paper would not be fully developed in the subsequent draft of the Transport Bill.

The Bill was published in late December 1967 and contained many controversial features, perhaps the most fundamental of which was the proposed removal of the public right of navigation that had been enshrined in the majority of individual canal Acts. It also excluded a large number of waterways from the list scheduled for proper maintenance. These included parts of the Kennet and Avon, the Caldon, the Ashton, the Erewash, most of the BCN, as well as the then unnavigable Pocklington and Bridgwater and Taunton Canals. On a brighter note, the Bill proposed the creation of an Amenity Advisory Council to consider the future of these canals and provided the opportunity for local authorities to contribute financially towards the cost of maintaining their local waterways. However, the Bill also incorporated proposals for the closure of the Ashton and Lower Peak Forest Canals, which were then the subject of a Court case promoted by the IWA. and other local organisations who were supported by the riparian local authorities. This claimed the BWB had failed in its statutory obligation to maintain the Ashton Canal. The IWA members were made aware of the proposals made in the Bill through a circular sent to each of them in March 1968. It sought

their help to fight the other possible canal closures that the Bill might precipitate. To pursue its own policy of restoration, the IWA also formed a committee to review the draft Bill so that constructive representations could be made to the Ministry of Transport, in the hope that the most damaging features it included, which prejudiced the future of the waterways, would be modified.

Some of the growing IWA fears were quickly allayed when J. Morris MP, Joint Parliamentary Secretary to the Ministry of Transport, attended the IWA annual dinner on 6 January 1968. He assured those present that:

"... even with the stabilised network ... the Government recognises that there is room for some additions to it. There are some stretches of waterway at present unnavigable where restoration would be economically justified; we wish to encourage such work."

This attitude of revival was exemplified in the work of the Erewash Preservation Committee, led by R. Torrington, which had by then started to organise clearance of parts of the Erewash Canal as well as promoting a local petition calling for its retention.

The theme of revival was similarly the basis of a proposal made by M. Dower, of the Dartington Amenity Research Trust, regarding the Grand Western Canal. In a report on the recreational potential of the canal he

Royal Military Iden Canal lock used as a drainage sluice

suggested that it could be restored for amenity use for £20,000 and indicated that a Government grant might be available to finance the work.

In the same vein the agreement of the Severn River Authority to the principle of new navigation works, weirs and approach channels, being installed on the derelict Upper Avon in order to restore use between Stratford and Evesham, paved the way for a private Bill envisaged by the Upper Avon Navigation Trust. To finance this work the Trust launched a major appeal for funds in early 1968.

On a far smaller scale, anglers who used the Crumlin Arm of the Monmouthshire Canal, started their own local campaign to have part of the local canal restored. They later formed the Risca, Magor and St Mellons Canal Preservation Society, at a public meeting in Risca on 9 May 1968, to promote the restoration of the canal, gaining guidance and assistance from the adjacent Newport Canal Society. The new Canal Preservation Society held its first volunteer working party to clear a section of the Crumlin Arm on 1 March 1969, although the work was planned much earlier.

By mid-1968 the "Navvies" movement was rapidly gaining strength. IWA members were told, in the *Bulletin* of May 1968, that:

"Voluntary work is fast becoming a most important part of the waterways scene. For not only does it do an immense amount of good to the navigations themselves ... but provides incredible publicity ... and gives vent to the feelings of frustration felt by the enthusiasts when seeing some priceless route being allowed to crumble, decay and in all too many cases be vandalised."

The article continued by listing restoration work being undertaken on the following waterways: Ashton Canal, Basingstoke Canal, Caldon Canal, Chesterfield Canal, Erewash Canal, River Stour, Kennet and Avon Canal (five sites), Lancaster Canal, Peak Forest Canal, Shropshire Union Canal, Welford Arm, River Wey, with four groups travelling to other waterways where work was required.

Apart from their volunteer work, the IWA members continued to organise protest cruises to fight to retain and revive those canals under risk of closure. Perhaps the most successful of these was a 24-hour cruise over much of the Birmingham Canal Navigations, commencing on 30 March 1968. In much the same way a protest cruise was organised along the lowest pound of the Basingstoke Canal, at Easter 1968, to demonstrate the pressing need for the waterway to be restored. These were particularly pertinent as Mrs Barbara Castle MP, had by then been replaced by Richard Marsh MP, as Minister of Transport,

and the Transport Bill was due for imminent debate.

The waterways section of the Transport Bill was debated by a Parliamentary Committee on 1 May 1968, and during the debate the membership list of the Inland Waterways Amenity Advisory Council (IWAAC) was announced. The chairman was named as I. Harrington and members included Cobb, Munk and Streat of the IWA. The Minister, in making the appointments, indicated that the group would commence work in advance of the Transport Act, as an informal review body and would investigate proposals for restoration and promotion to Cruiseway status of those sections of the canals within the "Remainder" category.

During the period June to December 1968 IWAAC members inspected the following canals: Slough Arm, Grand Union Canal, Caldon Canal, Kennet and Avon Canal, Grand Western Canal, Dudley Tunnel and the Erewash Canal, and discussed their future with interested local organisations. With the brighter prospect of a new future for many local canals which were supported by local restoration proposals, various individual canal societies were formed at this time. They included the Caldon and Pocklington Canal Societies, who immediately started to prepare restoration proposals for submission to IWAAC.

As IWAAC began its review, so the provisions of the Countryside Act came into force on 3 August 1968. The Act created the Countryside Commission and authorised the facility of grants to local authorities in approved cases in respect of expenditure for the provision of Country Parks. It also authorised the development of waterways within or adjacent to the National Parks. This feature was later used to finance the full restoration of the Brecon and Abergavenny Canal. Although the "Commercial" and "Cruiseways" under the control of BWB were excluded from the provisions of the Countryside Act it applied to the "Remainder" waterways, and thus gave a further stimulus to their revival.

To ensure that the urban canals received equal consideration, the IWA and the Peak Forest Canal Society sought BWB permission to clear sections of the semi-derelict Ashton Canal as part of an even larger local renovation scheme called "Operation Spring Clean". Co-ordinated by Palmer, editor of *Navvies Notebook*, a major canal clearance working party, code-named "Operation Ashton", was launched. It had the threefold objectives of: (1) Showing the local authorities the value of the canal; (2) proving that a large co-ordinated voluntary working party could be arranged; and (3) showing what volunteers could do *en masse*, in contrast to the work of smaller teams of professionals.

The working party took place on 21–22 September 1968 and over 600 volunteers attended. It gained considerable publicity for the waterways restoration movement and proved, without doubt, the considerable impact such a co-ordinated volunteer operation could have.

Whilst this major restoration project was being planned, two other developments connected with waterways revival, as part of a growing interest in industrial archaeology, were also beginning to develop. The first was the foundation of the Ironbridge Gorge Trust, which included the projected restoration of the Hay Incline and Coalport Canal as part of the Blists Hill Museum site. The second was a scheme for the complete restoration of Buxworth Basin, promoted by the IWPS, to show the full extent of the former Peak Forest railway and canal interchange.

In a similar way, the IWA Midlands Branch, organised a Waterways Conference at Birmingham University on 12–13 July 1968 with the aim of evaluating the many different ways in which the BCN system could be revived to the benefit of those who lived in the area. This was pertinent as a large number of the waterways in the BCN system were given an interim status when the 1968 Transport Act received Royal Assent on 25 October 1968. The Act guaranteed the retention of the canals in their existing state for a period of three years, whilst their future was reviewed. In an effort to further develop local interest in their revival, the IWA planned its national rally of boats in Birmingham in July 1969.

As interest developed in reviving the major waterways so the potential future of various other derelict canals also came under review. One of these was the Wey and Arun Canal, which had been abandoned in 1876. This attracted the interest of some local enthusiasts during 1968 and, after further research, they formed the Wey and Arun Canal Society in 1970 to more formally promote, in the longer term, its complete restoration.

It was within this growing wave of interest in the revival of the waterways that the IWA set out its strategy for 1969 under the theme, "Safeguarding Britain's Waterways." Each of the eight IWA branches were allocated waterways in their region which were designated for restoration. For each the IWA members were asked to work in conjunction with the local waterway groups. This had a two-fold effect. Firstly, for those waterways that did not have a local protection group, it stimulated local enthusiasts to form one, as was the case of the Worcester and Birmingham Canal and the adjacent Droitwich Canal. Whilst secondly, for other waterways not already the subject of formal restoration proposals, it provoked further consideration of their future potential. It equally created a growing public awareness of the potential of the derelict waterways, which in its turn gave rise to the inauguration of other restoration groups. This was the case with the derelict Driffield Navigation and the slumbering Royal Military Canal.

As part of this strategy for the promotion of the various restoration campaigns, the IWA launched a National Restoration Fund appeal with a target of £50,000. It was planned that the money collected should be available to contribute towards the costs of restoring waterways in any part of the country. Preliminary projects to receive contributions from the fund were the Ashton Canal, the Kennet and Avon Canal and the Upper Avon Navigation.

The first success from the renewed vigour of the restoration campaign came with the official reopening of the Welford Arm by F. Price, the BWB Chairman, on 17 May 1969, at a rally of boats which had been organised by the Old Union Canals Society that had participated in the restoration work. A second success was a commitment by Bath City Council to allocate £7,500 towards the restoration of the Kennet and Avon Canal in the town, over a three-year period commencing in 1970. The third success was the announcement by the BWB that they proposed to establish a working party to study and report on the future of the BCN. Representatives of the local canal societies and the IWA were invited to join this group.

There was equal progress on another front. After a joint meeting between the BWB, Stoke-on-Trent City Council and the Staffordshire County Council, agreement was reached that the Councils would contribute towards the full restoration of the Caldon Canal. The work of the Caldon Canal Society in promoting the local campaign over the preceding years was thus finally reaping its reward. In much the same way the future of the Bridgwater and Taunton Canal seemed more assured when the Somerset County Council indicated they would consider a recommendation that it be designated a Linear Country Park.

To capitalise on the growing Local and County Authority interest in reviving the canals, the IWA organised a "Waterways in Planning" conference in London on 15–16 October 1969. In particular the restoration potential of the Slough Arm, the Basingstoke Canal and the Kennet and Avon Canal were fully reviewed and the support of the authorities concerned carefully developed. The strength of feeling developed by the meeting gave added impetus to the work of IWAAC in reviewing the waterways concerned.

Another event that gave impetus to one particular restoration scheme was a major "Dig" at Welshpool on the. Montgomery Arm of the Shropshire Union Canal. The event was organised by the Shropshire Union Canal Society at the request of the Welshpool By-Pass

Action Committee, which had been formed to oppose a proposal to use the bed of the canal as the route for a new road. The "Dig" was a considerable success and later paved the way for the inauguration of a formal Montgomery Canal restoration campaign.

For the waterway restorationists, 1969 provided a year of consolidation. In 1967 there were 11 working groups, in 1968 the number had risen to 16, and by the close of 1969 the number had risen to 23, with over 200 volunteers being mustered for the two major "Digs" at Marple and Welshpool.

The year 1970 offered a new challenge to this growing band, which became more formally known as the Waterway Recovery Group. 1970 was European Conservation Year and the IWA stated that its contribution would be the organisation of a restoration campaign for the derelict waterways. To add weight to its aims the IWA announced on 19 January 1970 that it would provide £10,000 and unlimited voluntary labour for the restoration of the Ashton Canal.

To further promote the restoration of the Ashton Canal the IWA organised a conference entitled, "Waterways in the Urban Scene" at Manchester University on 8–9 April 1970. The conference included sessions on "The Price of Neglect", "Restoration", "Amenity Uses" and "Counting the Cost". The speakers included L. Scott,

(chairman of *The Guardian*), I. Harrington, (chairman of IWAAC) and M.P. Winstanley MP, all of whom added their weight to the restoration campaign.

The IWA also decided to try to prevent the passage of a draft BWB Bill through Parliament which included a clause relieving the Board from the responsibility of maintaining a certain depth of water in the Grantham Canal. Ultimately, as the result of the acceptance of an amendment to the Bill, the prospect for the longer-term restoration of the Grantham Canal became enhanced, and this in turn led to the formation of the Grantham Canal Society to promote the restoration scheme.

As the year 1970 progressed so did two separate commercial restoration proposals. The first was a proposal to restore the Leven Canal, as part of a scheme for a marina and associated recreational development. The second was the restoration of the old Engine Arm of the Oxford Canal, as a pleasure boat mooring. Both schemes offered a new dimension to the waterway restoration campaign.

In a similar way a Civic Trust Award for the Farmer's Bridge canal-side redevelopment scheme in Birmingham added another aspect to the role of the restoration movement. It also provided a showpiece to which other local authority representatives, in doubt about the amenity value of waterways, could be brought. One of

Derelict Monmouthshire Canal at Malpas Lock

Canal work at St John's Lock, Woking

the first of such groups was a party from the Manchester area who were shown the development by members of the IWA and Peak Forest Canal Society as part of their campaign to gain local authority support for the reopening of the "Cheshire Canal Ring". The Farmers' Bridge scheme also did much to convince members of Droitwich New Town Development Committee of the value of restoring the Droitwich Canal as an integral part of the New Town's development plan.

By mid 1970 the growing interest in canals had led to the production of a *Canal Enthusiasts Handbook: 1970–71,* which provided a reference volume for those interested in the inland waterways. It also offered an analysis of the various waterway museums and associated ventures, all of which generated a further public interest in canals. This interest was further enhanced by the reopening of Ports Creek on 19 April 1970, which was once part of the London to Portsmouth inland waterway until the creek had become blocked in 1939. Its restoration and reopening was the result of a joint IWA and local residents" campaign that was inaugurated in l963.

Of even greater significance was a press conference called by IWAAC, on 26 June 1970, to outline its preliminary recommendations to the BWB about the future of the "Remainder" waterways. These included proposals for the restoration and upgrading

to "Cruiseway" status of the following canals: Dudley Canal, Caldon Canal, Erewash Canal, Kennet and Avon Canal, Grand Western Canal, Slough Arm of the Grand Union Canal, Ashton Canal, Pocklington Canal and the Cromford Canal. The comprehensiveness of the list and the weight of the IWAAC support gave the waterways enthusiasts added heart to more critically develop their own political campaign, which had once again been put in the balance with the defeat of the Labour Government in the June 1970 general election.

The change of Government provided a timely opportunity for the waterways enthusiasts to review the substantial progress that had been made over the preceding years. At the January 1966 IWA council meeting it was said that, "mass closures are now in sight"; by mid 1970 only some of the "Remainder" waterways were in jeopardy – for the majority the future seemed assured.

Map 5 depicts the further spread of restoration schemes during the period 1965 to 1970. The majority of these were waterways defined as being in the "Remainder" category in the 1968 Transport Act. In the light of the facility within the Act for local authorities to contribute to the cost of restoring individual canals perhaps the most significant development during this period was the substantial growth in the number of local waterway societies, many of which organised volunteer working parties to clear the rubbish from the canals they sought to revive. The growing awareness of the value of these volunteers to the promotion of the national restoration campaign led to the production of the *Navvies Notebook* by a co-ordinating body under the leadership of Palmer, which became the Waterway Recovery Group in 1970. The impact of the volunteer "Digs", first at Ashton, and subsequently at Marple, Welshpool and Dudley supported by the *Navvies Notebook,* did much to enhance the overall waterway restoration campaign and increase the public awareness of the amenity potential offered by the restored canals. The evergrowing number of waterway books that appeared between 1965 and 1970 still further developed a public interest in the heritage of the inland waterways and strengthened the growing commitment by local authorities to finance waterway restoration schemes.

VI 1971-75:

AMENITY DEVELOPMENT

The change from a Labour to a Conservative Government in June 1970 presented a new political perspective to the way in which the future of the inland waterways could develop. Reviewing the state of the nation at the time Harold Wilson commented:

"No incoming Prime Minister ... in living memory has taken over a stronger economic situation. I wanted to use ... the economic situation for building on what we have done ... now we hand over the means to do that, to somebody else."

Although there was evidence that the state of the national economy had begun to improve, and the first proof of the existence of North Sea oil gave the prospect of an even brighter hope for the 1980s, other potentially basic deficiencies in the national resource base gave cause for concern. Perhaps the most vital of these was the rapid growth in the demand for water, and the realisation by the authorities that existing conservation and distribution systems could not keep abreast of the rapid rate of increase in demand. Much of the extra water needed was required by the sophisticated industrial processes and the wide range of domestic equipment that was providing many members of the population with increased leisure time.

This leisure time, when combined with the extra hours gained from the shorter working week and the third week's paid holiday which was available to the majority of workers in 1971, provided a rapidly growing demand for increased leisure facilities. This, when added to the increased personal mobility offered by the higher level of car ownership, which had been a feature of the late 1960s, led to growing fears of the rapid destruction of the very environment that people sought to enjoy during their leisure timeIt was this fear, amongst others, which stimulated the development of a strong conservation lobby, which sought to protect the national heritage. This lobby placed a burden of additional financial demands on the newly elected Government as it began to evaluate its strategy for the years ahead.

One of the first steps to placate the lobby was the creation of a new Ministry for the Environment. This placed Government control of the waterways in the hands of the Secretary of State for the Environment, to whom BWB and IWAAC reported. To assist the Secretary of State in developing a policy for the waterways, the IWA prepared a memorandum on the matters that they considered to be of immediate importance.

These included a request that the guarantee to retain the "Remainder" waterways should be renewed for a further three years so that positive negotiations could continue. It also made the suggestion that the BWB

1.	Prees Branch (1971)	16.	Westport Canal (1972)
2.	Hazelstrine Arm (1971)	17.	Chichester & Arundel Canal (1973)
3.	Titford Canal (1971)	18.	Thames & Medway Canal (1974)
4.	Ivel Navigation (1971)	19.	Neath & Tennant Canals (1974)
5.	River Lark (1971)	20.	Higher Avon Navigation (1974)
6.	River Little Ouse (1971)	21.	Gipping Navigation (1974)
7.	Louth Canal (1971)	22.	Upper Trent Navigation (1974)
8.	Carlisle Canal (1972)	23.	Huddersfield Narrow Canal (1974)
9.	St Helens Canal (1972)	24.	Itchen Navigation (1975)
10.	Market Weighton Canal (1972)	25.	Saltisford Arm (1975)
11.	Lower Cromford Canal (1972)	26.	Wyrley & Essington Canal (1975)
12.	Slea Navigation (1972)	27.	Stafford Arm (1975)
13.	Bure Navigation (1972)	28.	Hatherton Branch (1975)
14.	Waveney Navigation (1972)	29.	Horncastle Canal (1975)
15.	Thames & Severn Canal (1972)	30.	Witham Navigable Drains (1975)

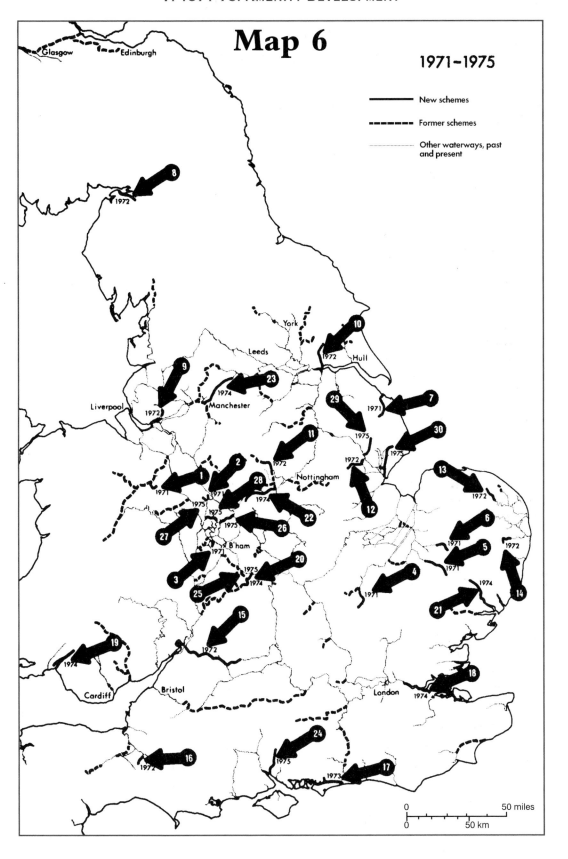

Map 6

1971–1975

——————	New schemes
– – – – –	Former schemes
··············	Other waterways, past and present

should be enlarged, both in power and representation, to include members from local government and bodies interested in environmental improvement. It similarly proposed that local authorities should contribute funds to the BWB, that could offset the costs of retaining the canals in their areas for recreational and amenity purposes. The memorandum was the opening move in the reappraisal of national waterways policy that subsequently followed.

The first official report of the situation of inland waterways was given to the Secretary of State when the BWB presented its 1970 annual report in early 1971. This noted the growing demand for water recreation and verified the more intensive use of the canals. It equally drew attention to the Board's restricted financial powers and lack of ability to deal constructively with the "Remainder" waterways. The report also recorded that a series of negotiations, with some 16 local authorities, had been developed during the past year with the aim of gaining financial support to secure the future of some of the "Remainder" lengths of canal. Little action had been taken in respect of other "Remainder" waterways.

The year 1971 was the IWA Silver Jubilee, and to sharpen its campaign to save the canals the IWA council designated it, "Remainder Waterways Campaign Year". The IWA set itself two tasks: to campaign for the restoration of the waterways in the "Remainder" category; and to raise money for the National Waterways Restoration Fund.

The campaign got off to a good start and the chairman, J. Humphries, told members in March 1971, of "an encouraging upsurge in public interest", noting that membership had increased by 20 per cent, over the past nine months to 6,337; that waterway authors were reporting a substantial increase in book sales; that several canal boat-hire companies had reported a 25 per cent rise in advance bookings; and that an increasing number of local authorities were asking the Association for advice in respect of potential restoration schemes. He concluded:

"1971 could be the turning point in many ways ... we are not yet on the crest of the wave, but I have a strong feeling that the tide is beginning to run our way."

In an effort to publicise the desirability of retaining and restoring the "Remainder" waterways the IWA scheduled a series of boat rallies during 1971 on the following canals:

9–12 April	Tame Valley Canal (BCN)
17–18 April	Rochdale Canal
23 May	Bridgwater and Taunton Canal
29–31 May	Endon, Caldon Canal
29–31 May	York, to support the Pocklington Canal and River Derwent restorations
29–31 May	Erewash Canal
12 June	Bidford, Upper Avon Navigation
26–27 June	Bristol for Southern Kennet and Avon Canal
13–16 August	Northampton, to support the Middle Level, Well Creek and Great Ouse
28–30 August	Sheffield for the South Yorkshire Navigation

At the time plans for these rallies were being made, so the first hopeful report for the future of one section of the "Remainder" waterways appeared. This was the report of the BCN Working Party entitled *Birmingham Canal Navigations*. It was submitted to the BWB on 11 December 1970 and published early in 1971. The report suggested that 66 miles of the 80-mile "Remainder" section of the BCN had a valuable future and that the canals could be restored for a total cost of approximately £47,500. The report noted that the majority of the 66 miles listed were currently navigable and no expenditure, other than routine maintenance, would be involved in retaining them. The recommendations for the BCN canals to be retained were made within four priority groups and none of the £47,500 required for restoration was needed for the first two of these categories, which the working party recommended for immediate upgrading to "Cruiseway" status. For the remainder of the canals it suggested that further discussions should be developed with the local authorities concerned, with the view to their restoration to "Cruiseway standard, on the cost-sharing basis which was envisaged in the 1968 Transport Act. This proposal was quickly adopted for two of the canals listed in the Priority 3 category and plans proceeded for the restoration of the Dudley Tunnel Branch and the Titford Canal, financed in part by the local authorities concerned.

In much the same way a Local Authority Joint Committee, covering both the Ashton and Lower Peak Forest Canals, started to actively review costings proposed by the BWB for the restoration of the two local canals which were needed to complete the "Cheshire Canal Ring". Such was the local commitment that the town clerk of Manchester, who acted as secretary to the group, started to explore what other Government grants might be available to help cover the costs of the restoration work.

Rather different problems confronted the North-Eastern Branch of the IWA in their quest to restore the River Derwent as a through navigation. In an effort to overcome the legal problems involved in obtaining rights to restore and operate the locks on the river a new charitable company, the Yorkshire Derwent Trust Ltd, was formed. The trust entered into negotiations with the River Authority during 1971 and these ultimately led to the trust receiving a deed of grant permitting them to proceed with the restoration work. To assist the trust in raising the necessary finance for the project, the Yorkshire Derwent Society was formed to offer its members the chance to actively pursue their restoration ideals.

Those interested in waterway restoration saw possible problems ahead when they heard that Harrington, the active IWAAC chairman who was undertaking a review of the "Remainder" waterways, was to be replaced as both a member of the BWB and also as chairman of the advisory council. These fears were, to a degree, allayed when H. Stockwell, vice-chairman and chairman of K&ACT, was elected in his place. In much the same way various invitations for the IWA chairman to visit the DOE in early 1971 and see the minister about the future of the waterways at first had an ominous ring, but were later proved constructive in shaping the policy that evolved.

The most useful early advances towards restoration during 1971 came from a number of grants made by the IWA from the National Waterway Restoration Fund, to assist in financing various restoration projects. Offers of £10,000 each were made to promote the restoration of

Reopening of Ashton Canal in 1974

the Ashton Canal and for work on the Upper Avon, with smaller sums being donated to the Kennet and Avon, Rochdale, Caldon and Montgomery Canals to assist the local restoration campaigns. Perhaps the most tangible action came when a member of the association, who wished to remain anonymous, offered to pay the cost of re-gating the first of the closed locks on the River Derwent at Elvington.

One area of the country where little co-ordinated action had evolved to promote a restoration campaign, was Scotland, where the IWA had less than 30 active members. To remedy this situation an associated organisation, called the Scottish Inland Waterways Association, was founded in Edinburgh in early 1971. The first task of the new group was to fight a proposal to infill part of the Union Canal, although it also had an interest in reopening the Forth and Clyde Canal.

As the year 1971 progressed, so the first of a series of restoration advances became a reality with the reopening of phase one of the Upper Avon restoration scheme. A section of the Upper Avon, between Evesham and Bidford Bridge, was formally declared open on 12 June 1971, when some 20 craft passed along a new navigation channel under Bidford Bridge. The thoughts of those present then turned to restoring the next stretch of the river through to Stratford but the problem of finance loomed as the greatest obstacle. This problem was, to a degree, dispelled when the Department of the Environment offered a contribution of £25,000 towards the estimated cost of £250,000 for completely reopening the river between Evesham and Stratford, which was the missing link in a potential circular cruising route through the Midlands for the growing number of holiday craft.

The problems created by the growing number of pleasure craft led to the initiation of three other restoration schemes during 1971. The first was the revival of the derelict Hazelstrine Arm of the Staffordshire and Worcestershire Canal. This was promoted to provide an alternative mooring and club base for the Stafford Boat Club, who were forced to vacate their previous moorings when the lease expired and BWB indicated that it wished to relet the site as a base for a boat-hire operator. The second and third schemes were of a similar nature. A plan to reopen the Louth Canal was envisaged as part of a project to create a boat marina at Louth, whilst the restoration of part of the Prees Branch of the Shropshire Union Canal was similarly connected with a new marina development. Only the latter scheme finally reached fruition because of the immediate local demand for extra boat moorings.

One other restoration plan was promoted in 1971. This was a longer-term scheme for reopening the former navigations of the Rivers Ivel, Lark and Little

Ouse. All were tributaries of the Great Ouse and had been associated with the Ouse Navigation system. The plans were proposed when the Great Ouse River Authority contractors commenced work on a new river-flow gauging station on the river at Roxton, as part of a major flood control scheme. The first stage of the River Authority project envisaged the construction of four new weirs and locks, at Roxton, Great Barford, Willington and Castle Mills, which, when completed, would reopen the former navigation on the river through to Bedford. The Great Ouse Restoration Society agreed to contribute £5,000 towards the navigation works for each of these new locks as its own contribution to the scheme. The firm prospect of the restored Ouse Navigation being fully operational by 1978 led some members of the Restoration Society to formulate longer-term plans for other extensions to their cruising waters. They believed that the revival of the former navigations of the Ivel, Lark and Little Ouse offered the greatest likelihood of longer-term success, with a prospect of similar River Authority participation in the schemes. These plans were later developed by a sub-committee of the East Anglian Waterways Association, who tried to generate further support from the local authorities and communities concerned.

On 20 August 1971, a long-awaited IWAAC report on the potential of the *Remainder Waterways* was published. The report was the culmination of three years work by members of the council and made various proposals to the Secretary of State for the Environment, suggesting that he should take positive action by upgrading some of the "Remainder" canals to "Cruiseways". The report detailed the various inspections undertaken by the council and made firm proposals for restoration action on many waterways they had visited. The report emphasised that many of the waterways mentioned had been included within the terms of a three-year guarantee for their retention, which was made in the *Transport Act* 1968. The publication of the list of waterways that IWAAC proposed should be retained and revived raised enthusiasts' hopes for their future. From the restorationists' viewpoint, the report made many welcome proposals, particularly with its suggestion that the Dudley Tunnel and Parkhead Locks should be restored with local authority help. In other instances, such as the Bridgwater and Taunton Canal and the Forth and Clyde and Union Canals, the suggestions fell far below expectations, with only minimal retention of short stretches being recommended instead of a larger-scale revival that the IWA had proposed.

The report, however, gave added hope for some future revival of parts of the St Helens Canal, as a water park in the Warrington New Town development plans and,

more particularly, added weight to the growing local lobby, led by the Shropshire Union Canal Society, for the complete restoration of the derelict Montgomery Branch of the Shropshire Union Canal.

IWA members were advised of the report's findings in November 1971 and were also told of the reopening of two of the sections of the waterways mentioned. The first was the reopening of Cottingwith Lock, on the Pocklington Canal, on 17 July 1971. This was mainly due to the efforts of the Pocklington Canal Amenity Society who were supported by the local councils. The other was the reopening of one of the flight of Widcombe Locks on the Kennet and Avon Canal at Bath on 5 September 1971. Both events gave added impetus to the restoration campaign and added further pressure for action on the IWAAC proposals.

As the IWAAC report was being considered by the authorities concerned, so various other features relating to the revival of a more general interest in the waterways were beginning to develop. The first of these was the growing public debate, in Manchester, over the cost and amenity value of a section of the Rochdale Canal that had been infilled and used as a shallow water park. Local public opinion was rapidly changing in its attitude towards the scheme, which had proved substantially more expensive than the restoration of the canal as an integral part of a new estate, on the style of the contemporary Farmers Bridge development in Birmingham.

The second was the inauguration of the North-West Museum of Inland Navigation at Ellesmere Port on 8 October 1971. This scheme was co-ordinated by D. Owen, the director of the Manchester Museum, to meet the demands of growing local interest in the inland waterways and the boats that used them. The third was the growing interest of the Derbyshire County Council in taking over the upper reaches of the Cromford Canal and restoring it as part of the larger High Peak Park amenity development scheme.

Each of these features highlighted the spread and growth of public commitment towards a revival of the waterways. This revival was also showing itself in a direct commitment to action by the growing number of volunteer work sites on various canals that were being organised throughout the country. Many of these were recorded in *Navvies Notebook* of January 1971, which also announced the launching of an embryo Droitwich Canal Trust at an inaugural working party on the Droitwich Canal on 13–14 March 1971. Similarly the renamed *Navvies,* in October 1971, announced the first of a series of working parties on the Grantham Canal at Hickling Basin. To further develop this spread of interest, various of the local waterway societies started to issue cruising and walking guides dealing with their own particular canal. Perhaps the best example of these was the booklet entitled *The Erewash Canal,* published by the Erewash Canal Preservation and Development Association in 1971.

This rapid surge of interest in the promotion of many small waterway restoration schemes was partially checked on 2 December 1971, when the Department of the Environment published Circular 92/71: *Reorganisation of Water and Sewage Services: Government Proposals and Arrangements for Consultation.* The main feature proposed was that of the creation of ten new all-purpose Regional Water Authorities on 1 April 1974. The circular also suggested that the new Water Authorities should take over the responsibility for the inland waterways, in their respective areas, from the BWB, which would subsequently be abolished. Immediate fears about the proposals were expressed by the IWA, who noted that the plans made for the restoration of many "Remainder" waterways, and their subsequent upgrading to "Cruiseway" status, could well be lost in the new debate.

To combat this potential loss, the IWA initiated an immediate membership drive and held a conference in Birmingham on 22 January 1972 to discuss the proposals made in the circular. The meeting ended with delegates passing a resolution for submission to the Government urging that:

(1) A National Waterways Authority should be established controlling all inland navigations, with an adequate income to maintain properly and to modernise the system for amenity and transport use.

(2) The Government should fulfil its pre-election pledge to restore the public"s right of navigation.

(3) Local authorities should be strongly encouraged to help financially in the restoration of derelict waterways. One other beneficial impact of the circular was the strengthening of local efforts to get viable restoration schemes under way. Perhaps the greatest advance in this respect was made on 15 December 1971, when a firm agreement was reached between BwB, the IWA and the riparian local authorities to restore the Ashton and Lower Peak Forest Canals. Each of the parties concerned was to contribute financially to the restoration costs involved. To inaugurate this project the Waterway Recovery Group, led by Palmer, decided to organise a major effort to show the local population just what could be done by co-ordinated volunteer action. The code name "Ashtac" was given to the "Dig", which was held on 25–26 March 1972, when over 1,000 volunteers from throughout the British Isles descended on Ashton and started to clear rubbish from the canal.

The commitment of the volunteers at Ashton was praised by BWB who subsequently published a broadsheet, *Co-operation '72,* outlining the full extent of

Restored Hay Incline

the waterway restoration work achieved in conjunction with the volunteers and local authorities since the introduction of the more liberal provisions of the 1968 Transport Act. The broadsheet carried an account of the progress made in respect of many of the "Remainder" canals, and offered a diary defining the critical dates of the advances made. The review concluded with a sub-section entitled: "Voluntary Effort – Showing People Care", which confirmed:

The work carried out by voluntary canal societies and organisations has played an important part in bringing about the present situation in which a number of waterways are to be fully restored to navigation.

The theme of the value of volunteers was also taken up in a report, *Fifty Million Volunteers,* presented to the Secretary of State for the Environment in February 1972. The report noted the growing value of the work of volunteers as a natural expression of their interest in the community and the environment. It suggested that the Government should both recognise the role of the voluntary movements, and provide the means within which they could improve their efficiency and thus play a more vital part in improving the environment. As an example of the voluntary work, the report referred to the IWA efforts in restoring canals and it noted: "The contribution of the Association and its affiliated groups in 1971 alone amounted to 7,500 days' work in the field.18

In February 1972 the Government announced "Operation Eyesore" under which local authorities could obtain exchequer grants of up to 85 per cent, to remedy local eyesores. The aim of the scheme was twofold; to provide jobs in assisted areas, and to improve the local environment. The scheme provided an ideal opportunity for local authorities to gain finance to restore semi-derelict canals. Funds from the scheme ultimately proved to be the key factor in the development of the Ashton, Lower Peak Forest and Caldon Canal restoration schemes.

The publicity of the agreement to restore the Ashton and Peak Forest Canals and the Caldon Canal, was quickly followed by an announcement of a similar scheme on the Dudley Canal. This included a commitment by the Dudley Corporation that they would not only provide 50 per cent of the finance required for the restoration work but would also landscape the land at the Park Head end of Dudley Tunnel as part of a major scheme to improve the derelict area. In much the same way the East Riding County Council revealed their plans for contributions towards the cost of restoring the Pocklington Canal in March 1972.

Perhaps the most rapid action to retain a waterway was made by the Market Weighton Civic Trust in early 1972, when they heard that the entrance lock of the Market Weighton Canal was faced with demolition. The Trust's Canal Restoration Committee took action to get the whole lock structure designated as an Ancient Monument. This was rapidly achieved. They then started to prepare plans for the restoration of the derelict upper reaches of the canal. The action of volunteer groups stimulated the BWB to make their own restoration proposals, the most promising of which was a plan that included the restoration of the upper two locks of the Ripon Canal, and the reopening of the Ripon Town Basin as a marina. This offered a prospect of the revival of the most northerly point in the interconnected national waterway system.

One other indicator of public attitudes of the time was the growing number of waterway orientated books that had appeared by 1972. One of these was a compendium offering details of the forgotten and lesser-known canal navigations. It was entitled, *Lost Canals of England and Wales.* The book, by R. Russell, detailed the current state of some 78 derelict canals. It stimulated various enthusiasts to review again the future potential of many of the waterways that were formerly considered lost. Amongst those waterways mentioned were the Carlisle Canal, the Stroudwater Navigation and the Thames and Severn Canal, the Sleaford Navigation and the Westport Canal. All of these became the centre of new restoration schemes as the year 1972 progressed.

Perhaps the most significant of these was a restoration proposal for the Stroudwater Navigation, which later embraced the connected Thames and Severn Canal. This restoration project was formulated by the newly formed Stroudwater Canal Society, which later became the Stroudwater, Thames and Severn Canal Trust. Other schemes that were projected in 1972 were those for the revival of the derelict upper reaches of the Bure and Waveney Navigations, stimulated by the East Anglian Waterways Association; and for the restoration of the Lower Cromford Canal, which was promoted by the Erewash Canal Preservation and Development Association as part of its longer-term aims. Volunteer navvies also moved to other sites to assist with special restoration projects. The most unusual of these was the restoration of the Hay Incline, at Coalport, situated within the Blists Hill Museum complex.

Two other unique projects were also under way by 1972. The first was the scheme to reopen the Wey and Arun Canal by the canal society of the same name. The Surrey-based members of the society held their first working party at Bramley in January 1972 and, to further develop the scheme, a second site, at Run Common, was inaugurated in April of the same year. Of a much more dramatic nature was a scheme to clear rubbish

Dudley Canal in 1970 (left) and after restoration (below)

from Well Creek, near Upwell, at a "Dig" codenamed "Fenatic" in October 1972. For this project plans were made by the Well Creek Trust to have the creek drained so that the clearance could take place. This was the first major volunteer working party on the Middle Level Navigations and denoted a further spread in the network of restoration schemes.

During 1972 the national debate grew over the merits and demerits of the Government proposals for abolishing the awB. At this time also the waterways enthusiasts gained their own independent national magazine, *Waterways World*. This provided enthusiasts with a regular means to keep up-to-date with developments on the inland waterways, and gave members of the general public a chance to read about the developments that were taking place on the canals. The October 1972 edition of *Waterways World* carried a report of the transfer of the upper Cromford Canal to Derbyshire County Council and of the consequent formation of the Cromford Canal Society to develop the associated restoration scheme. It also reported plans of Somerset County Council to improve the Bridgwater and Taunton Canal and recorded details of the Somerset Inland Waterways Society fight to get some of the fixed bridges across the canal removed. Both items stimulated considerable public support for the societies mentioned.

In much the same way, one of the longest-standing restoration schemes received a publicity boost on 12

August 1972 when the Duke of Bedford reopened Roxton Lock on the River Great Ouse. This was the first of four new locks to be built by the River Authority over the period 1972–78 as part of a major river-control scheme.

Similarly the formal start of the full restoration of the Caldon Canal, which was marked by a ceremony on 22 August 1972, gained considerable publicity. It was also used by the magazine as a means of publicising the BWB views about the proposals for the reorganisation of the waterways. These were contrasted with the very different problems faced by the Yorkshire Derwent Trust in reopening the River Derwent when Lord Feversham officially reopened Elvington Lock, on 27 August 1972, calling for the Government to inaugurate a "national park of waterways."

By the close of 1972, the dilemma over the future of the "Remainder" waterways was still unresolved. This was becoming the subject of ever-growing public concern, which was best shown by the rapid growth in the membership of the IWA. This had risen by 334 per cent, during 1972 and had nearly reached 10,000 by the close of the year.

Some fears were allayed when the draft of the 1973 Water Bill was published in January 1973. Although it did little to clarify the future of the "Remainder" waterways, it did offer a new lease of life for the BWB. The mounting pressure from the local authorities and waterways enthusiasts, and even the BWB itself, during 1972 had been sufficient to persuade the Government to modify its plan for the reorganisation of the country's water services, and the nationalised canals were excluded from the scheme. This did not, however, resolve the dilemma of finding additional resources to finance the growing number of restoration schemes. To assist in some way, the IWA launched an appeal to develop its National Waterways Restoration Fund to enable the Waterway Recovery Group to extend the range of machinery and equipment it held, which was available to assist more practically with the various volunteer schemes.

Two such schemes were making considerable headway by early 1973. The first was that projected by the Erewash Canal Preservation and Development Association to restore Great Northern Basin, at Langley Mill. The group had cleared the derelict basin by the close of 1972 and were undertaking the final landscaping work in readiness for a formal reopening ceremony on 26 May 1973. The second scheme, and perhaps the more important, was the Tunnel Reopening at Dudley (TRAD) by the chairman of BWB on 21 April 1973. This event was heralded as a significant advance for the restoration movement because it was the first time that an officially abandoned nationalised waterway had been restored to full working order. It was equally the first nationalised canal to be fully restored since the introduction of the 1968 Transport Act, which had authorised the facility for joint action between a local authority, a voluntary waterway organisation, and the BWB. A less formal reopening took place on the Kennet and Avon Canal at Wootton Rivers on 10 June 1973, when the four locks that linked the 15-mile Devizes Pound to the summit level were officially reopened. This also inaugurated a three-year restoration programme organised by the K&ACT entitled, "Project 76".

The success of these three reopenings coupled with the local example of the practical achievements of the Wey and Arun Canal Society in restoring sections of the Wey and Arun Canal, prompted waterways enthusiasts in Sussex to form the Sussex Canal Trust in July 1973, with the aim of preserving and ultimately restoring the former Portsmouth to Arundel Canal. Founder-members of the group were involved in organising a procession of small boats along the associated Chichester Canal, in June 1973, to celebrate the dredging of the Chichester Basin and the entrance channel by its owners, the West Sussex Council.

After a long gestation period, a modified version of the 1973 Water Act received Royal Assent on 18 July 1973. It placed a duty on the Secretary of State for the Environment to develop a national policy for water, which included "the use of inland water for recreation",

and "the use of inland water for navigation", but excluded the waterways operated by BWB. It authorised the establishment of the ten new Water Authorities who were responsible for general recreational provision, on 1 April 1974, and created a National Water Council. It also created a new body called the Water Space Amenity Commission, to act in an advisory capacity and to co-ordinate nature conservation and amenity development. The Act directed each of the Water Authorities to review the water resources within their areas and prepare plans for future developments. As a minor part of this planning remit, another potential restoration project was formulated by the research department of the Severn Trent Water Authority. This was a possible scheme for reopening the former Navigation on the Trent, between Nottingham and Burton, details of which were later published in *Motor Boat and Yachting* of October 1975.

In much the same way as the Water Authorities were considering potential schemes for development, IWA members were debating which of the other derelict waterways might be candidates for restoration. Two proposals that competed for attention were the adjacent derelict trans-Pennine links of the broad-gauge Rochdale Canal and the more heavily locked narrow-gauge Huddersfield Narrow Canal. Both projects were announced in the *Bulletin* of June 1973, and in 1974 two new independent canal societies were formed to promote the separate schemes.

At national level, a broader debate on the theme of "Sport and Leisure" was being developed by a Select Committee of the House of Lords. The Committee produced its *Second Report* on 25 July 1973. This paid particular attention to the value of the inland waterways, and noted:

"While demand for water recreation increases swiftly, the amount of available water increases only slowly ... In England and Wales, however, there is far too little amenity water available for the public."

The Committee recognised the value of restoring derelict or partly derelict waterways, and welcomed the positive approach of many local authorities. Their report also suggested that restoration should be given every encouragement. In particular it highlighted the anomalous position of the "Remainder" waterways in the development of new recreational facilities. The report concluded by recommending:

"Water recreation should be grant aided ... The British Waterways Board must have a substantial improvement in financial resources ..."

The status of "Remainder" waterways under the Transport Act 1968 should be reviewed."

Although the report was well received its recommendations did little to stimulate any immediate resolution of the problems that beset the waterways.

However, one member of the House of Lords, the Prince of Wales, did initiate some constructive action through the Prince of Wales" Committee. In October 1973 he announced a plan to restore a seven-mile stretch of the Montgomery Canal to amenity waterway standards. The scheme was co-ordinated by the Shropshire Union Canal Society and backed by the Variety Club of Great Britain, who were interested in the facilities the restored waterway could ultimately offer to handicapped children, as a recreational base.

As hope grew brighter for the restoration of the Montgomery Canal, so similar advances were made on the Basingstoke Canal. In 1972 an Officers Working Party was created to review the future of the canal after both of the County Councils concerned had resolved to purchase the 32-mile waterway. The report of the working party was published in mid 1973 and this recommended the full restoration to navigation of both the Surrey and Hampshire lengths of the canal. Full restoration was the most expensive of three alternative courses of action in relation to overall capital cost (£346,000), but offered the lowest longer-term net annual expenditure (£44,200). As the result of the evidence presented in the working party report both County Councils agreed to proceed with the compulsory purchase of their separate lengths of the canal and planned to restore them to navigable condition.

In mid-1973 the IWA created an Internal Review sub-committee to examine its own organisational structure, which was under severe stress through the 50 per cent increase in membership that had taken place between 1971–73 (5,500 to 11,000). The sub-committee produced a report in July 1973 which suggested that the Association should be reformed into six regions, under which it proposed that a second tier of 26 local branches should be created. These proposals were accepted and it was agreed the new structure should be operational by July 1974, except for the North-Eastern Region, which was able to bring the new arrangements into operation almost immediately. The formal creation of this new structure ultimately led to further restoration schemes being proposed during 1974–75, as the new branches began to review the restoration potential of the waterways in their respective areas.

Quite separately, practical progress on a long discussed restoration scheme was made on 23 October 1973 with the formal inauguration of the Droitwich Canals Trust. The groundwork for this advance had been carefully cultivated by local enthusiasts over the preceding decade. To launch the scheme with maximum local and national publicity, a major volunteer working party was promoted on 27–28 October 1973, code-named the "Droitwich Dig". The event was jointly organised by the Droitwich Canals Trust and the Waterway Recovery Group, who coordinated the work of the 500 volunteers that attended. The event gained television, radio and national newspaper coverage and was critically evaluated in an article in *Country Life* of 7 March 1974, which gained further support for the project and also for the national restoration campaign.

The extent of the national restoration campaign, in early 1973, was best defined in the *Canal Enthusiasts' Handbook,* No. 2, published in the autumn of that year. This provided a fairly comprehensive resume of each of the 28 major restoration schemes that were in progress at the time. It also provided a directory of some 60 clubs and societies that were directly associated with the revival of the inland waterways. A more comprehensive list of 194 waterway clubs and societies was, however, available in an *Address Book* (second edition) published by the BwB, which indicated the considerable extent of organised interest in the inland waterways at that time.

The year 1973 closed with a degree of optimism for the future of the canals. The number of pleasure boats on inland waterways had more than doubled between 1966 and 1972, and in 1973 over two million people had taken holidays on, or used, the inland waterways.

The IWA made its plans for 1974 looking to the future optimistically, but realising that lack of finance was going to provide the biggest stumbling block on the way ahead. Other unquantifiable features for 1974 were the reorganisation of local government, and the creation of the new Water Authorities, both on 1 April 1974. Each presented different problems yet both offered opportunities to the restoration movement. Perhaps the most significant of the advantages was that imposed by the time constraint for the changes. This was exemplified in the West Midlands where under local government reorganisation, the County Borough of Warley was due to amalgamate with West Bromwich to form a new authority, Sandwell. The Borough of Warley had been party to a plan to restore the Titford Canal and the associated Oldbury Locks as part of a derelict area redevelopment scheme. So that this work could be completed before Warley disappeared as a borough, plans for the Titford Canal restoration were substantially advanced and the restored canal became the first restoration scheme to be reopened in 1974. The ceremony took place on 30 March 1974 at a restoration rally organised by the BCN Society. The reopening of the canal, which was a joint effort between the BWB, the

Restored Grand Western Canal

Borough of Warley, and local volunteers, coordinated by the BCN Society, was the first of a series of reopenings that took place during the year. The reopening also came at a time when a new Labour Government had just been elected and were starting to grapple with the problems created by the miners" strike and the three-day working week, all of which placed greater constraints on the broader potential for development during the year ahead.

The national economic problems did not, however, deter the new Water Authorities from starting to review the rivers within their charge. One particular review undertaken was a survey by the Severn Trent Water Authority of the River Avon between Stratford and Warwick. Because this stretch of the river offered a potential new navigation route, the IWA contributed £250 towards the cost of the survey and in return received a copy of the resultant survey report. The evidence provided by this report was later used to promote a scheme to open the Higher Avon, which was evolved and promoted by a new body, led by Hutchings, called the Higher Avon Navigation Trust. With a view to promoting this and other potential restoration schemes, the IWA council decided to form a National Restoration Committee in April 1974 to ensure that all of the many local schemes were co-ordinated in the most effective way.

A major advance for the restoration movement took place on 1 April 1974, when an official test boat was able to successfully negotiate the restored sections of the Ashton and Lower Peak Forest Canals. The official reopening ceremony was conducted on 13 May 1974 by Denis Howell MP, Minister of State at the Department of the Environment. The event marked the culmination of a 13-year campaign to have the waterway restored and was the result of the combined efforts of BWB, the local authorities and the various local waterway groups. The total cost of the project was some £412,000, of which the greater part had come from Government grants under "Operation Eyesore". On a much smaller scale, but no less significant, was the reopening of Welshpool Town Lock by the Prince of Wales on 23 May 1974. This was the first tangible achievement in the scheme, supported by the Prince of Wales" Committee, to reopen a seven-mile section of the Montgomery Canal.

This event preceded what was to be the major reopening of 1974, when Queen Elizabeth the Queen Mother declared open the newly restored Upper Avon Navigation on 1 June. The project, organised by Hutchings, was certainly the largest restoration project of its kind ever undertaken. It involved the construction of nine new locks to reopen the 17-mile section of river, which had been closed to through navigation for over a century. All the funds required for the work were raised by public subscription, with the exception of a £25,000

DOE grant. Apart from showing the full extent of the capabilities of the restoration movement it also completed the missing link in a 110-mile circular inland waterway route through the Midlands. This in itself provided a substantial boost to the potential number of boating holidaymakers likely to use the restored waterway.

The reopening of this new route led some enthusiasts to review nostalgically a journey over another route through the Pennines that had long been closed. A series of articles on the last voyage through the Huddersfield Narrow Canal in 1948, undertaken by Aickman and others, appeared in *Waterways World* for April, May and June 1974. As the first of the articles appeared, so local enthusiasts, led by a large contingent from the Peak Forest Canal Society, decided to form the Huddersfield Canal Society to campaign for the eventual restoration of the canal.

At much the same time, the IWA and the Littleborough Civic Trust were reviewing the future potential of the other trans-Pennine link, the Rochdale Canal. As the result of a joint meeting in June 1974 the Rochdale Canal Society was formed with the longer-term aim of reopening the Rochdale Canal as a through route, and as an integral part of the proposed Pennine Park.

As the separate societies developed their restoration plans, so the eventual prospect of a more northerly circular canal route began to develop. In this case, however, the numerous obstructions on the two canals made both schemes far more difficult to achieve than the successful Upper Avon revival.

In the spring of 1974, the reconstituted Inland Waterways Amenity Advisory Council (IWAAC) gained a new chairman, J. Barratt who, as the former county planning officer for Staffordshire, had already been associated with local canal restoration on the Caldon Canal. The County Council and Stoke-on-Trent City Council jointly contributed some £50,000, much of which came from the "Operation Eyesore" scheme, to have the waterway restored. The work was undertaken mainly by BWB staff, but volunteers from the Caldon Canal Society assisted with the task. The restoration work was completed during 1974 and the restored waterway declared open at a ceremony at Cheddleton Wharf on 28 September 1974. An associated picnic site at the Froghall terminal basin, developed by the Staffordshire Planning Department, was opened at the same time and owed much to Barratt's planning ideals.

With this background of restoration and amenity planning, Barratt gave IWAAC a new lease of life and started to actively stimulate the revival of the waterways. One of the first actions he undertook was a survey of the Forth and Clyde, and Union Canals in Scotland, in June 1974. In a press release in advance of the visit he noted:

"... changes in public opinion about the future use and needs of the British Canal system have been reflected in the growing pressure in Scotland for a "new look" at the Forth and Clyde, and Union Canals before their potential is further eroded by development. This Council will be investigating what practical proposals it can contribute to assist all interested in the future of these two waterways."

This new attitude of IWAAC was much in accord with the approach adopted by Denis Howell, MP, the Minister for Sport, who told the House of Commons on 24 May 1974:

"... the canals are of tremendous importance in the development of leisure facilities as a whole I believe that we ought not to be closing canals but opening many more and even building new ones. I have made it clear to the authorities that it would seem to make more sense to dig canals to transport the water through canals which can be used for other purposes like boating and angling ..."

Devon County Council was the first to respond to the plea to reopen canals. On 13 July 1974 the restored section of the Grand Western Canal, between Tiverton and Loudwells, was declared open. A new horse-drawn passenger boat was named and took its first trip along the waterway that had become a Linear Country Park.

The commitment to reopening canals took a further step forward on 20 July 1974, when Lord Sandford formally declared open Hungerford Lock on the Kennet and Avon Canal. The repair of four locks, west of Kintbury, re-established the waterway link between Newbury and Hungerford and completed yet another phase in the Kennet and Avon Canal Trust's plan to re-link Devizes with Newbury via canal by the end of 1976.

Whilst the reopened section of the Kennet and Avon Canal had adequate water supplies, many other canals during 1974 were beginning to suffer from severe water shortages. The prospect of many of the canals used by pleasure craft being closed for the major part of the peak hire-craft season caused some alarm. Although the water shortage in some areas was due to drought, one other major cause was the rapid decay of the navigation equipment on the ageing canal network, with silting and bank erosion adding to the problem. To examine the full extent of this and the other problems of the waterways, the Government appointed a firm of consultants, Peter Fraenkel & Partners, to review the position and make a survey of the future maintenance requirements.

With these growing fears for the future of the Cruiseway system, IWAAC started to seek more solid assurances that those canals within the "Remainder" network, that had already been restored, would speedily be upgraded to "Cruiseway" status. To clarify the situation for the Minister, IWAAC prepared a report, *Upgrading of Remainder Waterways,* which was submitted to the Secretary of State on 10 September 1974. This detailed the restoration work that had already been completed on the:

Ashton Canal
Birmingham Canal Navigations
Caldon Canal
Erewash Canal
Kennet and Avon Canal
Monmouthshire & Brecon Canal
Peak Forest Canal
Slough Arm, Grand Union Canal
Welford Arm, Grand Union Canal

and recommended that all the waterways listed be given Cruiseway status in accordance with the provisions of the 1968 Transport Act.

This report was followed by a second, in October 1974. entitled *Scottish Waterways: Forth and Clyde Canal, Union Canal,* which provided a detailed review of the state of the two Scottish canals. The report indicated: "... we believe that these waterways have a wide potential, not only for recreation and leisure, but also to serve the commercial needs of the Scottish Lowlands. It concluded with the recommendation that: A detailed Scottish Lowlands Waterway study should be carried out immediately ... nothing further should be done or permitted to be done which would be contrary to coast to coast restoration."

These recommendations gave heart to the growing numbers of members of the Scottish Inland Waterways Association and their colleagues in the New Glasgow Society who were particularly interested in the Forth and Clyde Canal in Glasgow. The two groups united and jointly evolved plans to restore various sections of the waterways in conjunction with the local amenity groups.

In England and Wales the IWA regional and branch reorganisation scheme similarly revitalised the attitude of the waterways enthusiasts. One of the first tasks that the various new branches undertook was a review of the waterways within their area. In the South-East this led to a proposal that a section of the derelict Thames and Medway Canal should be restored for local amenity and recreational use. Subsequently a new Thames and Medway Canal Society was formed to bring the project into effect. In much the same way the Ipswich Branch of the IWA Eastern Region reviewed the derelict Ipswich and Stowmarket Navigation, the River Gipping, and started to promote a similar restoration scheme. Whilst in South Wales the merits of the Neath and Tennant Canals were not overlooked and, as the result of local efforts, a Neath and Tennant Canals Society was formed to promote a local restoration scheme.

Some of the new regions were less well endowed with members and this retarded the progress made in the review of local waterways. After a slow start the new Lincolnshire Branch put forward its own projects for longer-term consideration during 1975. The most promising of these was the restoration of East Fen Lock, which offered access to the extensive network of the Witham Navigable Drains. As a secondary scheme the revival of the derelict Horncastle Canal was proposed as this also offered longer-term promise once the number of pleasure craft using the Witham had increased sufficiently to make the scheme a viable proposition.

The IWA held its 1974 National Rally of Boats at Nottingham. Its prime aim was to influence local authority support for the Grantham Canal restoration scheme, which was in the process of being developed. A new booklet, *The Grantham Canal Today,* outlining the restoration plans, was on sale at the rally site. It detailed how some of the major problems of restoration could economically be overcome by the construction of a new link to the Trent through restored gravel workings. The rally also added weight to the growing interest in a proposal for restoring the lower section of the Cromford Canal, which was then in an embryo stage. The rally similarly enabled the Severn Trent Water Authority research staff to make some initial soundings regarding their own plans to ultimately reopen navigation on the Trent, between Nottingham and Burton upon Trent. The Nottingham rally was used also to set the scene for the National Rally at York the following year, which was aimed at drawing public attention to the various restoration schemes to revive the East Yorkshire waterways. Some 600 boats ultimately reached Nottingham and they did much to convince the City and County Councils of the amenity value of their local waterways.

Another general election, in October 1974, gave waterway enthusiasts a chance to reiterate their aims to the national political parties. The IWA sent telegrams to each of the three major political parties seeking their assurance that they would actively promote waterway restoration if elected and equally show goodwill by upgrading the restored "Remainder" waterways to "Cruiseway" status. When the Labour Party was re-elected, the Secretary of State for the Environment was pressed for a favourable reply.

The IWA similarly addressed members of the reformed Parliamentary Waterways Group and asked that they review the prospects for the waterways during 1975. One of the themes discussed at the meeting was a proposal for a Waterways Bill, which Lord Feversham hoped to introduce in the House of Lords during January 1975. The main aim of the Bill was to facilitate the restoration and reopening of those navigations that were without an official navigation authority. If passed, it would simplify the reopening of the Yorkshire Derwent, the Basingstoke Canal and the Driffield Navigation amongst others, and would save the heavy costs that were likely to be incurred by promoting separate private Bills for each of the waterways to be reopened." The projected Bill seemingly offered a potential way ahead for many restoration plans. The Department of the Environment was, however, unwilling to back the Bill and, after some debate, it was withdrawn.

A second development in 1975, of equal significance, was the preparation of the new county structure plans by each of the area planning authorities. These provided another means for the waterways enthusiasts to promote longer-term restoration projects. IWA members were told of the potential of such action in March 1975, and urged to ensure that their local waterways were duly noted in the structure plans. Two potential restoration schemes were directly developed in relation to the

West Midlands structure plan. The first was a scheme to restore the former Hatherton Branch of the Staffordshire and Worcestershire Canal as a Linear Park. This scheme involved the construction of a new by pass link canal to avoid the opencast mine-workings that had obliterated part of the former canal line. The second, which later proved non-viable, was a plan to restore the derelict Litchfield section of the Wyrley and Essington Canal. Members of the IWA Midlands Branch and the BCN society separately examined these schemes and put forward their ideas to the West Midlands planning team for consideration.

Three other schemes for waterway restoration were also developed, but for different reasons, although each of them was connected in the longer term with the development plans. The first was a scheme to revive the Saltisford Arm of the Grand Union Canal, at Warwick, as a linear pleasure-boat mooring. This was promoted in early 1975 by the IWA, South Warwickshire Branch, and arose as the result of their survey of the waterway needs in their region. The second was a scheme to restore the derelict Stafford Branch of the Staffordshire and Worcestershire Canal. This was promoted by members of the local canal society as a long-term solution to the ever-growing congestion on the canal. Both these schemes were put forward for further review by the authorities concerned.

Opening of Flatford Lock in 1975

A third project that developed in 1975 was related to a motorway plan. This was a longer-term scheme for the restoration of the derelict Itchen Navigation. Interest in this project was promoted by two separate groups, the Winchester Tenants and Residents Association, and the local IWA branch. Both were concerned that the navigation might be irretrievably obliterated near Winchester by the proposed route of the M3 motorway extension. To fight to preserve the navigation and seek its ultimate restoration, the two groups later joined forces and were instrumental in the formation of the Itchen Navigation Preservation Society.

In an effort to promote a co-ordinated approach to safeguard the waterways, IWAAC offered a policy statement entitled, *Recreational Framework for Britain's Canals.* This suggested that certain basic provisions for the revival and development of canals should be included in the new structure plans. Barratt, in introducing the statement, called for, "... canal users to produce joint action studies for their waterways", which would effectively conserve and improve their scenic, architectural and historic character. One of the first

effects of this suggestion was the action of Macclesfield Borough Council in designating the whole of the Macclesfield Canal a Conservation Area in June 1975. The council subsequently published a report outlining how it proposed to improve the canal. A second effect was the designation of the whole of the Staffordshire and Worcestershire Canal as a Conservation Area in 1978.

In quite a separate way, the restorationists' ideals received a further boost, when the BWB agreed that the Waterway Recovery Group could prepare a restoration scheme to renovate the remaining four-mile derelict section of the Montgomery Canal. The BWB permission was granted subject to an engineering survey being made by an independent consultant so that the extent of the work to be undertaken could be officially agreed. This was the first occasion that such permission had been given for a group to undertake unsupervised restoration work and marked a further step forward in the official acceptance of the value of the volunteer navvy.

To enable members of the public to appreciate more readily the full extent of the waterway system, *The Shell Book of Inland Waterways* by H. McKnight, was published

Sleaford Navigation Society members

in mid 1975. This added to the ever growing number of waterway books that had by then appeared, and provided details of every aspect of waterway life. The first major waterway event of 1975 was the reopening of Flatford Lock on the River Stour on Easter Monday. The work had been undertaken by the River Stour Trust, who planned to reopen a second lock, at Stratford St Mary, as their contribution to the European Architectural Heritage Year of 1976. The achievement in restoring Flatford Lock was the first major breakthrough in a campaign that had extended over 30 years.

Over Easter 1975, the first test boats were able to complete the journey through the restored Well Creek. The completion of repairs to Marmont Priory Lock by the Middle Level Commissioners and clearance of the creek by volunteers organised by the Well Creek Trust, had enabled it to be reopened after a closure of several years. By mid-1975, the growing national financial stringency was beginning to cause the IWA council some concern. To ensure that the restoration of the waterways was co-ordinated in the most effective way, the IWA council decided to create a Restoration Committee with the main aim of promoting the restoration of as many waterways as possible. Palmer, the Waterway Recovery Group leader, was asked to chair the new Committee and draw up a list of priorities for action.

Surprisingly IWAAC had a similar view, and on 25 September 1975 produced its own statement: *Priorities for Action on Waterways of the British Waterways Board*. This defined a strategy for the future. The report reviewed the various aspects of the waterways including: the user market; key priorities for expenditure; ancillary priorities for action; and additional revenue sources. In submitting the report to the Minister of State for the Environment, the IWAAC chairman, Barratt, recorded that the waterways were:

"A national asset which supports the active recreation needs of more than a million people every year and provides an amenity for many more."

The report recommended that:
"All classes of waterways are maintained in a sufficient condition to enable their speedy development to match the demands made upon them in a more favourable economic climate..."

and, in particular, for the "Remainder" waterways it asked that: "Nothing further should be done or permitted to be done or tolerated by default, to the nation's Remainder waterways which would be contrary to their ultimate restoration for navigation."

The IWAAC Priorities report set out a national overview of a theme that had been prompted by an earlier fact-finding inspection of the upper reaches of the Lancaster Canal, which was the subject of a continuing restoration campaign by the Lancaster Canal Trust. The trust prepared a report for IWAAC as the result of their visit which outlined the possibilities involved in the case for the waterway's restoration. This prompted IWAAC to issue a *News Release* on 28 July 1975 stating:

"Even in a time of economic stringency it is important that all the local and national canal-based organisations ... come together to prepare a Recreation Action Plan ... which will not only retain its character and beauty but at the same time use its opportunities to give maximum pleasure to all."

This attitude was more sharply defined when IWAAC considered a proposal by the Huddersfield Canal Society for the restoration of the Huddersfield Narrow Canal. In this case the Council suggested a Three Point Charter: (1) "Stop the Rot"; (2) "Take the Chances that Come"; and (3) "Plan for the Future".

Surrey County Council, together with Hampshire County Council, were quick to adopt this attitude when they formally gained control of their section of the Basingstoke Canal in mid 1975 and announced that they would be restoring the waterway to full navigable standards over the following five years, in conjunction with volunteers from the Surrey and Hampshire Canal Society.

In August 1975 the Government produced a white paper, *Sport and Recreation* (Cmnd 6200), which accepted that recreation should be regarded as "one of the community's everyday needs" and noted that provision for it "is part of the general fabric of social services". The report suggested, that even in a time of financial stringency, the resources that were available should be developed in the most cost-effective way. The white paper commended the voluntary associations, but indicated it was the role of Government to co-ordinate and give a lead to planning the use of resources within the community.

At the time the white paper was issued, the Manpower Services Commission were considering the idea of a Job Creation Scheme. An article on the proposal appeared in the *Daily Express* of 17 July 1975 and suggested that it could be used for, amongst other things, the renovation and clearance of rivers and canals. The same theme was reiterated in a letter to *The Times* of 9 August 1975, and an article in *Waterways World* of September 1975 noted: "As economic problems increase, voluntary work on waterways grows in importance – both for restoration and maintenance."

The article went on to describe the range of waterway restoration work being undertaken at that time by some 29 groups spread throughout the country. The theme of job opportunities on the inland waterways was equally advocated by IWAAC, who suggested that the Job Creation Scheme, launched by the Manpower Services Commission in October 1975, could well be used to revive the "Remainder" waterways. In this respect they suggested that: "Extra manpower here might well have a dramatic effect on their recovery and their future use by the community." These suggestions gradually bore fruit and eventually over 20 canal restoration projects, employing some 500 young people at a cost of approximately one-million pounds, were accepted under the Job Creation Scheme. These included restoration projects on the following canals:

Basingstoke Canal
Birmingham Canal Navigations
Coventry Canal
Cromford Canal
Droitwich Canal
Kennet and Avon Canal
Neath and Tennant Canal
Monmouthshire Canal
Rochdale Canal
Royal Military Canal
Shropshire Union Canal
Union Canal (Scotland)
Thames and Severn Canal.

The future prospects of the waterway restoration movement thus took on a new light at a time when the depressed British economic climate seemed likely to sound a death knell for many other national development projects. By the close of 1975 it at last appeared to be accepted that canals, once deemed lost and gone forever, could be again resurrected with State aid and by the efforts of voluntary workers. In an aim to develop the co-ordination of the voluntary workers, the leaders of the Waterway Recovery Group reviewed their strategy at the close of 1975 and made plans for 1976. Their attitude was best defined by Palmer in *Navvies* of February 1976, when he noted:

"As usual a crisis has a silver lining. I do hope that the current one will have the effect of making us all more aware of what is at stake and improve co-operation between us all to enable us to meet the very significant challenge that lies ahead."

To convert this strategy into a positive action the Scottish Inland Waterways Association started to issue its own working party coordination magazine, *MacNavvies,* in December 1975, with the aim of projecting a cohesive influence among the various restoration groups in Scotland. During the period 1971–75 the waterway restoration movement had spread its net still further. This is best shown by Map 6, and the list below that places the schemes in chronological order.

1971	Hazelstrine Arm, Staffordshire and Worcestershire Canal.
	Louth Canal.
	Prees Branch, Shropshire Union Canal.
	Rivers Ivel, Lark and Little Ouse
	Titford Canal
1972	Carlisle Canal
	Lower Cromford Canal
	Rivers Bure and Waveney
	Sleaford Canal
	Stroudwater and Thames and Severn Canals
	St Helens Canal
	Westport Canal
1973	Sussex Canal (Portsmouth and Arundel)
1974	Higher Avon Navigation
	Huddersfield Narrow Canal
	Ipswich and Stowmarket Navigation (River Gipping)
	Neath and Tennant Canals
	River Trent (Nottingham to Burton)
	Thames and Medway Canal
1975	Hatherton Branch, Staffordshire and Worcestershire Canal
	Horncastle Canal
	Itchen Navigation
	Saltisford Arm, Grand Union Canal
	Stafford Arm, Staffordshire and Worcestershire Canal
	Witham Navigable Drains
	Wyrely and Essington Canal (Litchfield Section)

The advances made had come both in the restoration of minor canal arms, and the revival of major trunk waterways. Perhaps the most significant in the latter group was the Thames and Severn Canal restoration scheme, which had made rapid advances during its inaugural years, and for which the potential reopening date of 1989 was being optimistically proposed.

By the close of 1975, the first impact of the role of the new Water Authorities, formed in April 1974, had also begun to show itself on the restoration scene, the most tangible evidence being the rapid strides made in reopening navigation on the Great Ouse, between Roxton and Great Barford, as part of a flood control scheme. Other plans, such as the restoration of the Westport Canal and the revival of navigation on the Trent, between Nottingham and Burton, showed potential as projects for future development.

The issue of a consultative document, *Review of the Water Industry in England and Wales,* by the Department of the Environment in early 1976, gave a firm indication of the advances that might be expected from this area in future years with the proposal to create a new National Water Authority to co-ordinate national development plans.

Perhaps the most hopeful aspect of the whole period rests on the various plans for the future that were made. The development of the county structure plans and the later IWA regional reorganisation, both gave birth to ideas for the third-phase restoration schemes, which included reopening the Higher Avon, between Stratford and Warwick; the Huddersfield Narrow Canal; and the lower reaches of the Cromford Canal. All of these schemes were aimed at providing an enlarged waterway network offering interesting cruising canals for the growing band of people taking inland waterways holidays. Yet at the same time they developed local amenity facilities for the people who lived in the area through which they passed. Above all else, by the close of 1975, the canals of Britain were more readily accepted as a worthwhile asset and as a valuable part of the national heritage, worthy of conservation.

Above: Wey and Arun Shell Award

Left: Wey and Arun Canal during restoration

VII 1976-78:
FUTURE UNCERTAIN

The years 1976–78 saw Britain struggling from crisis to crisis. Many problems arose because the economy was beset with high levels of inflation and the country with increasingly high rates of unemployment. Even the weather created problems when first the countryside was stricken with drought in 1976 and then, in subsequent years, subject to higher than average summer rainfall. Everybody in their own way had to ride out the storms.

These same storms were particularly difficult for the waterway restoration movement. They caused it both to slow its momentum and persuaded advocates to review their longer-term aspirations. Fortunately some of the Government's palliatives to overcome the nation's ills were directly beneficial to the restoration scene. Others, however, created potential difficulties for the way ahead.

The IWA Chairman, J. Heap, saw 1976 as a perilous year. In a New Year message he told members:

"The waterways of this country cannot be allowed to rot again as they were in the past … we must all pull together to see that Britain's grave financial state is not allowed to do irreparable damage to the waterways of this country."

His fears were rapidly justified when far-reaching Government expenditure cuts were announced in February and July 1976. Each successively reduced the amount of cash available at the "official" level to assist with restoration schemes. This lack of finance was most vividly demonstrated when BWB announced that the Brecon and Abergavenny Canal, an officially restored waterway which had been closed in March 1975 by a serious breach, would remain closed until "more favourable economic times".

The crippling effects of inflation were similarly reducing the amount that volunteers could achieve with the cash they were able to raise. To combat this in some way, various voluntary restoration groups, such as the Stroudwater, Thames and Severn Canal Trust and the Droitwich Canals Trust, re-launched their national appeals for funds to enable them to maintain their existing work programmes.

The cash crisis did not, however, deter David Hutchings and others from forming the Higher Avon Navigation Trust in early 1976 and publishing details of their scheme for through navigation between Stratford and Warwick at an estimated cost of £300,000. Neither did the cash

crisis dissuade IWA members from reiterating their ideals. A sample survey of members' attitudes published in early 1976 showed that their order of priorities were: (1) persuading Government to improve waterways for recreation; (2) persuading Government to make more use of water transport; and (3) restoring derelict waterways.

These ideals were rapidly put to the test in making comments on the Government's consultative document, A *Review of the Water Industry in England and Wales*, when it was issued in February 1976. The amalgamation of the British Waterways Board together with other navigation authorities to form part of a large national body responsible for all aspects of the water industry, including navigation, was among the proposals in the document. This feature had serious implications for the development of existing and future restoration schemes. In this context, Aickman reminded volunteers in *Navvies No. 62*:

"It really is useless to assemble even a hundred diggers when there is no clear political, legal and organisational infrastructure for restoring the navigation and for administering it subsequently. The political problems are almost always vastly greater than the mechanical and engineering problems …"

The IWA council used their response to the consultative document as a means to draw attention to the existing problems faced by restored waterways within the nationalised network and to reiterate their plea for the re-establishment of the public right of navigation, which had been removed by the 1968 Transport Act.

Of even greater importance to restorationists was a pilot Bill promoted by the Anglian Water Authority. This was destined to be the forerunner of similar waterways Bills in preparation by other Regional Water Authorities. Its most contentious clause was one giving the Authority, through the Secretary of State, the power to extinguish or vary navigation rights. Such a clause in all Water Authority Bills was potentially restrictive for future restoration schemes. The Anglian Water Authority Bill, in particular, had a direct bearing on the aims of the River Stour Trust and their efforts to restore and reopen the lower reaches of the river for navigation.

The IWA and the River Stour Trust jointly petitioned against the Bill. Their views were heard by a Select Committee of the House of Lords in May 1976 and, as

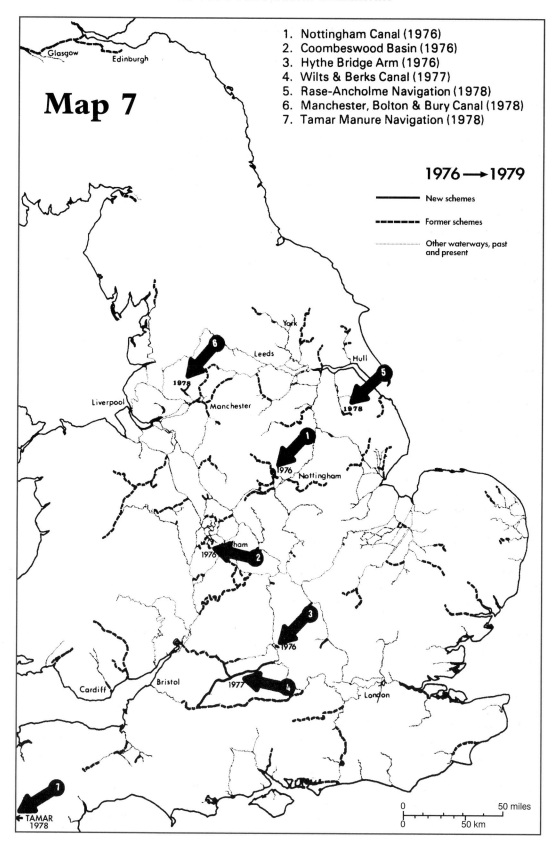

Map 7

1. Nottingham Canal (1976)
2. Coombeswood Basin (1976)
3. Hythe Bridge Arm (1976)
4. Wilts & Berks Canal (1977)
5. Rase-Ancholme Navigation (1978)
6. Manchester, Bolton & Bury Canal (1978)
7. Tamar Manure Navigation (1978)

1976 ⟶ 1979

——————— New schemes

- - - - - - - Former schemes

.... Other waterways, past and present

a result, the Bill was subsequently modified to preserve navigation rights.

The success of amending the Anglian Water Authority Bill did not, however, ease the problems of the River Stour Trust. As their contribution to the 1976 Constable Bicentenary they planned to restore the derelict lock at Stratford St Mary. Preliminary site clearance commenced on 7 December 1975 with the view to renovating the lock in the following spring. However, when the Trust sought the permission from the Anglian Water Authority to proceed with the project, this permission was refused on the grounds that the Trust had no legal right or interest in the lock or its approach channel. The decision came as a complete shock to the Trust, who had previously consulted local Water Authority officials about their plans. It also provided yet another barrier to their restoration aims.

The longer-term plans of the Slough Canal Group and the Grand Union Canal Society also suffered a setback in April 1976 when the Slough Council formally rejected their scheme for a link between the Slough Arm and the River Thames. The aim of the group was the construction of a new two-mile canal which would offer a short non-tidal link with the navigable Thames. Not only would this have brought more traffic to the Slough Arm, itself restored by BWB after a campaign by the group, but would have also reduced by some 28 miles the journey of Thames craft wishing to reach the canal network, by opening a safe new circular canal route for cruising craft.

Refusals elsewhere did not, however, deter the Huddersfield Canal Society from launching their own detailed proposals for a complete restoration scheme in a booklet, *The Huddersfield Canal – A Unique Waterway*, published in early 1976. The booklet, which presented the society's arguments and detailed the way in which various obstructions could be overcome, was circulated to the local authorities and other interested parties to gain their backing.

Support for other restoration projects was developed by different means. In an effort to persuade more people to use the Witham Navigable Drains the local IWA branch offered a plaque for all boats that passed through Cowbridge Lock. Their ultimate aim was to gain sufficient traffic to justify the reopening of the derelict East Fen Lock which provided access to additional extensive cruising waterways. In a similar way the Lancaster Canal Trust began to promote the idea of constructing slipways to facilitate the entry of craft to the truncated upper reaches of the Lancaster Canal. These slipways were ultimately installed and first used at a boat rally over Easter 1978.

Perhaps the most successful scheme in 1976 was that proposed by the IWA Oxford Branch for the restoration of the Hythe Bridge Arm of the Oxford Canal. The scheme had first been proposed in 1973 when the local IWA branch started to campaign for the improvement of the area and suggested using the arm for short-term moorings near the centre of Oxford. Both BWB and Oxford City council ultimately gave their permission for restoration work to proceed subject to the availability of finance. Volunteers offered to undertake all the tree clearance and landscape work to upgrade the surroundings of the arm, and work commenced in February 1976. This was completed by May 1977, allowing a BWB dredger to clear the arm itself. Work was finally completed in October 1977 allowing boats to use the quarter-mile arm again after a lapse of 17 years.

In an effort to preserve and promote the use of the truncated Dudley No. 2 Canal, a group of Birmingham IWA members formed an organisation to restore Hawne Basin at the terminus of the three-mile navigable line. The basin was formerly an interchange basin owned by British Rail who ceased using it in 1967. The area surrounding the basin was subsequently designated for light industrial development and British Rail planned to sell the basin site. The group, who became the Coombeswood Canal Company in 1976, entered into negotiations with Dudley Council and detailed their scheme to restore the basin and operate it as a moorings and boating centre. Dudley Council gave the scheme their support and subsequently placed a compulsory purchase order on the basin. To publicise its aims, the group held a fund-raising event at the basin in September 1977 followed by a sponsored walk. Formal proceedings in the restoration were delayed until the autumn of 1978 because the compulsory purchase order went to a Court of Appeal to resolve a dispute over land values. However, provided no other objections are raised, phase one of the restoration should be completed by mid 1979, with boats again mooring in Hawne Basin after a lapse of 12 years.

Just as the Birmingham group saw a future for their local canal, so a group of enthusiasts in Nottingham saw a future role for part of the derelict Nottingham Canal. In September 1976 they formed the Nottingham Canal Society to maintain and ultimately restore the canal. One of their first tasks was a survey of the canal which was completed by the close of 1976. Negotiations were then opened with Broxtowe District Council, who owned the canal, to gain their support. During 1977 the group were able to persuade the council of the value of their plans for amenity development, and with the council's backing volunteers from the group started preliminary clearance work. Longer-term plans were made to re-link the canal with the adjacent Erewash Canal, which had also been the subject of an earlier restoration scheme, "when the economic climate became more amenable." Thus another restoration project got under way in the Erewash Valley, gaining strength from the local history of successful canal restoration achievements.

In much the same way as the Broxtowe District Council backed the Nottingham Canal Society, the Gravesham Council added their support to the aims of the newly-formed Thames and Medway Canal Society. In February 1976 the council produced a report on the canal, *The Thames and Medway Canal – A Study of Recreational Potential,* which supported the idea of restoring a three-mile section of the canal as a recreational water space provided rights of access could be obtained.

Although the economic climate of 1976 was bleak, canal restoration schemes had other official support in the form of the Job Creation Programme. At first the majority of projects were on the non-nationalised canals. A sum of over £17,000 was allocated to the Stroudwater, Thames and Severn Canals Trust to enable them to employ 20 young people for six months from April 1976; over £19,000 was granted to the Droitwich Canal Trust to cover the cost of 15 workers for six months from September 1976; and £40,000 was granted to the Rochdale Canal Society for phase one of a scheme to revive the Rochdale town centre section

of the Rochdale Canal. This scheme was subsequently extended in September 1976 with a further £208,000 grant to create some 150 additional jobs.

Perhaps the most significant breakthrough came on 1 October 1976 when approval was given for a project on a BWB-administered canal. The scheme concerned was the rebuilding of the infamous dry section on the Kennet and Avon Canal between Limpley Stoke and Avoncliffe. The £238,000 grant, which had to be supplemented by a £75,000 donation for construction materials from the Kennet and Avon Canal Trust and a £28,000 provision by BWB for plant and fuel, gave a major boost to the longer-term aim of reopening the whole Kennet and Avon Canal, as it provided the means of overcoming one of the three major obstacles to achieving this aim.

The year 1976 also had its successes marked by the reopening of various stretches of restored waterway. The most notable of these were the opening of two new locks on the Great Ouse at Great Barford and Willington on 12 June; the reopening of the Widcombe flight of locks on the Kennet and Avon Canal on 4 June, and the reopening of the Tyle Mill and Towney locks on the same canal on 23 May. Each in their own way marked a milestone for the local restoration campaigners and gave impetus to the longer-term projects of reopening both

Thames and Medway restoration open day

93

Widcombe Kennet and Avon Canal before and after restoration

the major waterways to through navigation.

Even so, in 1976 setbacks abounded for other restoration ideals. One of the greatest problems countrywide was the physical lack of water caused by the drought. Various sections of canal were closed as summit levels were drained to provide water for the lower reaches of the network. This action in turn prevented hire-craft operators from offering a full range of holidays on the inland waterways, the potential customers of which often later became supporters of their various local restoration campaigns.

However, it was other imposed measures that more directly retarded the restoration campaigns. Perhaps the most critical of these was a decision by the Welsh Office to construct a new bypass road at Arddleen with a culvert across the Montgomery Canal not offering navigable headroom for craft. The plan seemed to place an insurmountable barrier in the way of the longer-term proposals to restore the whole of the Montgomery Canal, part of which had already been reopened under a scheme supported by the Prince of Wales. The IWA and the Shropshire Union Canal Society jointly set out

to dissuade the Welsh Office from going ahead with the road scheme and sought ways to overcome the impasse. The battle continued throughout 1977 and by mid-1978 an engineering solution was found which in part resolved the problems. Even so, the additional costs involved provided a further delaying factor to the canal's restoration plans.

It was in recognition of this fighting spirit that a new Restoration Trophy was donated by the Stroudwater, Thames and Severn Canal Trust Ltd in September 1976. Its purpose was to recognise the person who had contributed most during the year to restoration nationally. The first person to receive the trophy was Graham Palmer, leader of the Waterway Recovery Group and chairman of the IWA Restoration Committee. The award was made for Palmer's efforts in organising the Stratford "Blitz", a series of volunteer working parties held to upgrade the southern Stratford Canal which had been restored in the early 1960s and reopened in 1964.

The award was opportune, as the Waterway Recovery Group journal *Navvies*, edited by Palmer, celebrated its tenth birthday in October 1976. The editorial of the

Thames and Severn Canal restoration

anniversary edition recalled how the body of subscribers had grown from 70 to over 2,500 in the ten-year period and that it "… has gone some way to assisting the explosion of interest in canal and river restoration". Palmer concluded:"The next few years will be the critical ones, if we let up, or allow complacency to overtake us, we will have lost, and there is no going back."

This set the theme for the restoration movement's work for 1977. To follow up this message came a call for support for a new group interested in preserving and restoring some sections of the derelict Wiltshire and Berkshire Canal. Letters were sent to the editors of the waterway magazines seeking readers' support. As the result, a steering committee was created to formulate the aims of the new group and an inaugural meeting was subsequently called at Swindon on 8 October 1977. This led to the formation of the Wiltshire and Berkshire Canal Amenity Group to safeguard the future of the remains of the canal. Subsequently the group started to organise working parties to restore a section of the canal at Kingshill, Swindon, with the aim of creating a small linear water park.

At the same time as the new group got under way, existing groups each fought to retain and develop their own sections of the local canal. Their actions were partly co-ordinated when the Waterways Recovery Group held an Organisers' Conference in Stratford on 30 April 1977. Over 50 delegates attended and agreed to a general policy of combined self-help.

This idea of self-help was further encouraged when Shell UK Oil Ltd announced an award scheme of £6,000 to encourage enthusiasts throughout the country to improve and restore Britain's inland waterways. The scheme opened on 1 May 1977, and by November some 84 applications had been made for awards. After adjudication some 68 awards were made. The largest was a grant of £400 to the Polmont Conservation Unit in Scotland for work in clearing the Union Canal, whilst two further awards of £275 each were made to two other groups on the Union Canal to assist in clearing the Linlithgow section and Lochrin Basin in Edinburgh. The Scottish awards were timely as the Union Canals Development Group, which was made up of local authority, central government and BWB representatives, published a report in April 1977 which noted that the current recreational use of the Union Canal fell far short of its potential. Whilst the report accepted in the short term that financial constraints restricted the range of options, it envisaged, in the longer term, that the waterway could be redeveloped for navigation. In this context, it praised the work of the Linlithgow Union Canal Society who had already cleared part of the canal and had introduced a trip boat on it, as well as opening a canal museum in a former canal building. The press were well represented at the conference to launch the report and from the publicity they gave it showed there was a keen interest in reviving the Scottish canal.

National attention was drawn to the future of the inland waterways in July 1977 when the Government published its proposals for their future control in a white paper (Cmnd 6876), *The Water Industry in England and Wales: The Next Step*. Whilst the proposals dropped the

Castle Mills lock cut, Great Ouse, reopened

Bridgwater and Taunton Canal restoration

earlier plan of wholesale nationalisation of all independent waterways, it was made clear that the envisaged new National Water Authority would be primarily concerned with water-supply and that recreation and commerce would take second place. The potential dismembering of the BWB and its absorption into the new body proposed in the white paper caused restorationists some concern. More particularly, their fears for the future of the inland waterways were governed by the statement that a study by independent consulting engineers, Peter Fraenkel & Partners, had identified a waterway maintenance backlog amounting to over thirty-seven million pounds at 1974 prices (worth over sixty million pounds in 1977) and in this context the white paper stated:

"This makes it essential to take a new look at methods of making the system viable, which must involve considering for individual waterways the cost of maintaining them in relation to the benefits they provide…"

The Government, fortunately, did not rush into an evaluation of individual waterways but as part of a programme to boost the ailing construction industry allocated five million pounds to BWB for urgent repair work in November 1977 when it finally published the Fraenkel Report.

Government money also flowed to restoration schemes in other ways. The major contribution came through the second phase grants from the Manpower Services Commission's Job Creation Schemes. These included finance for the Bridgwater and Taunton Canal to clear the canal through the centre of Bridgwater; a £35,408 grant for the Basingstoke Canal; and £20,000 for restoring the upper section of the Market Weighton Canal to complement a £750,000 Yorkshire Water Authority project to restore the entrance lock and revive the lower reaches.

The Job Creation finance bore fruit in one of the canal reopenings of 1977. This was the completion of phase one of a new Black Country Museum project at Dudley on 1 October 1977. A canal arm was restored as part of the museum complex and a replica boat yard constructed adjacent to it. The scheme complemented the earlier Dudley Canal Tunnel restoration project and provided a new base for the electrically powered trip boat which, in August 1977, took the twenty-five thousandth visitor through the restored canal tunnel – a major milestone since the Dudley Canal Trust began the trips in 1964.

Other reopenings of 1977 included the introduction of a trip boat on a short restored section of the Grantham Canal at Hickling on 24 May by the Grantham Canal

Restoration Society, to draw support for their longer-term aim of reopening the entire 33-mile waterway. There was also the reopening of the rebuilt lock, necessitated by decay through age, at Tewkesbury on the Lower Avon Navigation at Easter 1977, which relinked the popular cruising route of the Avon Ring. At much the same time, the completion of the restoration work on Bethel's Bridge on the Driffield Navigation again allowed large craft access to the middle reaches of the navigation.

On 23 July, the Thames and Severn Canal Trust held a ceremony to commemorate the restoration of the Eastern Portal of Sapperton Tunnel. And, on 28 August, four miles and seven locks on the Kennet and Avon Canal west of Hungerford were officially reopened, thus completing a further phase of the ultimate plan to reopen the entire waterway between Reading and Bath by the early 1980s.

Whilst reopenings were taking place on some waterways, the regeneration of aims for the revival of others were being reiterated. One such scheme was that published by the Shrewsbury and Newport Canals Group, which had been formed in April 1976. They published a feasibility study outlining the restoration potential of the Newport Branch in early 1977 and started to restore part of the canal and rebuild an access bridge later in the year.

In a slightly different way, the Chesterfield Canal Society, formed in September 1976, started to promote its aims for the restoration of the derelict upper reaches of the Chesterfield Canal. In conjunction with the local IWA branch and the Retford and Worksop Boat Club, the group staged a boat rally to commemorate the bicentenary of the canal. The event attracted some 150 boats and over 21,000 people and did much to promote the society's plan to restore Morse Lock, the first derelict lock above Worksop and the current head of navigation.

"Deepcut Dig", Basingstoke Canal restoration

Restoration was also in mind when the Sleaford Navigation Society was formed on 4 November 1977. The group set out both to develop the earlier work of the Sleaford Civic Society in rejuvenating the canal-head in Sleaford and planned to ultimately revive the whole Sleaford Navigation. Members also hoped to generate wider interest in the amenity offered by the Lincolnshire waterways, by acting as a research unit to collate historical details of the little-known Lincolnshire navigations and to publish their findings.

Just as these new societies started to make their way, so existing societies continued to carry forward their plans. The Caldon Canal Society returned to the business of physical canal restoration in mid-1977 when BWB reached agreement with the local authorities for financing the restoration of the Leek Arm of the Caldon Canal. In July 1977 working parties from the society started to clear the banks of the canal in readiness for the arrival of a BWB dredger.

Most waterway restoration groups entered into the spirit of the Jubilee Year but the theme of the Jubilee was only commemorated in one restoration development in 1977. This was the opening of the new Jubilee Dry Dock at Great Northern Basin at the head of the Erewash Canal. The dock, built by the Langley Mill Boat Company, was part of a longer-term restoration project for the whole of the Lower Cromford Canal. The project took some 10,000 man-hours, almost entirely at weekends and evenings, and greatly enlarged the facilities offered by the restored basin. Associated with the development of the dock, a further short section of the Lower Cromford Canal was re-excavated to provide additional boat moorings and access to the next stage of the restoration development, which was planned when finance became available.

Perhaps the major event of the restoration calendar of 1977 was the Waterway Recovery Group "Deepcut Dig". Some 600 volunteers turned out in periods of torrential rain on 8–9 October to clear some twelve derelict locks on the Surrey section of the Basingstoke Canal. It was estimated that the clearance work undertaken would have taken normal working parties a year and the effort was valued at nearly £8,000 by Surrey County Council, the owners of that part of the canal.

On a much smaller scale, but of equal significance locally, was a canal clearance operation launched by the Huddersfield Canal Society in September 1977, as part of their campaign to reopen the Huddersfield Narrow Canal. Volunteers cleared some 60 tons of rubbish from the first lock on the canal. The working party proved to be the centre of attraction of a boat rally held over the same weekend and gained further public support for the society's longer-term aims.

To capitalise on the considerable public interest in watching others work, Graham Palmer, organiser of the Waterway Recovery Group, decided to launch a "Sponsor a Navvy" campaign at the close of 1977. The major aim was to ensure that experienced volunteers were available to attend the various annual summer work camps without personally bearing the full financial sacrifice involved.

Just as individuals were short of cash, the problems of lack of finance for the waterways in general continued to loom large in 1978. The only slight note for optimism was cast by the announcement of four major extensions to the Manpower Services Commission Job Creation Programme. The most enlightened of these was a scheme sponsored by Kennet District Council and the BWB for the restoration of the Caen flight of 29 locks at Devizes. The project embraced the renovation of the lock chambers and side pounds, but excluded the replacement lock-gates, and involved a capital expenditure of £170,000, of which £45,000 had to be found by BWB. The Kennet and Avon Canal Trust committed itself to a £300,000 fund-raising project to finance the purchase and fitting of the new lock-gates required to complete the scheme. BWB also committed itself to a four-year programme for the complete restoration of the remaining derelict sections of the canal between Bath and Newbury by 1981; leaving only the problem of a fixed swing-bridge at Aldermaston and the replacement of the turf-sided locks as the remaining barriers to the complete restoration of the through route from London to Bristol.

The second major scheme was a commitment to the final phase of the reopening of the Brecon and Abergavenny Canal by Easter 1979. The fourth phase of the Job Creation Scheme included the complete relining of suspect areas of the canal in the vicinity of the earlier breach and involved a Manpower Services Commission grant of £93,000. The Welsh Development Agency provided a donation of £126,000, and BWB met the balance of £59,000.

The third project was on the Basingstoke Canal, where a further cash grant of £140,000 extended the current Job Creation Project for the whole of 1978. Here an additional grant of £45,000 for building materials was made by the Surrey County Council as part of their longer-term commitment to renovate the whole canal by 1983.

The fourth project during 1978 was the extension of the Job Creation work on the Rochdale Canal both in central Rochdale and at Sowerby Bridge. This provided further momentum to the longer-term aim of reopening the whole waterway as a further trans-Pennine link.

The year 1978 had its share of reopenings of restored lengths of waterway. The most significant of these was the official opening of the new Castle Mills Lock on the Great Ouse on 28 April. This provided the last link in the project to reopen the river to navigation between Bedford and the sea. A celebration to commemorate the event was staged in Bedford on 28–29 May and was the culmination of the thirty-year campaign waged by the Great Ouse Restoration Society to reopen the river between Tempsford and Bedford. It was also the first major restoration scheme completed by a Water Authority. On a more minor scale, yet equally significant, were the formal reopening of Claverton Pumping Station on the Kennet and Avon Canal, to provide a regular supply of water to the restored Limpley Stoke section of the canal; and the reopening of the partially restored Westport Canal, a two-mile extension of the River Parrett Navigation. Full through navigation was not, however, possible to Westport because a lowered bridge prevented large craft from negotiating the entire length of the waterway.

Not quite in the same class, but a reopening in its own way, was the inauguration of the trip boat *John Pinkerton* on 20 May 1978 along a section of the restored Basingstoke Canal at Odiham. This was the first boat of any significant size to operate over this section for 65 years – and was the first real step in getting the Basingstoke Canal back to being an active navigation. Whilst successes were achieved in some parts more problems loomed in others. One was a plan for a new road that would pass directly through the partially restored Buxworth Basin site on the Peak Forest Canal. Another was a new road plan which would obliterate part of the newly-restored section of the Neath Canal. Both required active campaigns to persuade the respective public inquiries that the canals were worth saving and that the roads could go elsewhere.

Perhaps both the road problems were symptoms of the wider political conflict over the future of the canals that erupted in 1978 when the Government's whole attitude towards the waterways came under severe criticism by the House of Commons Select Committee on Nationalised Industries. Their fourth report, published on 27 February 1978, again raised the thorny question of who should pay for the upkeep of the canals. This was a dilemma that seemed unanswerable in the tight economic climate of 1978. Thus, as expected, the Government's reply in a white paper, *British Waterways Board*, was far from helpful. Whilst it indicated that "the Government is seeking to achieve a stable and healthy future for Britain's Canals", it similarly gave no reassurance that a high priority could be given to ensure that the necessary finance would be made available. However, as an act of good faith, the

Government indicated that ten million pounds in grants, for urgent maintenance work during the period 1978–80, had already been approved and that a further review of the most practical, sensible and economical method of maintaining the waterways would be made.

Although at national level the political future of the canals was still in doubt, a more constructive policy was being pursued by some local authorities. Perhaps the most progressive of these was the West Midlands County Council who were developing a master plan for the Birmingham Canal Network with the aim of co-ordinating and seeking to exploit the recreation and leisure potential of the waterways of their area. Thus, when the IWA national rally was held at the Titford Pools, a restored canal in Birmingham in August 1978, many saw the event "as a harbinger of better times to come." In much the same way the Greater Manchester Council's non-encroachment policy for the derelict waterways of its area offered a similar feeling of hope for the future of the derelict canals.

To capitalise on this feeling of hope, the IWA nationally launched a further recruitment drive with a target membership of 15,000 by the close of 1978. It equally called on each of its current 14,500 members to take whatever action they could to preserve and develop a flourishing and integrated inland waterways network. And, in the light of the future election, to canvass political support for the revival of the waterways from the three main parties. At the same time it launched its first national lottery to raise funds for its National Waterways Restoration and Development Fund, setting a target of £50,000 from this major fundraising scheme. Members were, however, warned that unless they continued to vocally promote the restoration campaign, all the gains that had been made could be lost.

The period 1976–78 closed as it had opened, as a time of uncertainty for the country as well as the canals. As a result the momentum of new restoration proposals had markedly slowed down, as is shown by Map 7. In 1976 only three new schemes came forward, two connected with pleasure-craft mooring sites at Coombeswood, Birmingham, and Hythe Bridge, Oxford, and one, at Nottingham, for the revival of a length of derelict canal. The year 1977 saw one new scheme put forward, that for the revival of sections of the long-derelict Wiltshire and Berkshire Canal.

Apart from the long-awaited formal Government approval for the reconstruction and upgrading of the Sheffield and South Yorkshire Navigation, there were only three other tentative plans published for longer-term restoration and development schemes in 1978. The first, in the South-West, was promoted by the local IWA branch. This envisaged the restoration of the single derelict lock on the old Tamar Manure Navigation, near Gunnislake, and the reopening of the Gunnislake Wharf area. A second scheme, in Lincolnshire, was proposed by the newly formed Rase–Ancholme Navigation Trust. This encompassed the upgrading of the Bishopbridge section of the existing Ancholme Navigation and, in the much longer term, the construction of an extension, by means of the creation of three new locks on the River Rase, through West Rasen to Market Rasen. The third project was in the North-West, where Bolton Council decided to restore a short section of the derelict Manchester, Bolton and Bury Canal, between Little Lever and Kearsley, as a recreational amenity. No plans were made, however, to revive the remainder of the canal, parts of which had been dry since a breach in the 1930s.

By the close of 1978 the extent of the range of potential restoration projects seemed likely to have been exhausted. Even so, the continuing growth of interest in the inland waterways had already led to the introduction of a second specialist magazine, *Canal and Riverboat*, in February 1978, which offered yet another means of stimulating wider public interest and support for the canals and the existing range of restoration schemes.

During the post-war canal restoration era, over 80 separate restoration schemes were nationally promoted. And, in much the same way as the earlier canal era, some schemes were more viable than others; these were ultimately the ones most likely to succeed. Of the remainder, only time will tell. Their longer-term prospects are, however, enhanced by the fact that people now have more leisure time to spare, and are showing a greater concern for the whole environment in which they live. This, coupled with a greater public willingness to fight for local amenities, should enhance the chances of successful completion of the major projects currently under way. Lack of finance will be second only to politics as the barrier to the way ahead.

Rochdale Canal
restoration

VIII 1979-1985:
EVERY CLOUD HAS A SILVER LINING

The "winter of discontent" brought new problems for the Callaghan government and national strikes served to take their mind off wider issues. Even a concordat between the Government and the TUC failed to reassure the general public. As a result, when James Callaghan went to the country on 3 May 1979 his government was defeated. Margaret Thatcher was elected Prime Minister and so started the decade of the "Thatcher years" with the moves towards privatisation that ensued.

Just as the Labour government fought for its survival, so the restoration movement had its first major challenge from new highways, a theme that came to provide canal restorers with many headaches over the following decades. The initial consultation exercise began over the proposed route of the M66 motorway in the Rochdale area. This threatened to block the Rochdale Canal and seemed likely to remove any longer-term hope for its complete restoration. Over 1,000 letters were sent to the Department of Transport objecting to the proposed low-level crossing. Another issue was also emerging, that of the "nature conservation" lobby. Grand Union Canal Society members organised a cruise along the Wendover Arm in late 1978 to the head of the navigation at Little Tringford Pumping Station. They feared that if boats did not use the Arm it might be dedicated to nature conservation and boats prevented from navigating along it.

Elsewhere, options looked brighter. The long running saga of the 'lost' Driffield Navigation Commissioners was finally resolved by the Charities Commissioners and the Driffield Navigation Amenities Association were able to again create a quorate governing body. On the Stroudwater Navigation, the Proprietors were able to grant the Thames and Severn Canals Trust permission to restore the Pike Mill Bridge to Ryeford section for potential trip-boat use.

Things were not, however, going so well for the IWPS. They alerted supporters that a new road plan threatened to destroy the tramway track leading to the Basin, as well as the lime-kilns, coupled with the creation of a temporary contactors road through the middle of the Basin area.

A Parliamentary Select Committee reviewing the state of the waterways recommended the Government provide British Waterways Board with the necessary £60m identified in the Fraenkel Report to remedy the backlog of health and safety maintenance works.

However, the editorial in the March 1979 *Waterways World* perhaps summed up the situation: "Whilst Government and Unions continue to haggle, the waterways continue to fall into disrepair. There is little prospect of the Braunston, Netherton or Kings Norton tunnels opening this year"

The tightness of the economy led Powys Council to apply to the High Court for a "writ mandamus" to clarify the position of the bridges on the Montgomery Canal in order to save money. Powys Council wanted to lower bridge No. 96 to overcome a weight limit problem rather than rebuild it. Enthusiasts were asked to write objecting to the proposal, which would add yet another barrier to restoring this idyllic rural waterway. At much the same time the Huddersfield Canal Society were seeking to overcome some of the barriers blocking their canal. They commented on the fact that "authorities spent money destroying the navigation means that someone [now] has got to admit that expenditure was a mistake. It is a big mistake for anyone to make". In the meantime they were seeking a site for a trip-boat operation to gain public support. The Society accepted that the "restoration is one of the biggest projects at present, so it perhaps is not surprising that progress is slow!"

Over the border in Scotland, enthusiasts were also concerned with a major road scheme for an Edinburgh Outer City Bypass that threatened to block the Union Canal. This was especially worrying in that the two major trip-boat operators could be affected, Ronnie Rusack's *Pride of Union* from Ratho, and the Linlithgow-based *Victorian*. Here again enthusiasts were called upon to lodge their objections.

In April 1979 an editorial in *Waterways World* concluded that "Britain's inland waterway system is in a worse state today than it has ever been. First priority is to settle the pay dispute [BW employees were working to rule and refusing to allow volunteers to work on the Board's waterways] and to get work on the waterways back to normal." It was also imperative to make certain BWB's £5m extra money for 5 years, promised in Cmnd 7439, was delivered and spent on the backlog of maintenance.

At this time David Hutchings and colleagues were seeking to promote a Higher Avon Navigation Bill. Parliament agreed that the 1751 Act did apply to the Higher Avon. However, it was suggested that further negotiations were required to see if the objectors' concerns could be resolved. As a consequence, the

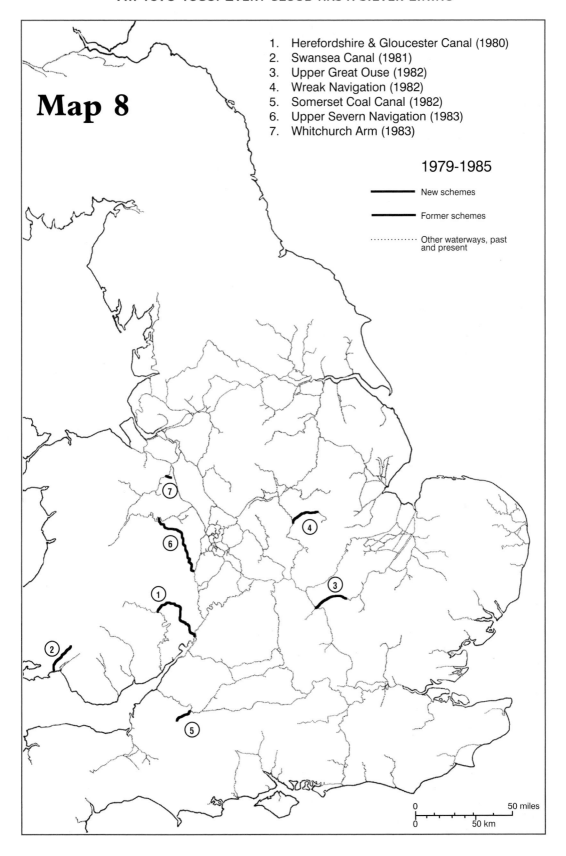

Map 8

1. Herefordshire & Gloucester Canal (1980)
2. Swansea Canal (1981)
3. Upper Great Ouse (1982)
4. Wreak Navigation (1982)
5. Somerset Coal Canal (1982)
6. Upper Severn Navigation (1983)
7. Whitchurch Arm (1983)

1979-1985

———— New schemes

———— Former schemes

············ Other waterways, past and present

Higher Avon Navigation Trust decided to withdraw their Bill temporarily, to allow time for further discussions to take place.

During this period, when the economy was tight, various restoration groups felt it necessary to appeal to their members for funds to complete scheduled tasks. Three such requests exemplify that trend. One was the River Stour Trust's appeal for funds to restore the Sudbury Basin area and the Granary Warehouse. The second was an appeal by the Pocklington Canal Amenity Society, who sought to replace three fixed swing bridges that offered farm access over their waterway. The third, and perhaps the largest, was by the Kennet and Avon Canal Trust for new lock-gates for the Devizes flight. Here a Manpower Services Commission Job Creation scheme had restored the structure of all but two of the 29 lock chambers and most of the connecting pounds but the scheme had not included the provision and fitting of new gates. The trust sought the £300,000 required to complete the task.

Not all schemes had such universal support. A letter to *Waterways World*, May 1979, in respect of the Foxton Incline Plane restoration scheme, indicated "it is a bold idea and worth a gamble for an independent viability study". Taking a gamble generally was not a strong point of government. It was pleasing that, on 24 April 1979, Peter Shore MP finally unveiled the plaque to commemorate the start of the Sheffield and South Yorkshire Waterway Improvement scheme, due to be completed in 1981, some 18 years after it was conceived! This would offer access to 700-ton craft to Doncaster and 400-ton craft to Rotherham and hopefully enable them to compete for bulk traffic on that route.

The survival of the waterways was a constant battle. It was not surprising that BWB were forced to lodge a notice of appeal against the court decision to allow Powys council to proceed with plans to culvert Bridge 96 on the Montgomery Canal. The BW appeal was based on the fact that restoration was already underway and various lengths were open to navigation.

Similarly, when the Derwent Trust received a copy of a report "The Yorkshire Derwent – a case for conservation", they too realised they might have a battle on their hands. The Trust saw the report as ill-founded and overtly biased towards anglers, farmers and naturalists.

One "silver lining" for the waterways came when, at long last, the government released extra funds to facilitate the repair works on some of the then closed waterways. Some of these had already been reopened and major works on Braunston Tunnel were underway, with the work there due for completion in the spring of 1980.

Enthusiasts in East Anglia were also hopeful of success, when the Anglian Water Authority Recreation Advisory Committee, proposed that a two-mile section of the River Lark, between Judes Ferry and Mildenhall, should be dredged and made navigable. This led them to turn their attention to the next section upstream of Mildenhall to Bury St Edmunds. It was interesting to note that in the midst of this twelve-mile section the derelict lock at Icklington was still in working order.

The appointment of the new Conservative Government, in May 1979, raised the question of what its attitude would be towards the waterways; especially to the then proposed Vale of Belvoir coalfield, and its potential affect on the Grantham Canal, but also for the prospect of creating a new waterway to service the proposed new mines. This was to become a long-running saga, as those for and against the scheme took sides. It also caused conflicts major within the IWA.

At the other end of the scale of plans was a scheme by the Severn and Canal Carrying Company, the proprietors of which had purchased the three-mile long Coombe Hill Canal in September 1978. By mid-1979 they had started to renovate the Wharf Buildings and the southern end of the canal and indicated they would be seeking planning permission to run a horse-drawn trip boat along the canal once it had been dredged. Subsequently it was heard planning permission was refused on access grounds.

As 1979 progressed, the Government started to declare its intentions for the waterways. Following enthusiasts' concerns that BWB might be disbanded and the waterways divided between the regional water authorities, the Government announced that BWB would remain an independent entity. In Scotland future prospects also became clear, when Lothian Regional Council indicated it had agreed to provide an aqueduct to carry the Union Canal over the proposed Edinburgh City Centre bypass in the vicinity of Sighthill. Likewise, a threat to the Thames and Severn Canal was lifted when Gloucestershire County Council indicated it would, after extensive local lobbying, rebuild a bridge over the canal at Daneway that had been damaged by heavy lorries, even though the cost of rebuilding was twice that of a causeway across the derelict canal.

In the North-West the Lancaster Canal Trust and the Lancaster Canal boat club joined forces to sponsor a survey to identify possible routes to link their canal to the national network. These identified the potential use of Savick Brook as the route offering the greatest potential.

On the political front, Michael Heseltine indicated he wished to have a "purge" of quangos. IWAAC was one of those identified. This led to concern that, if it were removed, it would take away a valuable avenue of advice to the government on waterways matters. Fortunately it was later learnt that IWAAC had been given a reprieve as any legislation on quangos was likely to be delayed until at least November 1980 at the earliest.

Towards the end of 1979 the Coombeswood Canal Trust published its prospectus, with a plan to restore Hawne Basin. They announced a rally in the basin over Easter 1980. On a larger scale, a scheme was proposed by the local authorities of Widnes, Warrington and St Helens to give a facelift to the St Helens Canal (Sankey Brook Navigation) and a pilot scheme began to clean up and improve some sections of the canal line in November 1979. This work was to be funded by a Derelict Land Grant, a source of cash used extensively by many waterway restorers over the next decade. The council's ultimate aim was to develop the waterway route as a linear park from Widnes docks, through Warrington to St Helens, offering facilities for water recreation as well as winter berths for craft at Spike Island.

An article appeared in *Waterways World* in December 1979 detailing the state of the Ipswich and Stowmarket Navigation. It concluded that the "tiny Ipswich branch

of the IWA has the ambition of wanting to restore the river to full navigation for pleasure purposes, which they accept must be a long-term proposal". In the meantime the Branch had already been undertaking towpath clearance work at the Ipswich end.

By the end of 1979 BWB had withdrawn its plans to create a new canal to service proposed the Vale of Belvoir coalfield as uneconomic, also dropping those for restoring the Wreak Navigation to service other pit heads. It was simply far cheaper to reconstitute former railway links in the area. Although the decision by BWB was clear cut, the outcome of the public enquiry into the whole concept of the new mines was not and the Grantham Canal Society needed to await the outcome of the inquiry to be sure their canal would not be affected by possible subsidence.

The year 1980 was, for canal restorers, one of some steps forward and some back. The Droitwich Barge Canal received a boost when Wychavon District Council allocated £200,000 for work on the canal in Vines Park, including a new route and the provision of a new mooring basin for 60 craft. In quite the reverse

Rochdale Canal restoration

direction, the Job Creation Scheme on the Market Weighton Canal, above Sodhouses Lock, came to a halt when the local council was reluctant to assist with the disposal of rubbish that had been dumped in the canal. The Rochdale Canal Society members were worried when they heard of plans to build a supermarket on the canal line at Sowerby Bridge and lobbied against it.

Some small rays of hope were felt when Shell announced a new set of awards. These included the Seagull Trust on the Union Canal, the K&A lock-gates appeal, Erewash– Great Northern basin lock-gates, a new swing bridge at Vines Park on the Droitwich, new gates for Thornton Lock on the Pocklington Canal, and a grant to the Driffield Navigation for restoration of a swing bridge. These helped to raise hopes.

The IWA itself was gravely concerned that proper funding for the waterways had not been provided and that the unwillingness of British Waterways staff to allow the use of volunteers continued to retard progress. It published a severe warning of the impending crisis in a 30-page study entitled *Waterways Survival – a report on the condition and status of Britain's waterways, past, present and future.* The report concluded: "If these recommendations are heeded and all concerned cooperate, together we can ensure not only the survival of the waterways as a national heritage, but also their expansion and development for the future. But if these recommendations are ignored, then the system is doomed to collapse and may be lost forever." Two years later the prophetic words came true when the culmination of years of neglect finally caught up. The network was decimated by ten major long-term safety stoppages, which combined to split the canal system into small cruising areas.

Whilst the national system was in trouble, some small achievements were being made locally. On the Montgomery Canal the Secretary of State proposed that the Shropshire County Structure Plan included a note that "the line of the canal should be protected". Likewise there was relief all round when the Government decided to accept the Inspector's findings that there should be adequate cruising headroom provided where the projected M66 motorway crossed the Rochdale Canal at Chadderton. A similar sigh of relief was heard when the Government gave IWAAC a further two-year reprieve. This new feeling of hope was mirrored when the group considering the restoration of the Portsmouth and Arundel Canal, through a society of the same name, set as their first target the Chichester Canal. In Wales, the Neath and Tennant Canal Society gained a Prince of Wales Award, for their work restoring the Aberdulais Basin. They also managed to protect their canal route from A465 trunk road improvement plans.

Not all was going smoothly elsewhere. An article in

Waterways World noted, with concern, that the line of the Manchester, Bolton and Bury Canal was being viewed for development especially in Salford. Likewise the long-proposed River Parret Barrage scheme, which offered the prospect of reopening a wide range of Somerset waterways, including the Tone, Yeo and Isle, as well as the connection to the Westport Canal, seemed less likely to get off the drawing board due to the adverse economic climate.

What caught the imagination of West Midlands politicians was the document *West Midlands Canals Strategy for the 1980s*, which offered a structured way forward to integrate the recreational value of the canals to various local redevelopment schemes.

Up in the North-West, John Hartley, of Northumberland College of Higher Education circulated his own thoughts for restoring the long-lost Carlisle Canal. He drew attention to the potential of the eleven-mile route, much of which had been taken over by a railway but was now disused, but recognised the high costs involved. He suggested a feasibility study, considering restoration, ought to be prepared in the hope of more affluent times ahead. Nothing further happened.

With more positive hopes for a brighter future for the Scottish Union Canal, Jane Clark was appointed as its project officer. Her role was to promote the reuse of the waterway route between Edinburgh to Falkirk, by linking up with local groups, councils and societies and investigating the prospect of creating a Union Canal Trust to actively coordinate and restore sections of the waterway for active use.

It is always interesting to see how canal restorers are able to persuade the Army of the training value of their projects A good example is when the Royal Engineers, Chepstow Army Apprentices, agreed to manufacture some lock-gates for the Droitwich Barge Canal.

In the east, the Sleaford Navigation Society got the Anglian Water Authority to look favourably on their aim to restore the Sleaford Navigation. This enabled the Society to start making positive plans to restore the first lock as well as the town basin. Showing support is vital for every scheme. Thus when thirty boats turned up to a rally at Hawne Basin, on the Dudley No.2 Canal, the Combeswood Canal Trust felt able to positively develop their plans to turn the former interchange basin into a marina with a full range of facilities.

News of another potential threat to restoration hopes, this time on the Yorkshire Derwent, appeared in an article in *Waterways World* in June 1980. This recorded a trip down the Derwent from Malton by dinghy. It recorded a false dawn for hopes of reopening the navigation in the 1970s, when the Yorkshire Water Authority itself offered to restore the waterway. Since that time a local group titled CONSYDER, ostensibly conservationists worried about extra boats damaging flora and fauna, had started to express their concerns publicly. This led the Water Authority to retract its original offer. By 1980, the Yorkshire Derwent Trust members again felt confident enough to believe that the present Water Authority Board might again be disposed to consider their aim to bring back pleasure boating on the river. It began to call for new Trust members who would be able to help with the actual physical work of rebuilding the locks. This gained some support, and a site was secured, but with little further progress.

Earlier restoration schemes were beginning to "show their age". One was the Avon navigation, where Welford Weir was in danger of collapse and a likely repair bill of between £20,000 and £40,000 was looming. The Severn Trent Water Authority offered £10,000 and the Countryside Commission stepped in to match the funding pound for pound. It fell to the Trust to find the balance to allow the repairs to proceed.

The other decaying canal was the Southern Stratford, where the National Trust were finding it hard to keep the previously restored structures sound. This led them to approach the DoE with a view to relinquishing their control of the navigation. This was an issue that took some considerable time to resolve.

Relationships were strained between the IWA and some canal societies. The IWA had taken the view that it felt unable to fight to protect the Grantham Canal at the Vale of Belvoir Mine Public Inquiry. Interestingly, IWAAC took the opposite approach. This presumed lack of a fighting spirit by the IWA led members of the Lancaster Canal Trust to propose a National Federation of Independent Canal Societies, to exert a stronger influence on the national scene. This move itself led to a critical editorial in *Waterways World*, which urged the IWA "to do more campaigning". This advice subsequently was rejected by the IWA General Secretary, John Taunton, who claimed that "nowadays a much more subtle approach is necessary". In reality the Association was fighting on other fronts by trying to remove clauses from the Anglian Water Authority Bill, which would have allowed them to close navigations, and by fighting the Middle Level Commissioners over the closure of Horseway Lock. Fortunately the IWA was able to head off complete defeat.

Forth and Clyde Canal restoration at Maryhill

Droitwich Canal restoration

Campaigning at a local level was more successful for others. The Rochdale Canal Society launched its "boats to Hebden Bridge" campaign. This was to raise funds for restoration between Sowerby Bridge and Hebden Bridge, a length on which they planned to run a trip boat in an effort to canvas for even more public support.

In Scotland, public support was growing fast for restoration of the Forth and Clyde Canal. In its first months the local society enlisted a membership of 16 councils and over 50 individual members and called for others to join. Nationally, many local councils' interest in the waterways were strengthened by an innovative IWAAC report *Inland Waterways – arteries for employment and spending*, which pointed out that "last year people spent £55m whilst enjoying the benefits of the inland waterways system". It estimated 17,000 people gained employment from being associated with the waterways network. At a time of economic stringency, the prospects of new jobs had considerable practical appeal.

Even though the economic outlook was not bright, this did not prevent idealists from publishing their longer-term plans. One was Ian Horsley, who had founded the Rase-Ancholme Navigation Trust in 1977. He set out his longer-term aims for new linkages from the Ancholme to Market Rasen, and on to Horncastle, and through to the Foss Dyke, so creating a northern Lincolnshire waterways network. This idea was well in advance of its time, especially in an area of low population with few enthusiasts to take it forward.

Longer-standing members of IWA were saddened to hear or Robert Aickman's death on 26 February 1981. While some disagreed with his approach, many more acknowledged the role he played in getting the waterways network back on the map and for the actions he took to start and maintain the vibrant waterway restoration movement that we have today. He personally was greatly upset by a BWB press release, in February 1979, which indicated that "in the interests of safety, some 15 major canal structures had to be closed". That anguish was compounded by a later press release, on 6 February 1981, just before his death, which warned of "long term interruptions to cruising in 1981". The campaign he started, and fought for so strongly, to get the Government to safeguard the heritage of the waterways, was far from won.

In early 1981 a newly formed Wandsworth Basin Restoration Society published its plans for the mouth of the River Wandle at Bell Lane Creek. One of their aims was to create safe moorings, by preventing the creek from drying out at low tide, with the creation of a half-tide barrier across the creek mouth. The Society gained planning permission for this work, but it was subsequently delayed. Their second phase was perhaps more difficult to achieve. This involved removing the weir that currently held back the River Wandle itself, so that craft could proceed unhindered up the river channel, under Armoury Way, as far as the High Street Bridge, Wandsworth, which had earlier been culverted. Here they proposed a new public garden, with a landing stage and a visitor mooring. This second phase subsequently did not materialise, but the half-tide weir was built and later fell into disuse.

Mid-1981 saw the start of what was to be one of the most difficult campaigns for both the IWA and for the River Derwent Trust, which had been planning to restore the River Derwent navigation. To gain public support the trust hoped to use a small donated boat to offer public trips along the regularly used section of the river at Malton, as far as Kirkham Weir. When their plans became public knowledge, the local conservation group, CONSYDER, wrote to the landowners along that section of the river, asking them to object on the grounds that there were no navigation rights. Four landowners did so. The Trust replied that they had been advised that rights of navigation still existed. Whereupon CONSYDER, through the landowners' solicitor, threatened they would sue for trespass if the trip boat were used, as a way of asserting their claim that the river was private.

Shortly before his death, Robert Aickman, who was chairman of the River Derwent Trust, commented: "there has been a massive change in public opinion – once we were on the side of angels – now Britain has gone mad". He simply could not understand why such a negative approach was being adopted by the conservation lobby.

The River Derwent Trust decided they needed to clarify their legal rights and sought a Relator Action from the Attorney General. To do this the Trust required both evidence and funds. The BCU and the Upper Derwent Boat Club, whose members had their personal craft on the river, provided the evidence and an appeal was made for donations to raise £10,000 to bring the case. Earlier the River Derwent Trust had taken a lease on a plot of land adjacent to Kirkham Weir on which they intended to build the necessary bypass lock. This lease was coming up for renewal in August 1981, so it was seen as important that the case was progressed

before that date. It turned out that the court hearing could not be scheduled until February 1985, which, on the other hand, gave the Trust more time to raise the necessary funds. They were able to submit their evidence in December 1984, but the landowners claimed they were not ready, so the case was postponed until July 1985. Both groups raised the stakes through their appeals for funding. The slogan "50p to keep the boats away" was promoted by conservationists, versus the wider "A River Derwent Appeal" by the Trust. When the case finally got to court the judge ruled that the action would be heard in two stages. The first would examine what rights of way existed on the River Derwent and whether the 1935 Revocation Order affected any of them. The second stage, if necessary, would examine whether a right of navigation has been created more recently by the use of the river over the last 50 years or so. The legal processes went on far longer than anyone had envisaged, and it was not until 19 December 1988 that a High Court judge ruled that there was "no right of navigation" on the Derwent up to Malton and placed an order for costs against the Trust, but leave was given for an appeal. The Trust, backed by the IWA, felt this ruling was unsatisfactory and agreed to fight on, on the basis that the 1932 Rights of Way Act did apply to waterways. Each party made a commitment to try to raise in total the £100,000 funding required to undertake the appeal. Again the hearing took a considerable time to arrange, and the appeal was not finally heard until July 1990. On this occasion the Court of Appeal overturned the previous ruling and confirmed, on 31 July 1990, that a right of navigation is considered to be established under the Rights of Way Act 1932 on a waterway that has been used by the public as a right of way for over 20 years. Although a right of appeal was refused, it did not mean the end of the saga, as the landowners decided to petition the House of Lords to hear their plea. This they did, but it could not be heard before the middle of October 1991, at the earliest. The House of Lords' decision was finally announced on 5 December 1991. The Law Lords overturned the Appeal Court's ruling and indicated that the 1932 Public Rights of Way Act did not apply to waterways. This was a devastating blow to both the River Derwent Trust and the IWA. Whilst their legal advisers felt it should be pursued still further, they reluctantly took the decision that they could not bear the likely costs involved. It was a sad day for the waterways.

By early 1981, economic constraints were beginning to be felt everywhere, not least on the waterways. Sir Frank Price, the BWB Chairman, lobbied the Government for sufficient funds to undertake the maintenance backlog on the canals and other inland waterways. He commented to the press that "The Board have never had sufficient funds to fulfil their statutory duty to maintain the canals." Subsequent BW chairmen continued to reiterate that concern.

At a time when public funding was desperately short, the advent of the Job Creation Scheme, run by the Manpower Services Commission to alleviate unemployment, which by then was up to 3 million, had a dramatic effect on restoration schemes. It enabled them to move away from weekend work parties manned by volunteers, to a full-time operation with skilled supervisors. The first three schemes to benefit were the Stroudwater, Thames and Severn Canal Trust, who gained 20 workers and a budget of £17,000, the Droitwich Canal, which gained 15 workers and £19,000, and the Rochdale Canal, with 52 workers and £40,000. The Basingstoke Canal similarly gained a team of Construction Industry Training Board apprentices to rebuild lock walls, and the Kennet and Avon Canal obtained one of the largest grant of £238,000, to tackle the longstanding problem of the dry section at Limpley Stoke.

It was not just money and trainees that helped the restoration movement. The MSC schemes themselves brought official recognition and approval of restoration, that had previously been lacking. This was best exemplified on the Rochdale Canal where secretary Brian Holden explained the hidden value. "The picture thus far was the foundation of a starry-eyed idealistic society that was attempting to restore a canal that was none of their business because it was privately owned. Suddenly, after two years of floundering about and wondering how to go about it without offending the private owners, we had 52 lads, paid for and administered by the local authority. This was a stroke of luck, since it brought in the local council, who had to obtain a licence from the [canal] company." At its peak, a total of 450 young people were employed by MSC on the Rochdale alone. Since no one was allowed to work for more than a year under the scheme, it meant thousands passed through it over the twelve-year period the scheme was in being, many taking away some knowledge and a new interest in canals.

This new way of working the system gave a fresh impetus to would-be resorationists. In the West Country, a Bridgwater and Taunton Canal Society was proposed. The aim of the group was to complement the work of the existing Somerset Inland Waterways Society and the local IWA Branch in getting the Bridgwater and Taunton canal fully reopened.

Likewise, a well-researched proposal to extend the navigation of the Thames, from Inglesham to Cricklade, was published by the Oxford and South Bucks Branch of the IWA at a public meeting in Cricklade on 11 May 1981. The background to the presentation was a feasibility study, undertaken by Sir Alexander Gibbs and partners, that envisaged three new locks at Hannington, Castle Easton and Water Eaton, to overcome the 16-foot difference in levels. It also suggested the River Churn could provide a new navigation link into the Thames and Severn Canal near Latton, the estimated cost being some £1.6m at 1980 prices. Subsequently a boat rally, "Lechlade 82", was held on 5 and 6 June 1982 to promote the project. In 1984, a "Token Ton" was carried from Coventry via the Lechlade Riverside Festival, to arrive at Cricklade Wharf on 16 June 1984. The special low-draft craft, the *Bold Adventurer*, duly delivered its load with much acclaim. Subsequently a local campaign, for a navigable culvert under the proposed Latton bypass, diverted attention from this scheme.

In April 1981 a rope failure closed the Anderton Lift. Subsequent checks identified serious flaws in the supporting beams. In consequence, the Boat Lift between the Trent and Mersey Canal and the River Weaver was closed until further notice. This was just one of the many key structures that subsequently failed, through underfunding of maintenance, so leading to a major closures crisis throughout the BWB waterway network.

Whilst the BWB system creaked through lack of cash, water authority navigations gained help from other sources. At Sudbury, on the River Stour, the 819th Civil Engineering Squadron of the US Air Force, which was based nearby, cleared a 100-yard arm of Sudbury Basin as part of a training exercise. At much the same time, the River Stour Trust itself set up a special fund to finance the building of a new lock at Great Cornard. However, on a less positive note, a Public Inquiry was held on 30 June 1981, to review the new River Byelaws, which proposed to restrict navigation on the River Stour to manually propelled craft only. The Trust went into battle, since it would negate all they were seeking to achieve.

Positive ideas often generate new opportunities. Thus when the Chelmsford branch of the IWA set out its scheme for building a new link canal from Springfield basin to the river above the weir, the idea was in principle accepted by Chelmsford Council and incorporated within their longer-term development plans.

Novel ideas were equally necessary to identify new ways of raising funds. The Kennet and Avon Canal Trust was able to attract attention by launching their "From Sea to Sea" appeal. They pointed out that only some fourteen locks and the completion of work on the Devizes flight was needed to enable the through navigation to be restored again. They launched this appeal just as a start was being made on regating the flight of 29 locks at Devizes. This initiative was further boosted on 29 August 1981 when the Crofton Locks up to the Crofton Pumping Station were reopened.

Enthusiasts were heartened when in mid-1981 they heard BWB had received permission to upgrade certain Remainder Waterways to Cruiseway status. These included the Ashton, Lower Peak Forest, Caldon and Erewash Canals. All of these had been restored in the 1970s, with financial assistance from the local authorities. It is remarkable to consider now that, even when these canals had been restored, others were at the same time in the process of being abandoned. One such waterway was the St Helens or Sankey Canal, where traffic ceased in 1959 and which was abandoned in 1963. Fortunately local councils were sympathetic to the aims of the Sankey Canal Society, which was formed to revive the waterway. Work started on reclaiming the canal, between Bewsey and Liverpool Road, Great Sankey, in October 1980. This was funded under a Derelict Land Grant scheme. A second stage project, from Great Sankey to Fiddlers Ferry, including restoration of the lock into the River Mersey, was also planned. Such Derelict Land Grants ultimately were to provide a great boost to the viability of various restoration schemes.

The Inland Waterways Association and others had been campaigning hard to ensure that the findings of the mid-1970s, particularly Peter Fraenkel and Partners' assessment of the maintenance backlog on the canal system, were not allowed to die, or even gather dust on Departmental shelves. They were thus very interested to hear that the DoE had commissioned the consultants Inbucon to investigate and identify ways in which waterways revenue might be increased. This study was later to bear some fruit. It also identified that proper funding for the waterways had not been overlooked.

Just as pressures were placed on central Government, local pressure was also bearing fruit elsewhere. A "Bridgwater and Taunton Interim Report" was published by BWB in mid-1981. This offered three options:

1.   Full restoration
2.   Interim Development
3.   No further development.

Its preliminary conclusion, accepted by the local councils, was that nothing in the interim should be done to prevent full restoration of the waterway.

Enthusiasts were keen to exploit similar opportunities elsewhere. An Upper River Ouse Navigation scheme was promoted in a *Waterways World* article, which suggested a new group should be formed to take over, where the Great Ouse Restoration Society had ceased, and campaign for a new link between Bedford and Wolverton on the Grand Union Canal. The East Anglian Waterways Association's legal advice was that the right of navigation existed on the river through to the Grand Union and beyond. Subsequent research by the Milton Keynes Branch of the IWA identified many low bridges that could affect the feasibility of such a river link. The discouraging attitude of Anglia Water Authority was also a consideration. It is interesting to note that this river development proposal never did get off the ground, but a much later Bedford to Milton Keynes direct link found far more national support.

The threat of new road schemes was always a great worry for canal restorers. Thus when the Stroudwater, Thames and Severn Canal Society heard of three proposals for a proposed East/West Stroud Bypass, two of which involved filling in the canal, they immediately asked activists to support the solution that protected the canal line. Initially it seemed Stroud Council would not heed the Society members' case, but their continual pressure brought about a change of heart and an alternative route was selected.

In Scotland the commitment towards the Lowland Canal was growing. The Forth and Clyde Canal Society looked after interests at the Glasgow end, whilst a second group, the Falkirk Canal Society, developed an interest in the eastern section and the Union Canal. The work of these two groups ultimately led to reports in the Glasgow press that more than £4 million could soon be spent to provide environmental and recreational improvements to the canal. The Forth and Clyde Society also purchased two old Clyde Ferries to provide boat trips along the canal at Bowling.

In January 1982 a report on the Union Canal was published that encouraged greater recreational use. The report suggested there was a need to develop further the Union Canal Project, set up in 1979, and it supported the aims of the Union Canal Trust, which was set up specifically to raise money for major restoration work such as the removal of obstructions to navigation.

South of the border, the prospect of major cash injections became apparent on the Rochdale Canal, where the MSC scheme was restoring the Hebden Bridge to Todmorden section of the canal, the cost of materials for the project being met by the local councils. In addition, a lock-gate workshop was set up in Halifax, in January 1982, under another MSC scheme.

There was long-awaited good news for the BWB Chairman, at the end of 1981, when the Government announced that their grant would be increased from £28.5 to £37.7 million for the period 1982/3. This enabled the Board to plan remedial works to overcome some of the major long-term stoppages, such as those at Blisworth and Preston Brook tunnels, as well as initial repairs to Boddington Reservoir.

In a small way, boaters themselves were helping to overcome the long-term neglect. For example, a crew of a pair of passing boats took it upon themselves to clear the entry of the then truncated and disused Saltisford Arm, at Warwick. Their effort subsequently led to the formation of the Saltisford Arm Trust by Dick Amende, which, in 1982, sought and gained support for a wider MSC scheme to complete the work of clearing and reactivating the waterway.

Prospects for the Huddersfield Canal similarly began to look brighter in early 1982, when the Greater Manchester Council agreed to pay the maintenance costs of the refurbished Upper Mill section. Also, West Yorkshire Metropolitan Council signed a lease on the Marsden Tunnel Cottages and Kirklees Metropolitan Council signed up to take over the maintenance of the towpath between Marsden and Huddersfield. This latter scheme offered restorers a model agreement for similar situations elsewhere.

It was a pity the Cwmbran Development Corporation did not have the same attitude, when they published plans for a new road along a quarter-mile of the Monmouthshire Canal at the village of Old Cwmbran. The Newport Canal Preservation Society put forward an alternative route, which protected the canal line, and asked enthusiasts to write to the Welsh Office to support their alternative plan. This ultimately led to the setting up of a Public Enquiry, in January 1983, at which Michael Handford, acting for both the IWA and the local groups, advocated the canal restorers' case. In doing so he produced a 1951 Development Corporation Master Plan, which showed the canal as restored. The Inquiry result, published in late 1983, allowed for a canal route, although slightly diverted, to be protected for possible future restoration.

Similar protection was provided for the Montgomery Canal in North Wales, when Powys Structure Plan was amended to include a statement: "No permission should be granted for any development inconsistent with the restoration of the canal north of Whitehorse Bridge No 120." Unfortunately, this was to a degree contradicted some weeks later when BWB, which was still strapped for cash, issued a statement: "Future restoration of the canal is uncertain. No new works to be commenced after work at Franklin and Carreghofa. Water is not available from the Llangollen Canal." The Montgomery Waterways Restoration Trust immediately asked for a meeting with the BWB Chairman, Sir Frank Price, and on 5 April 1982 agreed that an economic study should be undertaken of the viability of restoration and that the report should be ready by the end of October 1982. This then could be used to guide the future development of the canal.

In the North-West, the local IWA Branch and Lancaster Boat Club organised a trip from the Rufford branch of the Leeds and Liverpool Canal up the River Ribble to Preston Docks. They did this to publicise a preliminary survey they had made that identified a route, via Savick Brook, to create a link with the Lancaster Canal. The costs for the link were estimated at £1.5 million for the works and £1.5 million for the necessary land purchase. In much the same way ideas about restoring the Ripon Canal, from above Littlethorpe Lock to the basin in Ripon, were proposed by local IWA activists. To press their case, they got them written into the "River Ure and Ouse Recreational Subject Plan", subsequently published by the North Yorkshire County Council. Its officers suggested that restoration prospects would be more likely to be achieved with the formation of a restoration society to champion the scheme. This was too good a chance to miss. A public meeting was called jointly by the IWA and Ripon Motor Boat Club to carry this concept forward. The Ripon Canal Restoration Society was formed at a second meeting, in January 1983. At its first committee meeting the name was shortened to Ripon Canal Society with the aim of actively promoting the whole canal.

At much the same time, David Hutchings was undertaking a survey of the Upper River Severn, supported by the riparian local authorities, particularly Bewdley Council. He concluded it would not be difficult for boats again to reach Ironbridge and beyond. This led to a meeting in Bridgnorth, in December 1982, at which the local branch of the IWA agreed to assist in the formation of the Upper Severn Restoration Trust. At a subsequent meeting, in February 1983, some rowers and anglers objected to the scheme but, at the wish of the majority of those present, a steering committee was formed to create the trust as a non-profit charitable company.

As events took a step forward on the Upper Severn, lower down the river news broke that the Severn and Canal Carrying Company, who were planning to restore the Coombe Hill Canal, had gone into liquidation and that the canal was to be sold. Other local activists talked about forming a Coombe Hill Canal Trust to buy the canal, but this ultimately did not prove to be feasible.

A range of new options for alternative funding for the waterways emerged, when the Government published the Inbucon Report at the end of 1982. This suggested BWB should maximise their efforts to develop land-based amenities, car parks, pubs, etc., and to set out to encourage waterside housing, craft workshops and boat-based entertainments. Soon after publishing that report, the Waterways Minister confirmed that BWB's grant would be increased from £37.7m to £41.9m in

1983/4, of which some £8m was earmarked to reduce the longer-term maintenance backlog. At last the Government seemed to be responding positively to the persistent pressure from activists.

Gaining access to funding was also a concern of the Rochdale Canal, where the private company who owned it could not themselves gain a Derelict Land Grant. In consequence, the Greater Manchester Council sought to take a lease on the canal to meet the DoE's requirements to access that source of funding for restoration work. Following much the same approach, Whitchurch Town Council voted to sponsor a feasibility study, to evaluate the costs, benefits and problems of restoring the local and infilled Whitchurch Arm of the Llangollen. The study was undertaken for them jointly by Liverpool Polytechnic and the Aston University Civil Engineering Department.

Following the publication of articles in the local press on the history of the old Herefordshire and Gloucestershire Canal, a public meeting was called in Hereford on 13 April 1983 to form a society to encourage greater public awareness of the Hereford and Gloucester Canal. This society was quickly to emerge as a very active restoration group.

Many restoration societies were able to utilise Manpower Services Commission Job Creation and Youth Employment schemes to carry forward their waterway restoration schemes; so much so, that the British Waterways Board created a post of Co-ordinator of MSC Schemes. They listed between 30 and 40 projects, on various canals, employing more than 380 people. A good example of this was the Community Service Project at the Ripon Canal Head. Here the team used the materials provided by the local council, whilst the labour and supervision were paid for by MSC. Another example was where the MSC team had enabled the Rochdale Canal, between Hebden Bridge and Todmorden, to be reopened on 20 May 1983. In the same way, the West Leicestershire District Council submitted plans to restore a section of the Ashby Canal, in conjunction with a Museum project, at Moira. This envisaged using MSC labour for three years. Bradford

Huddersfield Narrow Canal pre-restoration

Metropolitan Council also hoped to join the MSC club, after a competition in the local paper came up with a scheme using MSC teams to restore the derelict Bradford Canal.

In an effort to make more thorough use of the MSC opportunity, the Monmouthshire, Brecon and Abergavenny Trust Ltd was formed, by local societies and the IWA, to restore the Monmouthshire Canal. This initiative was supported by Newport Borough Council, who was already using a 30-strong MSC team to restore another part of that waterway.

Concerns were raised in East Lincolnshire by the local IWA Branch when Anglian Water Authority indicated they were preparing to demolish some of the remaining lock structures on the Louth Canal. All those interested in preserving this waterway were invited to make contact with the local branch with a view to protecting the structures.

The Barnsley Canal Group was established in 1984. Its first act was to make a detailed survey of the remains of the canal to determine whether a campaign could be mounted to promote its restoration. An article appeared in *Waterways World* at about the same time detailing the route and obstructions on the Bradford Canal. It suggested restoration of at least part of the Bradford Canal was worthy of serious consideration. Little action locally ensued. In the spring of 1984, the Lark Valley Association was formed. It started to consider the restoration of the upper reaches of the River Lark, above Judes Ferry. They were later able to report some progress in convincing the local council of their case.

In the summer of 1984, the effects of the severe drought were beginning to hit a large number of canals. Overnight lock closures and severe timetabling restrictions on lock use during the day made it difficult for boaters to move around. That gloom was partially lifted when the Blisworth Tunnel was reopened in August 1984 and the Leek Tunnel restored in July of that year. It was also the time when Government announced that BWB had been give permission to promote a Private Bill, to obtain the powers to facilitate restoration of waterways, and also to allow for allocation of matching funds and financial support from the EEC regeneration budgets to waterway projects.

In South Wales, the Swansea Canal Society, formed in 1981, was also celebrating a grant from the Prince of Wales Committee to enable them to restore the Gurnos Aqueduct. In November 1984, the Scottish Inland Waterways Association held its first conference to discuss the history of the Lowland Canals and review how they might be revived. It was interesting that Prime Minister, Margaret Thatcher, made her first recorded canal trip in September 1984, as a guest of the Seagull

Trust, from their new base at Ratho on the Union Canal in Scotland.

By the end of 1984, enthusiasts were far more confident about the future for the nation's canals. In South Wales, the Monmouthshire, Brecon and Abergavenny Canals Trust commissioned an engineering study into rebuilding the lowered Crowne Bridge at Sebastopol. The Upper Severn Restoration Trust had received a survey of the River Severn, through to Shrewsbury, prepared by Waters and Partners, which identified the need for 21 locks and weirs that would add another 50 miles of navigable waterway.

In October 1984, locals formed the Macclesfield Canal Society to cater for those interested in that canal. Later in its life it too would be suggesting a new link to its canal. At about the same time the Wilts and Berks Canal Amenity Group published its plans for the staged restoration of their entire canal in a document entitled *Boats to Laycock and beyond*. In the same area, work began in November 1984 on restoring the first section of the Old Somerset Coal Canal at Dundas. This was a private venture to create new linear moorings. A more public show of strength by the restorers was the "Stratford Blitz" on the southern Stratford canal, where some 16 separate weekend working parties were organised by WRG volunteers to upgrade the waterway structures that had been restored earlier on a very tight budget and timetable. Likewise the Upper Avon Navigation Trust announced plans to rebuild Stratford New Lock, which was constructed before they knew what the final water levels were likely to be as the ground needed was not available for an intermediate lock someway downstream. It had consequently been built far too deep, with heavy gates that were difficult to operate.

In East Anglia, a major improvement scheme was being undertaken on Well Creek. This joint venture by Well Creek Trust, the Middle Level Commissioners and Shell UK, together with Cambridgeshire and Norfolk County Councils, involved an MSC scheme employing eight trainees, plus a supervisor, for one year. A similar MCS scheme was set up at Crofton on the K&A, as was one on the Barnsley Canal. These all made tangible progress.

In much the same way the Stroudwater, Thomas and Severn Canal Trust were finding that the proprietors, the local authorities and even parish councils were supportive of their plans to fully restore the Stroudwater Navigation and were exploring similar opportunities.

At this time, it was sad to see the demise of a third new waterways magazine, *Narrow Boat*, which did not survive its first year through lack of advertising revenue combined with low sales. That same fickleness was recorded elsewhere, when the Peak Forest Canal

Society, instrumental in reopening their canal over a decade earlier, was wound up through "lack of interest and general apathy on the part of members". Most had moved on to the nearby and more exciting Huddersfield Narrow Canal restoration work.

By May 1985, a new threat to the Rochdale Canal had emerged. This was yet another planned road scheme, this time for an extension to the M66 motorway, which cut across the Rochdale Canal at Chadderton. Society members were advised that a public enquiry would be held in 1986. The local activists, helped by Michael Hanford, a university lecturer well versed in such matters, started to plan their case. This road building threat did not deter others nearby from wishing to restore their derelict canal. The Sankey Canal Restoration Society, founded in March 1985, started to set out their canal revival plans.

David Hutchings, the stalwart campaigner, had two campaigns active in mid-1985. A leaflet, "The Avon Connection", was presented to Warwick District Council, who expressed interest in that scheme. Elsewhere, a "Bewdley or Bust" rally was being sponsored on the River Severn by the Severn Navigation Restoration Trust. High water levels on the river enabled a large flotilla to reach Bewdley, where "supporters" and "protesters" were out in equal numbers to either greet or jeer at the boats.

By then, a new Joint Steering Committee had been formed on the Huddersfield Narrow Canal to give impetus to the restoration of that waterway. It was seen by local activists that the prospect of fully restoring the Narrow Canal could really become a reality.

This forward thinking was evident elsewhere. The Fenland District Council published the "Nene-Ouse Navigation Link" prospectus that recommended a northern route across the Middle Level and suggested that a Middle Level Waterway Users Committee should be established to assist with the implementation of the Council's plan.

It was at this time that concerns about getting an acceptable balance between flora, fauna and navigation use came to the fore. To seek a resolution, an MSC scheme was created on the Montgomery Canal to record the current populations of flora and fauna, prior to further restoration activity. The project included an experiment of creating "off line" reserves in which rare or interesting plans could be accommodated. The first of these was at Rednal, a few miles south of Welsh Frankton. This innovative project was later to facilitate permission for further restoration work both on the Montgomery and later elsewhere on the system.

In late 1985, the Chesterfield Canal Society unveiled their plans for the western end of their canal. It suggested Derbyshire County Council should buy the Chesterfield to Staveley section of the Canal from BWB, and develop it for local amenity use. The Society saw this as the most efficient way, at that time, of getting that isolated length of the canal restored.

Set apart from the national network, in the North-East, a new lock, to take craft 80 feet long and 8 feet wide, together with a containing weir, was constructed at the mouth of the River Wansbeck, in Northumberland, in 1985. Whilst the lock was toll free, boaters had to pay for the use of the new stabilised river navigation upstream of the lock.

By the end of 1985, it had been learnt that the M66 Public Enquiry, at Chadderton, had been postponed until May 1986. This presented an ominous challenge for the year ahead.

New schemes during the period 1979 to 1985 included:

1. Herefordshire and Gloucestershire Canal
2. Upper Great Ouse
3. Wreak Navigation
4. Somerset Coal Canal
5. Swansea Canal
6. Upper Severn Navigation
7. Whitchurch Arm, Llangollen Canal.

Between 1979 and 1985, although the national financial climate had become difficult, more money was available for the waterways through schemes brought about to help stem the high levels of unemployment which beset the early Thatcher years. Dark clouds over the decline of the waterways network in some places were starting to have silver linings, with more people actively engaged restoring waterways full-time than in the past.

IX 1986-1990:
TOWARDS MAJOR RE-OPENINGS

The year 1986 opened with an air of greater and tangible commitment from local authorities towards their canals than they had offered in the past. This was exemplified by the willingness of the Greater Manchester Council to investigate possible designs for the removal of the then existing blockages in the Rochdale Canal and also for overcoming the M62 crossing at Failsworth. This local commitment to solving problems augured well for the likely council submissions to the forthcoming Public Inquiry into the M66 route.

On much the same theme was the sponsorship, by East Yorkshire Borough Council, of the work on two replacement swing bridges on the Pocklington Canal, the bridges themselves being provided by the Pocklington Canal Amenity Society, and Warwick District Council's willingness to set up an Officers' Working Party to investigate the advantages and disadvantages of the proposed Higher Avon scheme.

The vexatious issue of conservation versus restoration and rebuilding reared its head at Blists Hill on the tub-boat canal, where the Hay Incline had been partially restored. The debate arose over the possible creation of a replica engine house, rather than leaving the relics as they stood. This caused a heated debate, which was not easily resolved. However, the leaks that had dogged the partially restored Coalport Canal, at the foot of the incline, had been overcome by the use of modern rebuilding techniques. Plans were also made to re-excavate along the canal as far as the Coalport Bridge, to act as a tourist feature. A trip boat was introduced on the River Severn at Ironbridge, to capture the same tourist market. In a similar quest to attract tourists, the West Country Branch of the IWA started to look for a small trip boat which they could operate on the Bridgwater and Taunton Canal, to raise its public profile. They also set out to raise £20,000 to reinstate a swing bridge at Bathpool, near Taunton, which had been fixed, as well as the creation of a picnic site at Durston.

Opportunities to provide public facilities, that might also act as fund-raisers, were sought out by restoration groups. Perhaps the best example of this was the derelict Granary Warehouse at Sudbury Basin, which the River Stour Trust purchased to restore as a theatre, café and meeting venue. The land alongside it also offered the site to build a new slipway for visiting craft.

The issue of the true value to the community of a restored waterway was investigated by the Stratford-upon-Avon Canal Society, in their battle to ensure that their

canal was retained and refurbished. They identified that the Stratford Canal basin brought 21,000 visitors each year to the town, on 3,400 hire boats and 600 private craft. They calculated that boat crews spent a total of £400,000 in the town each year. In addition, £300,000 was paid to local boat yards for the hire of craft. Their report concluded that if the canal were again to fall into disrepair, it would cost the town £700,000 of lost income each year.

The two high-profile restoration projects of this period were the Basingstoke Canal and Kennet and Avon Canal restoration schemes. On the Kennet and Avon, electric back pumps were being installed at Bradford-on-Avon, with further pumps planned for Semington, Seend, Devizes and Wooton Rivers, to augment the potential deficit of water supplies when the canal was reopened. The Kennet and Avon Trust set itself the task of raising the necessary funds. On the Basingstoke Canal, Youth Training Scheme workers continued to restore the remaining derelict locks. New gates for them were constructed at the Deepcut Workshop. A report of progress to date noted that of the twelve locks still to be restored, only Locks No.2 and No.3, at West Byfleet, remained untouched. This enabled the Surrey and Hampshire Canal Society to set itself a target of 1988 as the year for the possible completion of the works.

Until 1985, the Grand Union Canal Society and the local IWA Branch co-ordinated the local activities on the Wendover Arm. By October 1985, interest in it had grown to the extent that a separate Wendover Arm Group was formed, with representatives from IWA, GUCS, Aylesbury Canal Society and local boat clubs. Its aim was to seek the full restoration of the Wendover Arm, from Tringford Pumping Station to Wendover. They identified a two-stage project. The first stage was from Tringford to the A41 road crossing, at Aston Clinton, and the second stage was the conservation of the waterway from the A41 to Wendover itself.

Further north, the Huddersfield Canal and the Rochdale Canal restoration projects were proceeding apace. Both of these schemes were being pushed forward by very supportive local councils. On the Huddersfield they were using MSC labour to reopen both ends of the canal, whilst on the Rochdale, West Yorkshire County Council were systematically removing blockages created by dropped bridges. This work was especially important as the Metropolitan County Councils, undertaking much of the works, were due to be abolished on 1 April

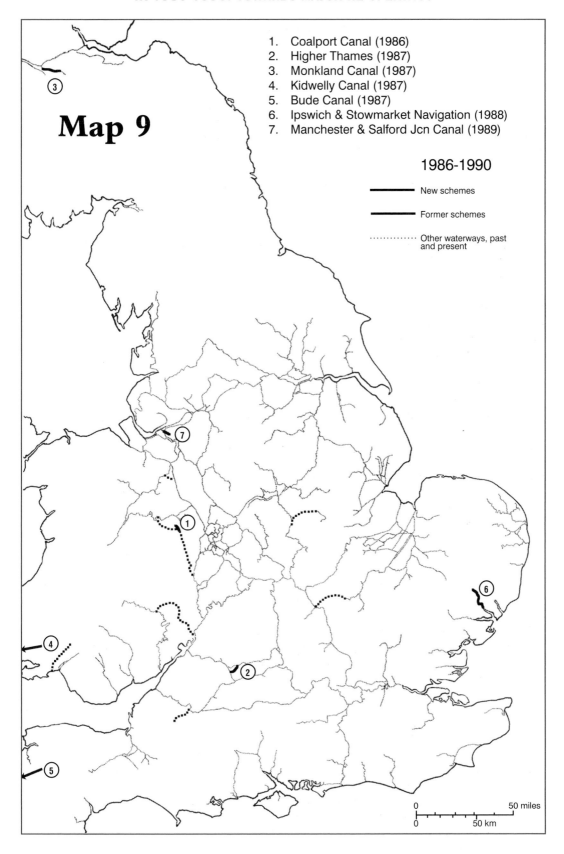

1. Coalport Canal (1986)
2. Higher Thames (1987)
3. Monkland Canal (1987)
4. Kidwelly Canal (1987)
5. Bude Canal (1987)
6. Ipswich & Stowmarket Navigation (1988)
7. Manchester & Salford Jcn Canal (1989)

Map 9

1986-1990

New schemes

Former schemes

Other waterways, past and present

0   50 miles
0   50 km

1986, with all the consequent disruption, caused by the re-allocation of functions that would ensue. The Greater Manchester Council acknowledged this problem by identifying a dowry specifically to finance the future restoration works on both canals in the following years.

Future planning was on the mind of members of the Lincolnshire and South Humberside Branch of IWA, when they prepared a report assessing the potential of restoring Gibson's Cut, which formed the first mile of the Horncastle Canal. It examined the possibility of creating a marina off the river in a basin. It also looked briefly at the longer-term possibility of restoring the Horncastle Canal itself.

Down south, the Higher Thames Trust held an open meeting at Cricklade Town Hall on 1 February 1986, to discuss draft Memoranda and Articles of Association. It was agreed to aim to formally launch the Trust as a Limited Company. To ensure that no stakeholders were omitted, it was proposed that the NFU, County Landowners and riparian local authorities also ought to be invited to join. This act of widening the opportunity for input by stakeholders gained considerable support. This was evident later in 1986, when landowners were approached by the nearby Wilts and Berks Canal Amenity Group, to get them onside for further work at Lacock. New leases were forthcoming to open up new work sites.

A "Save the Rochdale Canal" rally was organised at Chadderton to gain local support for the provision of navigable culverts under the planned M66 motorway. At this time, BWB were also undertaking their own consultation exercise, before putting forward a new Private Bill, to facilitate the restoration of the Montgomery Canal. At Foxton Locks, the Inclined Plane Trust was busily restoring the old Engine House for conversion to a museum. At Chelmsford, the local Waterways Advisory Group had been taking councillors on boat trips, in an effort to get their support for the IWA plans for "Springfield Basin and Beyond". On the Wendover, the Wendover Arm Group produced a document called "Water to Wendover", to seek support for their ideas. In Scotland, it was through a Report of Land Use Consultants that a short section of the Monkland Canal, at Coatbridge, was restored by the Local Council, as part of the Summerlee Heritage Park and Open Air Heritage Museum.

Although many of the earlier safety closures had been lifted, one problem was recurring. This was the erosion of the lock island at Linton Lock. It caused the closure of the lock again, until further notice, on 30 September 1986. The Linton Lock Commissioners simply had no means of raising the £20,000 needed for the repairs and had to make a public appeal for alternative sources of funding.

This appeal was led by the Secretary of the Ripon Canal Society, who indicated he planned to create a charitable trust to project-manage the appeal and organise the repair works. In subsequent discussions with BWB, they indicated they would be prepared to take over the lock, but could not do so until it was structurally sound and carried forward no debt. They indicated the DoE would not sanction such a takeover until they were given that assurance. Initial fund-raising for the works went well and the lock island was stabilised sufficiently for the lock to reopen on 31 July 1987. Unfortunately, a further landslip caused a second closure in the autumn of 1989. This time it was estimated it could cost up to £100,000 to fully resolve the problem, of which £50,000 was needed immediately. It took until August 1990 to raise the total of £92,000 finally required, with the repair work proceeding piecemeal. Even then, BW still felt unable to take over the structure, and in the summer of 1993 the Linton Lock Commissioners decided they needed to force the DoE's hand, and formally ask the Secretary of State for an Order, under Section 112 of the Transport Act, to remove their responsibilities. The DoE did not rise to this request. By December 1995, the Commissioners again were forced to seek BWB help, this time to put in a bid to the Heritage Lottery Fund to cover all the potential restoration costs. Finally, in June 1997, the Commissioners heard that they were successful with their lottery bid and that £765,000 would be made available, against the £1,019,000 needed to completely refurbish the structure. Work was commissioned and the lock was fully repaired and reopened on 15 May 1998. The whole saga of Linton Lock reached a conclusion on 20 October 1998, when the Secretary of State granted an order for the transfer of the lock to British Waterways, with the Commissioners finally being relieved of their responsibilities.

In mid-1986 enthusiasts at Whitchurch, with the backing of the Town Council, formed the Whitchurch Arm Trust to promote the reopening of the local canal arm off the Llangollen Canal. The Council proposed that the first three-quarters of a mile of the Arm be restored under the auspices of an umbrella body, the Whitchurch Waterways Trust. In the longer term, they envisaged a major rebuild of the second section of the Arm, to the town centre. Since much of the original route had been lost to development in the 1950s, a bypass route, which involved an inclined plane to lower boats into the valley, was proposed, to gain access to the town centre.

In October 1986, the first reconstructed section of the Droitwich Barge Canal was opened at Vines Park. This provided an extension to the cruising route for the Trust's trip boat *Sabrina*. A plaque was unveiled to record the MSC involvement with the reconstruction work necessary for opening this central feature for Droitwich.

Yorkshire Ouse, Linton Lock repaired & reopened

Droitwich Junction Canal, top flight locks, official reopening

The historic Bugsworth Basin came under threat from the revised route of the A6 around Whaley Bridge in late 1985. Fortunately the Inland Waterways Protection Society were able, through skilled negotiation, to protect all but a small corner of the basin complex, which they previously had got listed as an Ancient Monument in 1977. However, they still had much restoration work to do to clear the large basin area.

Considerable progress had been made on the Kennet and Avon restoration by the MSC. This progress was identified by the MSC chairman, Bryan Nicholson, when he reopened Aldermaston Wharf and the adjacent lock, in September 1986. Similar reopenings were taking place on the Rochdale Canal where three previously culverted bridges and two derelict locks were completed under a £1 million project financed by Calderdale Council, together with grants from the EEC and elsewhere. This same MSC team were by then continuing working along the canal towards Tuel Lane, at Sowerby Bridge, where a final complicated road crossing stood in the way of re-linking the canal to the Calder and Hebble Navigation.

Another reopening took place, in November 1986, with the completion of restoration work on Kyme Eau lock, on the Sleaford Navigation. The Society's next task was that of raising a low footbridge and constructing

a new winding hole at South Kyme. Thereafter, they planned to continue towards Sleaford, with the restoration of Cobblers and Haverholme locks.

At much the same time, BWB announced proposals to reopen twelve miles of the Forth and Clyde Canal, between Cloberhill and Kirkintilloch, together with the Glasgow Branch, from Stockinfield Junction to Port Dundas. They hoped to attract EC funding to cover part of the £2.3 million costs involved. The total scheme included re-gating the Maryhill Locks and Temple Lock, together with the replacement of the top gate at Cloberhill. The prospect of tourism was seen as a key driver in the proposals and BWB aimed to complete the works to coincide with the Glasgow Garden Festival due to be held in 1988.

The Montgomeryshire County Council were generous towards the Montgomery Canal, when they announced they would allocate £1 million for canal restoration works spread over the following five years. This announcement coincided with BWB submitting their Private Bill to Parliament to authorise the full restoration. All parties hoped it would become law by January 1987.

As we have seen before, not everything always goes smoothly with restoration efforts…. Trust members

Rochdale Canal, official reopening

were thus concerned to hear that the Monmouthshire, Brecon and Abergavenny Canals Trust had been forced into liquidation, with over £12,000 missing from the Trust's Bank Account. A former Chairman of the Trust was charged with theft, and subsequently found guilty. Although the Trust's Management Committee was able to detect the deficiency promptly, it was unfortunate that such a theft should involve the hard-won funds of a charity and be perpetrated by a man members had previously trusted.

Better news was heard in Northwich, where the local Vale Regional District Council were setting up the Anderton Boat Lift Trust as a mechanism for applying for matching funding from the EEC, once BWB indicated they were ready to proceed with their Lift restoration project. BWB finally announced the repair works would start shortly on what all envisaged could eventually become a major visitor attraction for the area.

Attracting visitors was also in the mind of Staffordshire Moorlands District Council when it called for a feasibility study into the possibility of providing a visitor-friendly terminus for the truncated Leek Arm of the Caldon Canal. The Council agreed to investigate ways of returning part of a local industrial estate, which had been built over the old line of the canal, or adjacent land, to bring the end of the canal back into the town. They saw the critical arbiter for the project would be the number of additional visitors to the town, and these would offer the payback for the investment involved.

Money opens many doors. It was thus most welcome when the IWA learnt that Humphrey Symonds, a former secretary of Shrewsbury and Border Counties Branch, had left a legacy of over £200,000, with the stipulation that it should be used for restoration work on the Montgomery Canal. The IWA indicated it would be used to provide materials and support for volunteer work on the waterway.

Restorers constantly needed to consider the interests of the "conservation lobby". Often a balance had to be struck. A note in the Poicklington Canal Amenity Society Magazine indicated: "Even the local anglers support restoration. The canal is so weed choked and shallow that they have handed back their lease because the existing condition is not adequate for their sport."

Different meanings can, of course, be placed on the word "conservation". In relation to the Kidwelly Canal, in the Gwenraeth Valley in West Wales, the conservation work under a Community Programme Scheme succeeded in clearing the overgrown canal basin area, revealing much of the structure still intact. The next stage planned was to extend the overgrowth clearance up the canal line, to provide a three-foot depth of water for rowing boats. When the project was completed, it was hoped one mile of the three-mile waterway would be restored.

The value of the recreational role of canals was the subject of an editorial in *Waterways World* in July 1987. This made the point, which had been confirmed by a Monopolies and Mergers Commission Report, that since the Government does not expect the National Parks to pay for themselves, why should the national amenity that is composed of the historic waterways system, and attracts visitors to the country from all over the world, be treated differently. This was the continuation of the long-lasting debate about levels of Government grant for the waterways. Like his predecessors, this was something that Sir Leslie Young's successor as BWB Chairman would have to address when Sir Leslie retired on 30 June 1987.

Before his formal retirement, he was able to be at the opening of the new aqueduct that had been built to convey the Union Canal over the new bypass around the east of Edinburgh. This new half-million pound structure enabled the Ratho boats to continue to reach the winding hole at Wester Hailes. It also maintained the pressure to get the blockage at Wester Hailes removed, so as to provide a clear through route to Edinburgh's Lochrin Basin.

The Kennet and Avon Canal Trust published its "Silver Jubilee" issue of *The Butty* in mid-1987, and within it was able to announce that it hoped to complete the full restoration of the canal by the end of 1989, with an official reopening in 1990. It was interesting to note that one of the factors cited, that had led to delays, had been the inability to recruit suitable local skilled labour for the various MSC schemes undertaking the refurbishment work.

Two new small projects emerged at this time. One was an attempt by the Old Paisley Society and Renfrew District Council to revive a small remaining section of the "lost" Paisley Canal, as part of a Paisley Heritage Town Trail, past the old Ferguslie Thread Mills. This they hoped could achieved as part of the Town's 500th anniversary celebrations in 1988. The other project was the clearance of a length of the Grand Western Canal, including the Nynehead Tub Boat Lift, which had been undergoing preliminary restoration by its new owners since they purchased in 1986. They hoped to clear the vegetation and re-water a 380yd section and to realign a footpath, to run along the towpath, so as to make the site more accessible.

In much the same vein, Stephen Parker wrote to the editor of *Waterways World*, in August 1987, about the mainly derelict Manchester, Bolton and Bury Canal. He indicated that "with very little work, these locks could easily be restored to their former glory. This canal offers

Manchester Bolton & Bury Canal, start of work

tremendous possibilities for all aspects of restoration and tourism… What I most need now, is help and advice to enable me to start a Society to commence restoration." That help was quickly offered and the Society was formed soon afterwards.

The Conservatives under Margaret Thatcher were returned to power in the 1987 General Election. Their manifesto indicated that they intended to create a National Rivers Authority. The proposals for this were subsequently published as a Government Consultation Paper, which indicated that the water industry itself would be privatised. Concerns were aroused as to the likely effect on the water authority navigations, some of which were in need of serious repair.

The new Government also gave the go-ahead for British Waterways Board to take over the Southern Section of the Stratford Canal from the National Trust. This transfer had been discussed earlier, between BWB and the National Trust, on 7 October 1986. The Secretary of State had been asked then to make an order to authorise it. The order was duly made for implementation on 1 April 1988, with the provision of a dowry of £1.5 million, over the following five years, to bring the canal up to standard.

On 19 July 1987, Brian Dice, the Chief Executive of BWB, formally reopened the Melbourne Arm of the Pocklington Canal. This was the culmination of a long campaign by PCAS. At the opening, the chairman of East Yorkshire Council pledged their full support, except

financially, for the further restoration of the canal. This project, however, rested on getting the approval of the Nature Conservancy Council.

The issue of getting approvals for works often required the preparation of detailed consultation reports. In 1987, the Severn Navigation Restoration Trust published three reports by independent experts. An Engineering Study identified that 16 locks and 15 new weirs would be required between Stourport and Ironbridge. The lock at Jack Fields offered passage around rapids, which the Trust believed should be preserved for ecological reasons and thus did not require a weir. A Hydrology Report confirmed there would be no detrimental effect from these works in times of flood, but they would offer substantial benefits for irrigation at times of drought. On the cost benefit front, the input of £2.79 million would generate 137 new full-time jobs, plus substantial benefits to agriculture, waterside property and recreation. Whilst these reports painted a good picture in themselves, actually convincing the opposition was the real battle that had to be won.

In contrast, North Yorkshire County Councillors were convinced that the extra £500,000 required to provide a high-level bridge on the new Ripon Bypass, over the canal, was a reasonable investment to make to allow the final half-mile of canal and the terminal basin to be restored. The final issue was that of negotiating with the services providers to get them to reroute their mains, so that the obstructing Little Thorpe Bridge, through

Montgomery Canal, Frankton Locks official reopening

which the mains were laid, could be removed. This was facilitated when Harrogate District Council allocated £70,000 towards these costs from their 1990/92 capital programme budget.

September 1987 saw two reopenings. The first was on the Kennet and Avon Canal at Aldermaston, where a major lift bridge, plus Aldermaston Lock and Padworth swing bridge, were opened on 9 September. This was followed, on 12 September, by the Frankton Locks on the Montgomery Canal. Here volunteers had contributed 12,000 man-hours to the task, which, the Prince of Wales noted in his message to those present, was valued at £200,000. This key event was followed with further good news for the Montgomery Canal. This was the Royal Assent to the BWB Act 1987, which allowed BW to actively remove obstructions from the canal and promote its restoration.

A restoration project of a different kind was developed in early 1988. This was the construction of a new link tunnel from Singing Cavern to Castle Mill Basin, under Dudley Hill. Dudley MB Council had allocated funds over the next two years to facilitate the construction,

which when completed would offer a circular route for the Black Country Museum electric trip boats that offered Dudley Tunnel tours.

Another restoration project in the West Midlands which received backing from the local IWA at this time was a plan to restore the Wyrley and Essington Canal from Ogley Junction to Huddlesford Junction. As a first step, the campaigners planned to get what was left of the line safeguarded, especially where the proposed Birmingham Northern Relief Road was to cross the canal. BWB, however, indicated it considered the project a lost cause, as it was too difficult and costly.

The new Manchester, Bolton and Bury Canal Society had positive news as it prepared its stand, at the former junction on the River Irwell, at the IWA Festival at Castlefield. A preliminary report on the feasibility of restoration, prepared by Richard Chester-Browne, indicated that there were no obstructions that could not be overcome. It concluded by pointing up the many advantages of restoration.

The advantages of restoration of their canal were recognised by the residents of Slaithwaite, on the Huddersfield Narrow Canal. At a Public Meeting in

1988, to discuss the scheme, they voted that the canal should be restored on its original route through the centre of the village. Kirklees Metropolitan Council backed that route and indicated it would contribute towards the costs involved.

In a separate effort to stimulate interest in the canals within its area, the West Country Branch of the IWA produced a series of walking guides. These included the Bude, Stover, Liskard & Looe, Chard, Westport, Grand Western and Dorset & Somerset canals.

Further good news for restorers came in mid-1988, when the Department of Transport announced it would provide a navigable culvert under the proposed Aston Clinton Bypass, where it crossed the Wendover Arm. The local group seized this opportunity and indicated they would form a Wendover Arm Trust to take forward the restoration project.

The death of Graham Palmer, on 19 July 1988, came as sad news to the Waterway Recovery Group members. He had been at the forefront of many of their early restoration efforts, especially those on the Ashton and Montgomery Canals. He would have been proud of the 90 volunteer navvies who worked for one week on the Droitwich Junction Canal entry locks, to clear them with a view to restoration. That scheme had two advantages. Firstly, when the M5 motorway was reconstructed, a navigable culvert had been secured under it. Secondly,

the route of the Junction Canal lay just within an area eligible for European Regional Development Funding grants, which could provide funding for the works.

Lock One on the Basingstoke Canal was reopened on 18 September 1988. This was the culmination of 130 weekend work parties for volunteers. However, delays in finally opening the remainder of the Basingstoke Canal looked inevitable. Various legal problems had to be resolved, but it was the recurring leaks, and the need to raise the towpath bank at Sheerwater, that were going to take some time to complete.

Image is often seen as an important factor for key organisations. It thus came as no surprise when the British Waterways Board announced it planned to drop the name "Board" from the start of 1989, and to be known as "British Waterways" in future. This seemed of little consequence for restorers, who happily went along with the idea.

The re-opening of the Kennet and Avon Canal came a step closer when, on 6 October 1988, the top locks at Crofton were reopened by the Vice-Chairman of British Waterways. He was able to confirm that the remaining restoration of just three locks and three bridges in Berkshire, plus the re-gating of the remaining Caen Hill Locks at Devizes, should enable the opening of through navigation by 1990.

Basingstoke Canal, official reopening

As things looked brighter for the K&A, those on the Montgomery Canal took a backward step. The Secretary of State for Wales, Peter Walker, announced on 24 November 1988 that he had not included any funds for Montgomery Restoration in his forward project allocations. This decision, in turn, denied access to a 40% European Regional Development Fund grant towards the works. This was in direct contrast to the prospects of the Ribble Link Trust, when they heard they would receive financial support for a study of their plans for the Link, from Trafalgar House and others. The same funders were also looking at a second stage, for reconnecting the Northern Reaches from Kendal to the main canal.

At about this time, the Wey and Arun Canal Trust set up a "Conservation Steering Group" with the aim of avoiding the problems that had emerged on the restored Basingstoke Canal. This similar issue was one of the tasks given to the full-time Field Officer, funded by IWA, to try to revive the restoration programme on the Montgomery Canal that now was without Welsh Office funding. A petition against that decision was delivered to the Welsh Office on 19 April 1989 asking the Secretary of State to reconsider.

Developers in Manchester came up with a novel restoration idea for the Manchester and Salford Junction Canal. This envisaged an electric-powered boat conveying visitors from the basement of the Granada Studios about 500 yards along the canal to the basement of the Great Northern Goods Warehouse, where a range of shops and entertainment facilities were proposed. The project hinged on whether the safety issues could be overcome. Various articles published at this time identified exactly how the scheme might work but nothing actually materialised in the longer term.

Articles also appeared about the site of the Old Runcorn Locks, which was being cleared for redevelopment by Chester County Council using funds provided by the Merseyside Task Force. They noted that the lock chambers still remained but were filled in, apart from the top two locks on the flight, which had been obliterated when the approach roads to the Runcorn and Widnes Bridge were built. Questions were asked of Hatton Borough Council about protecting the remainder of the flight for possible restoration. The same question was asked when an article appeared giving details of the remains of three derelict, and partially infilled, branches of the Ashton Canal. These were the Hollinwood and Fairbottom Branches and the Stockport Branch.

Major water shortages beset the canal system during the summer of 1989, with major restrictions and overnight lock closures. Worries about future water supplies did not deter the local authority planners at Sowerby Bridge from proposing the construction of a new deep lock at Tuel Lane, together with a tunnel under a road junction, to offer the long-awaited reconnection of the Rochdale Canal to the Calder and Hebble Navigation.

Central Government always seemed to work at a slow pace. The Environment Committee's fifth report on British Waterways was published on 9 August 1989. This indicated it was regrettable that BW could not absorb the navigation functions of the National Rivers Authority at that point in time, but recommended that the position should be reviewed again by the DoE in three years, with the view then of creating a single navigation authority embracing all the navigations currently run by BW and the water authorities. On the issue of safety-related work, the committee identified an outstanding and critical maintenance backlog costed at £40 to £45 million, plus another £160 million of work BW itself had identified as needing to be done. The issue of appropriate levels of funding for the waterways remains a continuing stumbling block even to this day.

In Cardiff, an unusual restoration project was being developed by Cardiff City Council. This was the rebuilding of the waterwheel and pump at Melingriffith, which once supplied water to the now infilled Glamorganshire Canal. This project was part of a wider area development scheme. It was hoped that the wheels would turn again by the end of that year.

At this time, Hampshire Council were in the process of purchasing an additional derelict length of the Basingstoke Canal, between the western end of Greywell Tunnel and Up Nately. This was purely to protect the historic remains, as the council had no funds available to fund any further restoration. The Surrey and Hampshire Canals Society were themselves concentrating their efforts on the final derelict lock site at Woodham. They confirmed they were still on target to reopen their canal, through to the River Wey, by 1990.

In the West Midlands a Rally was held by the IWA at Pelsall, to promote interest in the long-forgotten Hatherton Branch of the Wyrley and Essington Canal, which was another under threat from motorway developments. This led to the formation of the Ogley and Hatherton Restoration Society, initially, which subsequently became the Lichfield and Hatherton Canals Restoration Trust.

In mid-October 1989, Peter White of BW put forward proposals to Oxford Council for the restoration of the former Hythe Bridge Terminus of the Oxford Canal, which he suggested could offer a new focus for regeneration. This project continued to resurface, from time to time, over the next decade, but with little action. At the same time an article appeared in *Waterways World* highlighting the potential of the former Wreak Navigation. It noted that "today, it has the dubious honour of being one of the very few navigations without a society attempting to restore it". This stimulated the local Melton and District Civic Society to start the preparation of a feasibility study for reopening the navigation. They indicated, as a first phase, that they planned to clear the river in the town and possibly start a trip-boat operation down to the first lock at Eye Kettleby Mill and, if sufficient local support was forthcoming, investigate the formation of a restoration society. This ultimately emerged as the Melton & Oakham Waterways Society in 1997.

One of the final barriers to reopening the Basingstoke Canal to visiting boats arose at the November 1989 Management Committee meeting. This was the issue of the number of allowable boat movements and numbers of craft authorised to be on the canal. This concern arose as most of the canal was formally designated an SSSI (Site of Special Scientific Interest). The Canal Management Committee took the view that there should be at least 50 additional annual licences and an extra 200 short-term licences to cope with the potential demand, allowing a maximum of 80 short-term licences in any one month. Negotiations opened with the Nature Conservancy Council to that end.

In South Wales, further progress was being made on the Neath and Tennant Canals, where the local council let a contract for rebuilding four locks on the Neath Canal. Meanwhile the local society refurbished the Rheola aqueduct to lengthen the cruising opportunities for their trip boat.

By mid-1990, two of the longest-running restoration projects, the K&A and Basingstoke, were reaching their final goals. The K&A was to be completed by July 1990 and HM Queen Elizabeth II had agreed to reopen it in August 1990. Final arrangements also had been made on the Basingstoke, to overcome the outstanding works at Sheerwater. It was hoped the formal reopening could take place in late May or early June 1991. Clearly these were true landmarks for restorers and the reopening of the K&A by the Queen was the crowning of a long-sought-after dream. This was one of the initial restoration projects identified by the IWA in 1946.

There was no such longer-term dream of reopening the remainder of the Somerset Coal Canal, but the Avon Industrial Buildings Trust identified some of the structures as worthy of preservation. These included the Combe Hay Locks and the Midford Aqueduct, which they hoped to open for public inspection. In a similar way the Grand Western Trust had agreed at its first public meeting, in September 1998, to protect and preserve the Halburton section of the canal for education and leisure use. They persuaded Devon County Council to undertake the necessary repair and maintenance work.

The IWA had itself created a formal Restoration Committee in 1988. One of its first tasks was to produce an analysis of the current restoration schemes likely to benefit most from its backing. The list included :

Chesterfield Canal
Cromford Canal
Droitwich Barge Canal
Montgomery Canal
Neath and Tennant Canal
Sleaford Navigation
Thames and Severn Canal
Wendover Arm
Wey and Arun Canal
Wilts and Berks Canal

These were all the mainstream projects where tangible progress was being made by mid-1990, but were clearly in need of extra resources. It is interesting to see that the Huddersfield, Rochdale, K&A and Basingstoke were omitted; presumably because they had already secured viable funding streams and had local authority support.

Some smaller societies, where local activists were trying to make progress, were disappointed they were not included on the list. The Grantham Canal Society fell into this category. They remarked that, in common with many restoration societies on BW waterways, the Grantham had been frustrated in that during the last fifteen years they had not been allowed to mount voluntary working parties. Fortunately, that matter seemed to have been resolved, subject to final agreement with the Unions.

On the Huddersfield Canal, where society confidence was growing, a revised Management Structure was brought into play by setting up a Finance and Fund Raising group, a Promotions and Membership group and a Construction group. The society hoped this would assist them in their partner status, and consolidate their campaign to get the canal fully opened. Likewise, the less mainstream but equally important Pocklington Canal Amenity Society (formed in 1968) celebrated its 21st birthday by launching an appeal to raise the £50,000 needed to restore Walbut Lock and aimed to increase its membership to over 600.

As one group went forward, so another fell on hard times. This was exemplified by the demise of the Cromford Canal Society that went into voluntary liquidation in 1990. This fall arose mainly from an internal "power struggle" that had led to the dismissal of the canal manager, Simon Stoker, who was subsequently awarded damages by an industrial tribunal. Derbyshire County Council, who leased the canal to the Society, regained ownership and their rangers, from the adjacent High Peak Trail, were used for day-to-day management.

At this time, there was a whole series of "openings" taking place. These included Tapton Lock on the Chesterfield Canal on 29 April 1990. The new link tunnel under Dudley Hill, from Castle Mill basin to the Singing Cavern, was opened on 25 April. The eleven-mile section of the Forth and Clyde Canal, including Noilly Bridge, opened on 14 May 1990, and the launch of the trip boat *Thomas Dadford* on the Neath Canal took place on 12 July 1990. The crowning achievement was the "official" reopening of the Kennet and Avon Canal by Her Majesty The Queen at Devizes on 8 August 1990. This came just after the Derwent Trust had heard it had won its appeal, and that the application of the Rights of Way Act 1932 did apply to waterways. This long round of celebrations continued when it was heard that the Cotswold Canal Trust had received £30,000 from Ray Scott Finance Group plc for restoration works, and that the work was nearing completion on a £400,000 contract, let by Devon County Council, to repair the dry section of the Grand Western Canal. The Barnsley Canal Group also gained financial support from the Urban Programme Fund to restore the canal basin at Elsecar, and for an Engineering Survey of the remaining two miles of that branch.

The period ended with the news that the Nature Conservancy Council had postponed its designation of 25 miles of the Basingstoke Canal as an SSSI, in an effort to allow the Canal Manager to seek resolution of debate over restrictions on boat movements. This gave the Surrey and Hampshire Canal Society and the two County Council owners sufficient confidence to confirm that HRH Duke of Kent would reopen the canal on 10 May 1991. It was agreed the Canal Authority would commission research into the actual effects of increasing boat movements to the levels agreed by the Management Committee.

The period 1986 to 1990 saw the following schemes emerge:

1.	Coalport Canal
2.	Higher Thames
3.	Monkland Canal
4.	Kidwelly Canal
5.	Bude Canal
6.	Ipswich and Stowmarket Navigation
7.	Manchester and Salford Junction Canal.

What is perhaps the most remarkable thing about this period is that at a time of national financial stringency, the restoration movement had continued to grow in strength. Public money, in the form of job creation schemes and urban renewal grants, provided the means for much physical progress to be made. Full-time teams of supervised trainees, combined with local government finance for materials, enabled the major schemes to make considerable advances. The Queen's presence, showing the public's support, in reopening the K&A, gave other restorers that added stimulus to strive to complete their own local schemes.

X 1991–1996:

"A PERIOD OF POLITICAL CHANGE"

The year 1991 started with the political and economic climates hardly at their best. Following the Anti-Community Charge riots in London in 1990, Margaret Thatcher resigned as leader of the Conservative Party. John Major won the leadership contest and took over as Prime Minister. He had a lot to do to rebuild the confidence of his party and to bring about general stability. Yet it was interesting that when the Boat Show was held in London in January 1991, the attendance figures were up 12 per cent. Some pundits put this down to advertising the Inland Waterways display as the central attraction, and also to the growing awareness of the value of canals as "engines for regeneration".

This theme of regeneration was brought out in an Ecotec Report on the costs of completing the Rochdale Canal restoration, which it estimated at £15.9 million. This study also indicated that for a cost of £17.3m, the total benefits to be gained could be £30m. This offered a positive net value of £12.7m, as well as creating 1,028 jobs, either directly or indirectly. It was unfortunate that as this report was circulated, BW sent out another batch of redundancy notices to some of its staff, due to its own strained financial situation.

Volunteers, however, were available and committed to move other schemes forward. The Lapal Tunnel Trust was formed at this time to restore the remainder of the Dudley No.2 Line, from Hawne Basin to Selly Oak. Teams from the Lichfield and Hatherton Trust were working on two restoration sites, one at Meadow Lock, Cannock, and the other at Fossway Lane, near Lichfield. Both were visible and offered welcome publicity opportunities to attract new supporters.

In an effort to boost its flagging financial resources, BW linked with Sprint UK to create a cable network under towpaths around the UK. This project was a "win-win" scheme offering much-needed cash to BW, and ease of access to the cable contractors.

On the Huddersfield Narrow Canal, Anthony Burton inaugurated work on restoring Dungebooth Lock on 4 April 1991. It was announced to those present at the function that the Society's aim was to see through traffic on the canal by 4 April 2007. The Rochdale Canal Society also were looking forward to regenerating boat movement, and installed a slipway and winding hole above the Tuel Lane blockage, to facilitate access by trail boats.

The Basingstoke Canal was reopened by HRH The Duke of Kent on 10 May 1991. It was disappointing for locals that it had to close again three weeks later, due to lack of water, between Woking and the St John's Lock flight. This sharpened the resolve of the SCHS to press forward with their plans to install back-pumping facilities at key sites along the canal.

The Waterway Recovery Group celebrated its 21st Anniversary in 1991. It was also the year the 25th Anniversary Issue of *Navvies* was published. The volunteers celebrated both events in the only way possible, by holding a "Big Dig" on the Wilts and Berks Canal, near Wantage. Elsewhere canal restorers were preparing themselves for battles to avoid new road schemes from obstructing their canals. The Herefordshire and Gloucestershire Canal Society presented their evidence to the Inquiry into the proposed Hereford Bypass route. Their aim was to seek a navigable culvert to protect the canal line and facilitate future restoration.

In much the same vein, the Cotswold Canals Trust commissioned a study, by Sir William Halcrow and Partners, into the restoration of the eastern end of the Thames and Severn Canal. The Thames Region of the NRA provided 50 per cent of the £35,000 costs involved. Local authorities and several commercial organisations provided matched funding, with the IWA and the Canals Trust bridging the funding gap. The Trust were keen to have the study completed by the time they made their case to the Department of Transport for a navigable culvert under the proposed Latton Bypass.

When Tony Baldry MP, a waterways enthusiast, was given the job of Waterways Minister, he added new weight to resolving such problems, especially when he said in his first major public statement: "It is the restoration movement which gives me the greatest hope for the future. From the 1950s, when the prevailing vision was 'fill them in', we are now at a time when last year Her Majesty the Queen re-opened the Kennet and Avon Canal, and the Duke of Kent opened the Basingstoke Canal. These achievements are proof the waterways restoration movement is alive and well."

This spirit of moving forward was evident on the Bude Canal, which 100 years after it had closed was having new life put back into it. In February 1990, a group of enthusiasts formed the Bude Canal Society and in 1991 they were already planning WRG work camps to restore the lower section and locks. Prospects also looked rosier for the Cromford Canal, when, after a break of two years, following the demise of the Cromford Canal Society, the Middleton Top Engine Group held work parties to clean

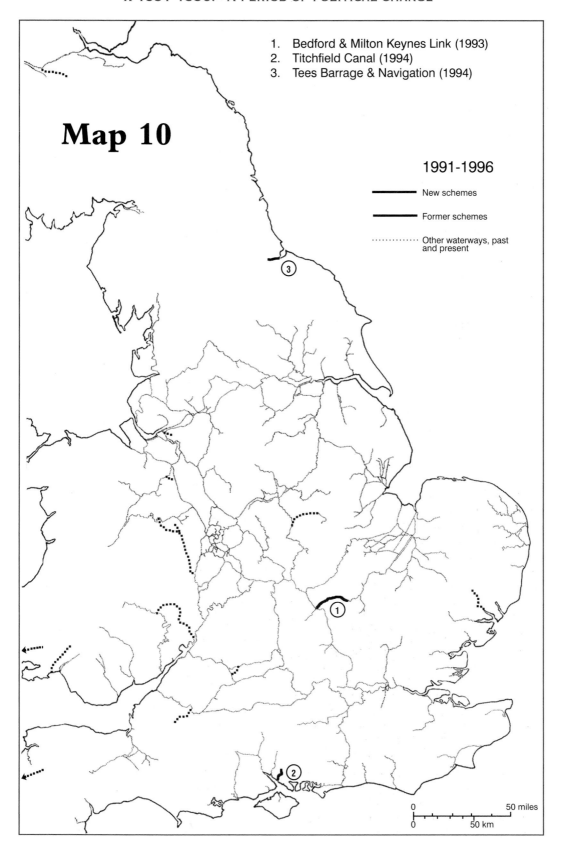

1. Bedford & Milton Keynes Link (1993)
2. Titchfield Canal (1994)
3. Tees Barrage & Navigation (1994)

Map 10

1991-1996

New schemes

Former schemes

Other waterways, past and present

0   50 miles

0   50 km

up the Leawood Pump and get it back into steam. This attracted visitors back to the dormant canal.

A new "boaters" group, the National Association of Boat Owners (NABO), was formed at the IWA National Festival in Dudley in August 1991. They specifically had the interests of narrow boat owners as their central focus, but provided another useful waterways lobbying group. Lobbying paid dividends for the River Stour Trust when they approached RTZ Corporation for help with funding the £30,000 repair of Flatford Lock. RTZ agreed to find the capital costs involved, provided the Stour Trust guaranteed to undertake future regular maintenance work. In much the same way, the Sankey Canal Restoration Society lobbied St Helens Council to include the restoration of the New Double Locks at Pocket Nook within a wider project to regenerate the centre of St Helens using funds from a Derelict Land Grant.

The Wendover Arm Trust sought, and gained, a UK 2000 grant for £2,000 to fund a feasibility study to evaluate the costs and problems of reopening Little Tring Bridge, which had been lowered in 1970. The study was also expected to cover the reinstatement of the canal, through to the new A41, Aston Clinton bypass route, where a new navigable culvert was to be constructed.

It was always felt by those involved that Restoration Society leaders ought to meet more regularly to explore issues of common concern. With this in mind, the Northern Canals Association was formed in early 1991, with two main functions:

1. A regular forum for the discussion of mutual problems
2. A means of getting to know those involved in other restoration schemes

At the inaugural meeting of the Northern Canals Association, Robin Higgs, chairman of the similarly constituted Southern Canals Association, explained how that organisation operated for the 25 societies actively involved. At the end of the meeting the following societies signed up as founder members of the Northern Canals Association: Huddersfield Canal Society; Pocklington Canal Amenity Society; Manchester, Bolton and Bury Canal Society, Rochdale Canal Society; Chesterfield Canal Society; Lancaster Canal Society; Sankey Canal Society; Barnsley Canal Society; IWPS Driffield Navigation Ltd; Ribble Link Trust; together with WRG [NW] and the IWA.

The year 1991 ended with Halton Borough Council engaging consultants to consider the future of the derelict and infilled Old Runcorn Locks. The Consultants were asked to review the potential of the flight as an environmental feature. The local council spokesperson indicated the council had had their attention drawn to the historic nature of the locks by an article by L.J. Boughey that had been published in *Waterways World* in 1986. Now the locks had been found the council were anxious not to "lose" them again.

The Chesterfield Canal, Western Section, was a centre of activity in 1991. Work on the section between Lock 1 and the Town Centre was being financed under a Derelict Land Grant. Lock 5, at Hollingwood, was under restoration by WRG. And at Rennishaw, a local Action Group were working on the canal through their village.

In January 1992 an editorial in *Waterways World* commented "there has never been so much legislation in the pipeline since the passing of the Transport Act in 1968. This will make 1992 a year when much campaigning has to be done." Apart from a BW General Powers Bill, a Transport and Works Bill had been promoted, and BW had asked the Government to have waterways added to it. There was also a proposal for an Environment Agency to be created, and rumours about changes to the status of IWAAC. Finally there was the DoE Review of the Navigation Authorities (NRA and BW) that had been promised, in 1989, by the Select Committee Report.

Vigilance was necessary at the local level as well. The Sankey Navigation Society had their attention drawn to an Auction Sale being mounted by BW, which included four lots of land that were infilled lengths of the St Helens Canal. The society were aware Warrington Council wished to take over the canal route and use a Derelict Land Grant to finance converting it to a cycleway, with longer-term provision for restoring the canal, and found it strange the lots were going up for auction. The society persuaded BW to withdraw the lots from the auction by getting the Shadow Environment Minister to raise questions with the DoE about the transaction.

In early 1992 it was heard that the rules relating to Derelict Land Grants were likely to be changed. A new Guidance Note, due to be issued, indicated that 100 per cent grants may be made available to restore derelict canals to navigable standards, instead of purely as an amenity as under the existing rules. DoE officials indicated to Rochdale Metropolitan Borough Council that grants of between £1.5m and £3m could be made available for their canal restoration projects, if the Council accorded them top priority.

Three new road schemes loomed at this time to cause canal restorers concern. One was the Latton Bypass, where the Department of Transport indicated it did not wish to provide a navigable culvert for the Thames and Severn Canal. The second was on the Ripon Bypass, where a public enquiry was set for 11 February 1992. The third was a proposed route for a new Preston Bypass, which would not offer navigable headroom over Savick Brook, the preferred route for the proposed Ribble Link. In all cases the local restoration groups drew up their battle plans. It seemed to all concerned, that one Government department was actively funding restoration as both a job creation as well as a local regeneration exercise, yet another was seeking to obstruct the selfsame projects.

One of the frustrations WRG volunteers often found was that when they turned up to works sites, there were neither materials nor relevant planning permissions to allow them to undertake the work. They considered these were matters that the Canal Society, on whose project they were hoping to work, should have resolved. This deficiency both wasted the volunteers' time and also did not help the societies to maintain the commitment of active volunteers. Waterway Recovery Group members developed the concept of "a guaranteed labour force for guaranteed work". The proposal was put to the Southern Canals Association by the three southern WRG groups and was accepted. This involved the societies having the funding etc. in place for a series of guaranteed work parties. This was to prove to be of benefit to all concerned. The first group of three projects were named as Thames and Severn Canal, Neath and Tennant Canal, and Wey and Arun Canal.

An unusual new navigation improvement scheme was proposed in 1992. This was the Tees Barrage, which would both have a lock alongside, and provide a canoe "white water" course in the weir stream. The aim was to open for navigation eleven miles of stabilised river, with water retained at high-tide level.

Further south, on the Pocklington Canal, restorers were finally given the go-ahead by English Nature to restore Walbut Lock, after months of negotiations. But English Nature remained unwilling to authorise navigation on the upper reaches that were still to be restored.

At a time when water shortages on the K&A and Basingstoke Canals were causing concern, the NRA produced a document, "Water Resources Development Strategy", which reviewed the options through to 2021. This sought ways of overcoming predicted shortfalls in public water supplies. The NRA set out to review possible solutions through a two-year research programme.

At Ripon, the by pass enquiry secretariat was advised of plans for the new bypass to be routed along an embankment, which would resolve the headroom problems for the canal. This was good news for the local restoration group. Less good news was announced, that Warrington Council had been forced to put on hold their plans for the St Helens Canal, due to an embargo on further Derelict Land Grants being made until after the forthcoming General Election. This, however, did not stop the Driffield Navigation Commissioners from restoring and re-gating the top lock on their navigation. Neither did it stop the Chelmsford Branch of the IWA from completing their work on clearing Springfield Basin and restoring the Basin entrance lock on the Chelmer and Blackwater Navigation.

Elsewhere in the press, a report on the Ulverston Canal, owned by Glaxo, noted that there was little doubt that the canal itself could be preserved, at least "in its present state, so long as Glaxochem themselves remain in the town, but it will be interesting to see whether the leisure industry can, as it has with so many others, restore its activity". Another article, in *Waterways World*, reported on the poor state of the River Rother navigation. It commented: "The Wey and Arun Canal has its own restoration society, why not the Rother? I am sure that at least moral support would be given by the landowners to such a proposal". However, the recession was still prevalent and that also was causing boat-builders to turn to building craft for the budget market. As such, it seemed unlikely any new restoration schemes would emerge for the time being.

The General Election took place in April 1992. John Major gained a further term of office, with a majority of 114. Some hoped this working majority might herald better times ahead. Such planning for the future was the aim of a working party, known as Somerset Navigations Officers Group. This was formed from representatives of the local authorities, NRA and BW, to consider the possibilities of reopening some of the "lost" waterways in the Somerset Levels to navigation. It also had a remit to review the options for a proposed River Parrett Barrage. Consultants were commissioned to undertake this work for the group.

With the election over, the Derelict Land Grants were back on the scene. However, the complicated application process meant that only two new grants were quickly approved. These were for the Rochdale Canal and the St Helens Canal, where both local councils were keen to proceed and had prioritised their application. Other schemes on the Rochdale and Huddersfield Narrow Canal were waiting in the wings.

The restorers of the Grantham Canal heard their good news with receipt of permission to remove a derelict railway embankment that blocked the canal in the Woolsthorpe locks. WRG work camps were promptly scheduled to undertake this task. Likewise, the Cotswold Canals Trust received a helpful report from Sir William Halcrow and Partners, on the restoration of the eastern end of their canal, through the Cotswold Water Park. The report concluded that there was no engineering reason why a navigable culvert could not be installed under the proposed Latton Bypass, and that the water supplies should not present any problems for the canal restorers.

This news was welcomed by the Trust's spokesman, Commander Nick Wright, who had recently joined the Cotswold Trust from the Kennet and Avon Canal Trust.

About this time various other changes were taking place. The Herefordshire and Gloucestershire Canal Society became a trust, and commenced a trip-boat operation on their first restored length of canal. Meanwhile, a Somerset Coal Canal Society was formed to focus interest on their canal. David Suchet, a well-known actor and boating enthusiast, drew the crowds for the reopening of Gallowstree Bridge on the Montgomery Canal on 7 June 1992. But, perhaps more significantly, restoration works had started on the Dudley Tunnel, which had closed in 1983 on safety grounds. The remedial works, which were likely to cost £1.8m, were being funded by a European Regional Development Fund grant, together with financial support from Dudley Metropolitan Borough Council and BW.

The issue of water shortages rose again during 1992, and gave BW the chance to put forward proposals for a National Water Transfer Network. This envisaged taking water from the North-West and Wales, and using the canals to deliver it to the Great Ouse and the Thames. For water transfer on a smaller scale, the Kennet and Avon Canal Trust recruited Terry Kemp, on secondment from BW, to mastermind plans to install back pumps, so that water could be lifted back along the canal to the summit level at Wooton Rivers. This three-year scheme, it was hoped, would resolve the water supply problems being experienced by the recently reopened waterway.

The Government announced its proposals for the creation of a new Environment Agency in July 1992. These proposed that the new agency would take over all the functions of the NRA together with HM Inspectorate of Pollution. It was planned it would come into being on 1 April 1995. It was also announced that 1993 would be designated "Industrial Heritage Year". BW indicated it would run a major publicity campaign, entitled "Canals 200", and stage 200 events around the country to attract more tourists.

At about this time, local enthusiasts got together to form the Buckingham Canal Society. They were concerned their canal might be truncated by a new local road plan. They considered that the time was right to foster local interest in preserving the remaining sections of the Buckingham Arm, as well as fighting the road scheme.

During 1992, the government came forward with a proposal, in a consultation paper, to create an Urban Navigation Agency, which would incorporate the Derelict Land Grants, City Grants and the system of regeneration grants administered by English Estates into a unified grants scheme. This caused restorers some concerns, especially those in the Huddersfield Canal Society, who had identified that the key to their canal's early restoration progress would be through such grants. Any new unified scheme would be likely to introduce delays.

Self-help was the route used by many canal restorers. Thus Swansea Canal Society member John Davis constructed a 23ft boat, based on drawings of the craft that originally used their canal. This offered to double up as both work boat and trip boat for the Society to clear the canal and also raise funds for their ongoing work. On the other hand Granada Studios, who owned the site of Lock 1 of the Manchester and Salford Junction Canal, had the lock re-excavated, at their expense, as a heritage feature.

The October 1992 edition of *Waterways World* had an article by John Liley about a boyhood "Rudyard Expedition". The map that was printed with the article identified a short overland route from the Caldon Canal feeder channel, via Rudyard Lake, to the Macclesfield Canal feeder that entered at the top of Bosley Locks. Whilst he used a portable dinghy for his trip, this gave others the idea of a possible longer-term new cruising ring by making the route he took completely navigable.

All too often, restorers were re-inventing the wheel because they did not have ready access to facts. The IWA Restoration Committee recognised that it would be valuable if they produced some Fact Sheets on relevant topics. In the summer of 1992 they published:

1. Derelict Land Grants and canal restoration
2. Powers of the Highways Authority to construct bridges and culverts
3. Managing consultancies on waterway restoration projects

The aim was to ease the task of individual restoration societies keeping up to date with the latest systems and practices. The IWA also produced a *Waterways Restoration Guide* listing details of all recorded societies and their restoration schemes.

A feasibility study for reconstructing the infilled length of the Ashby Canal was produced in the summer of 1992. The consultants, W.S. Atkins, identified there were no insuperable direct engineering obstacles to the reconstruction of the waterway through to Measham and Moira. It also recommended, for ecological reasons, that a broad canal construction was more appropriate, even through its likely cost was 7 per cent more.

The Sleaford Canal Society continued to make progress in 1992, and had nearly restored Cobblers Lock. The society was also exploring longer-term water supply issues. Their research brought to light the need for some £250,000 worth of flood protection work and embankment strengthening, to be undertaken on a section to Haverholm Lock. This required a further round of major fund-raising. Whilst the Sleaford Canal Society kept its team united, it was unfortunate that when some disaffected members of the nearby Grantham Canal Restoration Society felt out of sympathy with the direction the society was following, they decided to split away to form an independent Grantham Navigation Association This Association indicated it was unhappy with the rate of progress in restoring the canal, and published its own strategy, "Reopening the Grantham Canal", which identified business sponsors as the key drivers. The members indicated they did not plan to do the physical restoration work themselves.

In September 1992, in Germany, the grand opening of a completely new, wide, commercial waterway, linking the rivers Rhine, Main and Danube, took place. The project was financed on the basis of electricity sales from a series of hydro-electric generation plants constructed on the upper Danube. The whole scheme was a masterpiece of modern engineering. On a, far, far, smaller scale, was the plan for a new deep lock at Tuel Lane, on the Rochdale Canal, and a linked, curved, 100yd tunnel from the lock to the Calder and Hebble Canal. This project was to be financed from a £2.5m Derelict Land Grant. The project was due to start in the autumn of 1993, for completion in spring of 1995. What annoyed the enthusiasts initially was a penny-pinching proposal to only build the lock 57ft 6ins long, rather than 72ft long to take the standard 70ft narrow boats. In the end, careful design work by local council planners enabled the longer length to be engineered into the scheme.

The Pocklington Canal Amenity Society had to face up to another problem in September 1992 when Gardham Lock gates failed and the lock was closed. As the canal was a "remainder" waterway, BW felt unable to pay for the replacement of the gates. The society had to seek another solution. In the end, PCAS paid the £15,000 bill and, by prior agreement, gained reimbursement from East Yorkshire Borough Council. As the gates were a direct replacement, and not regarded as new work, English Heritage had no problems in approving the project to get the lock operational again.

The year 1992 ended with three pieces of good news. A developer of an estate adjoining the Chesterfield Canal had his planning permission refused, as the development would block access to restoring the canal. Further along the Chesterfield Canal line, a private owner got a Derelict Land Grant to restore a 500m section of the canal, between Killamarsh and Renshaw. The second came on 8 October, at a public meeting called by the Trent and Mersey Canal Society, when 300 local people confirm

their continued commitment to the full restoration of the Anderton Boat Lift. Approval of the restoration was now down to English Heritage approval and the availability of funds. The third, as part of the "Dig Deep" exercise, was when 250 navvies descended on the Wey and Arun Canal, at Billingshurst, to clear a section of the canal and rebuild three accommodation bridges.

The year 1993 started well for the Bude Canal Society, in that their discussions with Devon County Council and others seemed to support the formation of a Bude Canal Trust to manage the five-mile section of canal known locally as the "Bude Aqueduct". The society were also working with WRG on clearing the Merrifield and Hobbcott Inclines. In Nottinghamshire, the Groundwork Trust had applied for a Derelict Land Grant to fund an engineering survey to review the possibility of restoring the infilled section of the Cromford Canal between Ironville and Langley Mill. In Sussex, a report on the Portsmouth and Arundel Navigation envisaged no insurmountable problems to restoring the Chichester Canal, but it indicated that the long-abandoned section between Ford to Hunston had two major obstacles: a housing estate at Yapton and a railway line crossing the canal line on the level nearer the River Arun. No economically viable alternatives were readily available to solve these major obstructions.

The Lapal Canal Trust produced a Strategy Statement for the restoration of their Canal. This envisaged a two-stage process. The first was restoration from Hawne Basin to the northern mouth of Lapal Tunnel. This they hoped to complete by the bicentenary of the canal in 1998. The second stage, restoring the Lapal Tunnel itself, had no target date set. Not only were there technical difficulties to overcome, but it seemed likely the actual costs involved would be high.

In much the same way, the Lichfield and Hatherton Canals Trust published their own detailed proposals for restoring the Ogley Locks Branch, which for clarity, they called "The Lichfield Canal". They also set up a "Friends" organisation to develop their fund-raising profile and provide social activities for members.

In May 1993 proposals for a "Preston Land-bridge" were unveiled. This was a scheme whereby boats could be lifted out of the water at Preston Docks and conveyed by land to be relaunched in the Lancaster Canal. The organisers hoped this would stimulate greater interest in the longer term aim of creating a physical "Ribble Link" to offer all craft direct access to the Lancaster Canal from the main waterways network.

A major appeal for money was launched in the spring of 1992 to fund the restoration of the Aston Locks on the Montgomery Canal. Included in the fund-raising prospectus was raising money to provide the Linear

Nature Reserve Project, which was fundamental to allowing the locks to be reopened. This project offered a clear marker of one way in which potential conflicts with conservation interests might be overcome elsewhere. This happened at a time when English Nature designated 24 miles out of the 32-mile total of the Basingstoke Canal as an SSSI. In doing so, they suggested a proposed requirement that motorised boat traffic should not exceed 1,000 movements a year, and restricted weed cutting to a 19.5 ft wide central channel in the canal. These proposals were submitted for discussion, but with final agreement required by the autumn. To validate traffic flows along the Basingstoke Canal, an electronic counter was installed on the canal jointly by Hampshire County Council & English Nature.

The Wey and Arun Canal Trust received some good news when Sir William Halcrow and Partners presented their feasibility study on reopening the canal. This report concluded there were no obstacles that could not be overcome by modern engineering expertise, and that although the cost of the restoration was estimated at £12m, about 50 per cent of the work could be done by volunteers, thus making it more affordable.

Another feasibility study, funded by the Civic Trust, reviewed the prospect of restoring the Spike Island to Fiddlers Ferry section of the Sankey Canal The study offered a significant step forward, in that it recommended works involving removal of four fixed bridges and the need for dredging. Although this would cost in the region of £2.3m, much of this could be derived from available local grants.

The availability of grants was the way in which the Whitchurch Waterways Trust were able to reopen the first phase of the Whitchurch Arm on 10 October 1993. The trust then turned their attention to further fund-raising to facilitate the land purchase necessary to complete the second phase of their project, getting boats back to Whitchurch Town Centre.

Consultants called in to review the prospects for restoring the Union Canal, in Scotland, identified that the two biggest stumbling blocks were making the link to the Forth and Clyde Canal at Falkirk and reopening the infilled section at Wester Hailes. These could be overcome, but were likely to be very expensive engineering projects. This led BW to confirm that they, together with the riparian local authorities, were determined to see the reopening of the inland water route between Edinburgh and Glasgow and to state, optimistically, that the restoration would be completed in the first decade of the next century.

The newly created Urban Regeneration Agency took over responsibility for the administration of Derelict Land Grants in January 1994. This gave the Huddersfield Narrow Canal Joint Committee an opportunity to submit a report setting out their proposals for the entire restoration scheme. It was fully costed, and indicated they were looking for a rolling programme of grants, totalling £23m over the next nine years. Their report estimated that when completed, the canal would create 230 full-time jobs in tourism and increased spending amounting to £4.5m per year.

Bridgwater & Taunton, Bridgwater Basin, official reopening

Whilst there were high hopes for the Huddersfield Canal, prospects for Somerset Waterways development plans took a step back. The consultants investigating the proposed River Parrett Barrage indicated the Barrage would cost £11.3m. In addition, to open up the 100 miles of waterways, four new locks and several bridges would need to be reconstructed. The consultants concluded that the costs were too high to offer a reasonable return on such investment. Somerset Council accepted the report's finding and asked the Officers' Working Group to explore the opportunities for smaller-scale boating improvements and to consider other "generic" tourist activities. In the interim, all looked forward to the full reopening of the Bridgwater and Taunton Canal in June 1994.

Basingstoke and Deane Council agreed to invest £30,000 in an engineering study, to explore the feasibility of restoring the Basingstoke Canal back to the town centre. Here again, whilst it would be quite simple to restore the section from the town centre to Old Basing, the major obstacle was the M3 and the loss of the canal route either side of it. It thus seemed more practical and simple to restore part of the old towpath line, an approach which was supported by Basingstoke Heritage Trust. In the meantime, the SCHS continued their clearance work at Up Nateley, whilst on the main canal section the Joint Management Committee were able to reach a deal with English Nature to allow 1,300 boat movements a year along the whole canal. This gave the Basingstoke Canal Authority the opportunity to start on their seven-year programme to replace all 28 lock gates on the Deepcut Flight. Unfortunately, the timber used in these gates when they were restored had not been proved to stand the test of time, perhaps because they were out of water and dry for much of the restoration period.

Two significant Derelict Land Grants were received separately by the Sleaford Navigation and Grantham Canal Society. One was for a feasibility study of the Upper Reaches through to Sleaford Navigation Head, whilst on the Grantham Canal a £400,000 grant was agreed for restoring a 2.5-mile section of canal east of Hickling Basin.

Detailed plans, including costs, were developed at much the same period for the Derby Canal. These identified a cost of £17.3m for restoring the whole 14-mile route from the Erewash Canal through to the Trent and Mersey Canal. A Derby and Sandiacre Canal Company was formed to take this project forward, with a Derby and Sandiacre Canal Society being formed alongside it to engage volunteer inputs into the restoration scheme.

During 1994, tangible progress was also being made on various other restoration projects. On the

Monmouthshire Canal the replacement of a low-level culvert at Crowne Bridge, Sebastopol, was underway which would reopen the canal to enable boats to reach the top of the locks at Cwmbran. Construction had started on the Ripon Bypass, with the building of a new bridge over the canal to allow through navigation. On the Wey and Arun, Old Toat Bridge was restored in April 1994. The reopening of the whole Bridgwater and Taunton Canal was planned for June 1994.

An interesting development was taking place in 1994 on the previously restored Southern Stratford Canal at Lapworth, where there had been a water supply problem. To resolve unnecessary water loss, following the takeover of the canal by BW it was decided to put back the former link, below locks 20 and 21, to offer an "on the level" access between the GU and Southern Stratford Canals. It was hoped to complete the works by March 1995, in time for the cruising season. On the Basingstoke Canal itself, after various controversial designs were put forward and discarded, a simple aqueduct was proposed to take the canal over the Blackwater Valley Road at the Ash embankment. Work on this project was scheduled to start in September 1994 with a completion date of June 1995.

A feasibility study on the Droitwich Canals was revealed to a packed meeting in Worcester Town Hall in May 1994. It identified two major potential problems to restoration. The first was the A449 crossing, where NRA would not agree to the use of the adjacent alternative river route, and the second concerned the availability of water supplies, that might be needed to operate the canal, being drawn from the Worcester and Birmingham Canal. The local authorities indicated they were committed to the principle of the restoration scheme, but that the ability to raise the finance necessary was their primary concern. The Droitwich Canals Trust equally did not have the manpower or resources available to it to press ahead as quickly as some would have liked.

The Herefordshire and Gloucestershire Canal Society had the issue of availability of finance on their mind as well. Thus their key aim for 1994 was to get their finances onto a longer-term footing so as to be able to pay for a professional cost–benefit analysis and engineering study of their canal. They also knew they had to protect the canal line within the various local structure plans. In the meanwhile their volunteers were busy working at Cold Harbour Bridge and on the approach to Oxenhall Tunnel.

The little-known Titchfield Canal made the headlines in 1994, with the restoration of the sea lock which gave access to the two-mile canal. These restoration works were paid for by Hampshire County Council and Fareham Borough Council, with assistance from

English Nature. The sea lock, at Meon Marsh, was uncovered unexpectedly by county surveyors in 1988, whilst they were investigating an old bridge that they considered required remedial work. The Titchfield Historical Society provided the surveyors with details of the origin of the structure and, in view of its historic significance, arranged for it to be listed in February 1993. Subsequently, English Nature declared the canal, north of the lock, an SSSI. Although the land by the lock was in private ownership, the landowner was supportive of its restoration and thus the County Council organised the remedial work to be undertaken.

Remedial work on the Anderton Boat Lift finally got underway in October 1994. English Heritage offered a grant of £500,000, but this was less than the amount required for the complete restoration of the Lift back to its original form. The Anderton Lift Trust was left to raise the balance of over £500,000 that was needed to fully restore both caissons to their original operational standard.

Much the same outcome, of a need to contribute, was recorded in the Inspector's Report on the Latton Bypass Inquiry. Whilst agreeing a navigable culvert should be built at the same time as the road, he did not feel able to recommend how it should be funded. However, in publishing the report the Secretary of State decreed that the culvert could only be built if the Cotswold Canals Trust acquired the land necessary and also provided the necessary finance. The Trust was given two years to do so.

BW was planning ahead positively, when they announced their plans for a Millennium Link in Scotland, and indicated they planned to submit a bid to the new Millennium Commission for funds to fully restore both the Forth and Clyde and Union Canals. They were able to quote the benefits gained by the local community from reopening sections of the Huddersfield Narrow Canal. They noted that the public investment involved had brought in £51.8m of private funding, with 739 full-time equivalent jobs created at a public sector cost of £9,776 per job. They indicated this offered overall a leverage of 1:7 (for every £1 of public money, some £7 of private capital was invested in the area). This was in addition to the significant environmental and community benefits that had also evolved.

Although the Kennet and Avon Canal had been reopened in by the Queen in 1990, much remedial work still needed to be completed. A canal partnership comprising the Kennet & Avon Canal Trust, BW and the local authorities agreed to get together to make a National Lottery Heritage Memorial Fund bid to pay for the necessary structural improvements required to make the waterway more user-friendly. These works were finally completed in 1997.

A new style of waterway campaign was launched, in early 1995, by Brian Young of the IWA Cambridge Branch. His project later became known as the Bedford and Milton Keynes Link. He considered that the local plans to develop a Community Forest, at Marston Vale, sponsored by English Heritage, offered a new window of opportunity to launch a scheme to create a new waterway link. He suggested a new Bedford–Grand Union Navigation Trust should be formed to put together a bid, to the Millennium Commission, for the costs of a feasibility study to validate his plans to link the Grand Union Canal to the Great Ouse. At the same time he arranged for invitations to be sent out to all those who might wish to join the embryo trust.

The BW General Powers Bill received its Royal Assent on 16 January 1995, after a very rough passage through Parliament. It provided hope for restoration schemes in that it offered BW with greater flexibility to assist with such projects. Thus, when the first physical restoration work actually started on the Lichfield Canal, the Canals Trust hoped for a more positive attitude from BW; especially when they heard that the proposed M6 widening plans did not include a navigable culvert for the Hatherton Canal. The Trust had earlier submitted a series of papers to the public enquiry over the route of the Birmingham Northern Relief Road, making the case for the navigation channel to be protected. They now hoped BW would be more supportive in their next battle.

The serious winter floods on many northern rivers in early 1995, did not deter the Chesterfield Canal Society from submitting proposals to the NRA for an eight-mile section of the River Rother to be converted into a navigation channel, linking the Chesterfield Canal, at Killamarsh, to the Sheffield and South Yorkshire Navigation at Rotherham. At the same time, the Society saw a £4.5m restoration scheme launched on the Nottinghamshire length between Worksop and the county boundary at Ryton Aqueduct. This used the facility of a Derelict Land Grant, which was topped up by funds from British Coal. Over the county border, Rotherham Borough Council was planning to use similar funding to restore their section through to Norwood Tunnel mouth.

Progress was being made on the Huddersfield Narrow Canal. Staley Wharf was reopened on 23 April 1995, and a further grant of £2m was allocated to restore the Mossley to Stalybridge section. In South Wales, Crown Bridge, Sebastopol was opened on 15 April 1995, and when further dredging was completed, boats would again be able to reach the Cwmbran Locks from Brecon. On the Thames and Medway Canal, a half-million pound grant from English Partnerships had enabled the Society to completely clear a 5yd wide channel, from Gravesend to Shorne Mead, using Groundwork Kent, Thameside. The first 1.5 miles of the Montgomery Canal was also reopened, on 3 June 1995, and work started on the Phase Two Project, through to Queens Head.

The shortlist of recipients for Millennium Fund Grants was announced in June 1995. This included the Sankey Canal, Huddersfield Narrow, Wey and Arun, Rochdale Canal and the River Stour Trust. Rather surprisingly the Forth and Clyde and Union Canals bid from BW was unsuccessful. This was because it was felt the scheme had insufficient local public support.

The Environment Bill, setting up the new Environment Agency, that was destined to take over all the former NRA functions from April 1996, received Royal Assent on 20 July 1995. The Tees Tidal Barrage, and the new lock alongside, opened on 17 July 1995. On 27 July 1995 a new lock was opened at Brandon on the River Little Ouse, extending the navigation through to the Town Bridge in Brandon. The new aqueduct on the Basingstoke Canal, at the Ash Embankment, was officially opened on 29 July 1995. It had taken just nine months to build, at a cost of £1.27m. WRG celebrated its 25th anniversary with a major "Dig" at Latton, at the eastern end of the Thames and Severn Canal. This was held to bolster the case for the provision of a navigable culvert under the proposed new Latton Bypass.

In December 1995 the *Waterways World* editorial commented, "Perhaps everyone is getting a little blasé about the enormous amounts of money going into restoration schemes. Full credit should be given to the patient, behind the scenes negotiations between BW, local canal societies and relevant government departments." Whilst there seemingly was sufficient funding available, lack of water due to a very dry summer became critical for many canals towards the end of 1995. There were closures throughout the national network due to water supplies dwindling. The year ended with a welcome Christmas present for the River Stour Trust from the Millennium Commission. It confirmed approval of a £167,890 grant towards building the new Great Cornard Lock. In this scheme, the balance of funding was coming from local

Rochdale Canal, Tuel Lane, official reopening

councils and the trust's own Appeal fund. The Rochdale Canal Society also heard that, "in principle", they had gained £11.9m Millennium funding to complete their restoration plans, matched funding being required from Derelict Land Grants and the ERDF funds.

The New Year, 1996, saw the release of an IWAAC report, *Britain's Inland Waterways: An undervalued asset*. This was the first of a series of significant studies, produced by IWAAC, that considerably influenced government attitudes towards the waterways. Amongst other things, it highlighted the need for index-linked "grants in aid". It also indicated that there was considerable scope for the development of waterway-related businesses to enhance local investment along the canal sides.

Early in 1996, BW submitted a revised Millennium Link bid, to restore the Lowland Canals, to the Millennium Commission together with a 30,000 signature petition that was aimed at proving there was significant local support for the restoration scheme. They hoped this might allay the Commission's earlier concerns that the scheme was lacking local public support.

1996 was the year of the IWA's Silver Jubilee. Various plans were made to celebrate the event. Perhaps the most newsworthy of these was a plan for pieces of a "Jubilee Jigsaw" to be collected from around the country and put together at the World Canals Conference in Birmingham in June 1996, held in the new Birmingham International Conference Centre, in an area where a major canal-side regeneration project had been completed.

National concerns were expressed at this time that a proposed new Landfill Tax could be applied to dredging disposals. The IWA, RYA and BMF joined forces to lobby Government to ensure that dredgings were excluded from the scheme. At this time, another battle with the road builders emerged, regarding a proposal to put an embankment across the Derby Canal, where the planned Derby Bypass crossed the canal line at Swarkestone. Here again, the Department of Transport had suggested that the Canal Society should pay for the additional works necessary to provide a navigable culvert, the costs of which were disputed.

Early in 1996 plans were published for the creation of a new country park embracing part of the Louth Canal. This overall scheme was supported by the Louth Navigation Trust and the local Civic Trust, who were working together to promote the park project. At much the same time, they proposed a scheme to restore one of the Navigation Head warehouses in Louth.

During 1996, the Foxton Inclined Plane Trust were busy raising funds for the production of a Feasibility Study to consider the practicality of reconstructing the Plane. They publicised their appeal through a display in the Boiler House Museum they had created on the site.

On 11 April 1996 the first boat made its way through the brand new deep lock and adjacent tunnel at Tuel Lane on the Rochdale Canal. The official opening was held on 3 May. By then, work was underway on the new Chadderton M66 motorway interchange complex. The Rochdale Society hoped that their final agreement with the road builders, combined with the promised Millennium Commission funding, would soon ensure the western end of the Rochdale Canal, through to Manchester, could be reopened.

Ripon Canal reopening

In an effort to assist restoration groups to develop their plans in a more professional way, the IWA proposed the production of a "Restoration Handbook". The DoE saw considerable value in the project and offered a £15,000 grant to cover costs involved.

In a final bid to get Linton Lock fully restored, the Linton Lock Commissioners made an £800,000 funding submission to the National Heritage Memorial Fund. They believed that, if they were successful, the comprehensive repair works it would finance would resolve the longer-term problems of the erosion of the lock island and facilitate the transfer of the lock to BW.

In May 1996, the Stourbridge Navigation Trust publicised its proposals for the future enhancement of the Fens Branch and the associated Stourbridge Extension Canal. The proposal envisaged restoration of the currently un-navigable section of the canal, from Brockmoor Junction to the culverted Brockmoor Bridge, where a new winding hole was proposed.

After due consideration of the results of an earlier consultation exercise, the DoE Minister announced he had concluded that no major changes were required in the distribution of the navigation functions between BW and EA, but he suggested that closer working relationships should be developed, and also that BW should become a statutory planning consultee. This move was felt to be beneficial by the Higher Avon Navigation Trust when they proposed their new Leam Link Scheme. This envisaged using the River Leam as a route to link the Grand Union Canal at Leamington with the River Avon. In an effort to secure local support for their plans, a colour brochure outlining the scheme was widely distributed in the Warwick and Leamington area. The trust also commissioned an environmental impact study in respect of the project, in the hope that this would support any subsequent planning application.

In their efforts to keep their canal open the K&A Canal Trust raised funds for various back pumping stations at strategic locations along the canal. The critical back pumping facility at Devizes was inaugurated early in July 1996. At much the same time, water supply restrictions had closed the Camp Hill to Knowle section of the Grand Union Canal. Similar water shortages had also led to overnight restrictions on the Oxford Canal. Here again, improved back pumping options were being devised.

A basin and arm off the Rochdale Nine flight of locks, which was part of the old Manchester and Salford Junction Canal, was cleaned out, re-watered and reopened in late June 1996. This offered a wonderful backdrop to the new glass-fronted Bridgewater Hall, as well as a potential new mooring for passing craft.

Charles Hadfield, one of the founding members of the IWA, died on 6 August 1996. He was the last of the three key architects of the Association, the others being Rolt and Aickman. They, as individuals, might have passed away, but the association they founded was in very good heart and continuing to campaign under its new slogan, "Waterways for all". At its National AGM in 1996, Audrey Smith, its first woman National Chairman, made a stirring call for better funding for the waterways. She asked all IWA members to lobby their MPs to get "a proper level of grant provided". This call for better funding was reiterated when the IWA hosted a National Conference for Waterway Societies on 30 November 1996.

The period under review ended with a flurry of reopenings. The Ripon Canal Basin was reopened by David Currey, MP, on 8 September. The River Stour Trust reopened the repaired Flatford Lock and also the restored Granary Warehouse, at Sudbury Basin, as the Queens Theatre. A further section of the Montgomery Canal, between the Parry Aqueduct and Queens Head, was opened on 21 September 1996.

Towards the end of the year, the Kennet and Avon Canal Partnership heard that it had been granted £25m towards the £29m required to finish the remedial work on the canal. This offered the financial resources to allow them to plan a six-year programme of works needed to upgrade the canal to "cruising status". The Labour Party rounded of the year for waterway restorers with the production of its "Waterways Policy". It recorded that "waterways are a priceless part of our heritage". All who loved the waterways hoped that this was a good omen and that they would remember that statement if they were returned to office at the next General Election.

During the period 1991 to 1996, the following new waterway restoration and development schemes were promoted:

1. Bedford and Milton Keynes Link
2. Titchfield Canal
3. Tees Barrage

The IWA Annual Report for 1996, recorded that by then, some 37 sections of canal had been restored, covering 450 miles of waterway, and that another 138 restoration schemes were underway. This was a considerable achievement for an organisation formed to campaign for the conservation, use, maintenance, restoration and development of inland waterways just 50 years before.

XI 1997 TO 2001:
"MILLENNIUM FEVER"

The news of the substantial grants available through the Millennium Commission quickly became quickly known. Canal restorers took heart from the this marvellous opportunity, and they began to believe that some of those "impossible dreams" could become a reality. Likewise, the Labour Party took heart from the substantial gains they had made in the 1996 local elections. When John Major called an election on 1 May 1997, Tony Blair and his "New Labour" team also believed their time had come. They were proved correct. This was a period of review and change, which offered a positive lead up to the new millennium.

For many smaller restoration schemes, this time also offered them a chance to break new ground. Thus the local IWA Branch in Lincolnshire pressed East Lindsey District Council to fund a feasibility study to consider the opportunities for restoring the Horncastle Canal. At the same time, a consortium of six local authorities, plus BW, were putting together a funding bid to restore the Grantham Canal. The River Seven Navigation Restoration Trust also put forward their plan for the construction of a new single lock, to open up the navigation to above Bewdley. A new group of potential Sussex Ouse restorers were also doing battle with the EA, pressing them to check whether the 1814 Act had never been extinguished and that a right to navigate the river still existed. Not all developments were positive. On the Whitchurch Arm, the Trust sought to develop phase two of their project. But their bids to the Millennium Fund and the Rural Challenge Fund both failed and so their project went back on hold. Similarly, a Swansea Canal Society bid was turned down. This refusal stemmed from an objection raised by Associated British Ports, who ran Swansea Docks, who indicated they did not support a link through the port to the Neath and Tennant Canal. Even the news of these failures did not deter a suggestion from being made in *Waterways World* that the semi-completed historic remains of the Leominster Canal "ought to be a project for someone to investigate the possibility of restoration, perhaps using lottery funding".

Really positive news came in the spring of 1997, with the announcement of a £32 million Millennium Lottery Fund award to restore the Forth and Clyde and Union Canals in the Lowlands of Scotland. The Ribble Link Trust also heard they were to receive a £2.7m grant towards completing their project. On the other hand, the Grantham Canal scheme only received a £2.3m grant, from the European Single Regeneration Budget,

to restore the Cotgrave Colliery site. This award only covered a short part of the canal line, within the boundary of a new country park. They were disappointed by the failure of their larger bid, to build a new link to the River Trent. This proved to be another major setback for the Grantham restorers.

The prospect of the certain reopening of Ripon Canal Head, at Easter 1997, caused the Ripon Canal Society to review its future. At its 1997 AGM, a decision was taken to wind up the Society and to distribute any residual money it held to the Linton Lock repair fund. More positively, at much the same time the Sleaford Navigation Society converted itself into the Sleaford Navigational Trust, a registered charity, to help it drive forward its longer-term aims.

April 1997 saw initial moves taken to form a Leeds and Liverpool Canal Society. Its primary aim was to get the "remainder" section, into Liverpool, upgraded to "cruising" status. However, in the longer term it also wanted to ensure the link to Liverpool Docks remained protected.

Three canal projects were successful in the next Heritage Lottery round. These included the Linton Lock repairs (£765,000), the Stourbridge Trust's bid for reviving the Fens Branch, and another for the BCNS, for the Oaker Hill Branch upgrades.

The August 1997 edition of *Waterways World* contained an article about the Hollinwood Branch of the Ashton Canal, within the Daisy Nook Country Park. This identified a potential threat to the next section of the canal from a planned M66 extension. This perceived threat stimulated the local enthusiasts to consider whether a protection society was needed.

After months of delicate negotiations, a grant of £250,000 from Gloucester County Council and another £125,000 from North Wilts Council, the Minister for the Environment, Transport and the Regions announced that a navigable culvert would after all be provided under the Latton Bypass for the Thames and Severn Canal crossing. Sadly, this good news for the Cotswolds Canal Trust was offset by the decision by the Birmingham Northern Relief Road Inquiry Inspector that the contractors would not be required to provide navigable crossings for the Lichfield and Hatherton Canals, but if the Society so wished it could pay for them itself. This led to the announcement of a major appeal for funds by the actor David Suchet.

In the summer of 1997 the Caldon Canal Society

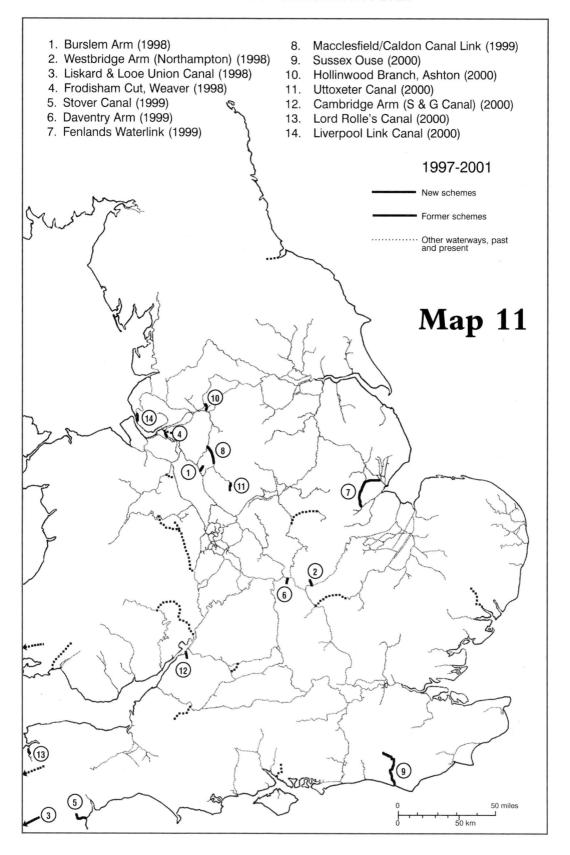

1. Burslem Arm (1998)
2. Westbridge Arm (Northampton) (1998)
3. Liskard & Looe Union Canal (1998)
4. Frodisham Cut, Weaver (1998)
5. Stover Canal (1999)
6. Daventry Arm (1999)
7. Fenlands Waterlink (1999)

8. Macclesfield/Caldon Canal Link (1999)
9. Sussex Ouse (2000)
10. Hollinwood Branch, Ashton (2000)
11. Uttoxeter Canal (2000)
12. Cambridge Arm (S & G Canal) (2000)
13. Lord Rolle's Canal (2000)
14. Liverpool Link Canal (2000)

1997-2001

—————— New schemes

—————— Former schemes

·············· Other waterways, past and present

Map 11

0   50 miles

0   50 km

announced its longer-term plans to extend the truncated Leek Arm by 720m, to a new terminus south of the "Pride of Moorlands" pub at Junction Road, Leek. Unfortunately, the cost-benefit calculations for this did not work out favourably and the project was put on the back burner.

At this time a novel scheme for a new water route was developed by the Lincolnshire Branch of the IWA and the EA. This proposed re-linking the South Forty Foot Drain to the River Witham via the Black Sluice at Boston, and thence creating a further new link from Guthron Gout into the River Glen. It was envisaged that this could lead to further extensions, reusing the River Welland, Bourne Eau and the Stamford Canal. An initial survey of the projected route by IWA members had reported favourably, and the IWA reported these findings when they responded to a consultation exercise, by EA, on the Welland, Local Plan.

Another new restoration proposal was put forward by the Leicester Branch of IWA, who were investigating forming a new local restoration society to cover both the Melton Mowbray Navigation and the Oakham Canal. Sadly, a nearby scheme to extend the Ashby Canal to Measham was stalled because negotiations to purchase a length of the former canal line from a local landowner had broken down. This meant that funding deadlines could not be met, and two funding packages that had been secured, worth over £1m, were lost. This failure to proceed with the purchase strengthened Leicestershire County Council's resolve to promote a Transport and Works Act Order, to give them the necessary compulsory purchase powers to enable the scheme to go ahead.

The summer of 1997 saw two more openings. The first was the completion of the new Great Cornard Lock on the River Stour on 15 September. The second, on 12 October, was the reopening of the Ocker Hill Arm of the BCN, and a new BW office. Work also started, in October 1997, on the long outstanding, comprehensive repairs to Linton Lock, with a completion date of April 1998. On the Lancaster Canal a Memorandum of Understanding, covering the Northern Reaches, was signed by both BW and the Northern Reaches Restoration Group. This set out how the restoration could proceed. Likewise, to get its systems right, the Rochdale Canal Trust was restructured to provide a potential vehicle for the takeover of canal ownership, so as to facilitate access to the full range of grants on offer that a private company, such as the then current canal owners, could not use.

One of the most significant developments on the restoration front in 1997 was the start of preparation, by IWAAC of a major review of "Waterways Restoration Priorities". This was the result of an earlier request from the Waterways Minister. On 26 September 1997, IWAAC set up a working group to assess all known waterway restoration schemes in the UK, with the aim of establishing a priority ranking listing. At first this proposal was viewed with great suspicion by the various societies, but after consultation the IWA recommended that all groups should assist IWAAC. This ensured the research could go forward positively. By the close of the first stage of the fact-finding process, some 70 responses had been received. When the IWAAC report was finally completed, on 16 July 1998, some 80 groups had responded. The Minister praised IWAAC for their work and indicated that some of the recommendations within their report had been taken "on board" in the Government's Transport White Paper, published on 20 July 1998. These included the concept of a Waterways Trust to draw in and distribute funds. It also considered the matter of the long-promised planning guidance on the protection of restoration routes in relation to the development of new highway schemes. The Minister also promised a complementary Government Policy Statement on inland waterways, taking forward the key themes from the earlier IWAAC report, *Britain's Inland Waterways: An Undeveloped Asset*.

What was especially helpful in the IWAAC Report was the division of restoration schemes into the immediacy of their funding requirements. The top tier included the three Millennium Projects, the Lowland Canals in Scotland, the Huddersfield Narrow Canal and the Rochdale Canal. In the second tier were a further 18 schemes that also needed funding in the short term (1–5 years), and 12 others which were ready for funding in the medium term (5–10 years). The third tier held a further 47 that would be ready for funding in the longer term (more than 10 years). Even with the strong steer given by the report, the Rochdale plans stalled due to the problems in negotiating the sale of the canal to a "secure owner". This hinged on the fact that the Millennium Commission rules required that their £11.3m grant could only be released to a scheme for "public benefit and not private profit". The Canal was then in private ownership. The Millennium Commission extended their deadline so that the purchase negotiations could continue. Ultimately, a last-minute deal was achieved by the riparian local authorities which met the Commission's rules.

Two other projects also had good news. In Louth, a Groundwork Lincolnshire general grant was deployed to refurbish the Canal Head Warehouse, to provide offices for themselves and the Louth Canal Trust, whilst in Sleaford, the Navigation Society gained a "spot listing" to prevent the demolition of the old warehouse by the canal head.

In Northampton, the local IWA cleared and reopened the Westbridge Arm in the town, that had become weeded and silted up, and in Stoke-on-Trent the Trent and Mersey Canal Society and the local IWA were working together to develop plans to restore the Burslem Arm. The scheme, known as the Burslem Port Project, which had been under consideration since 1997, envisaged restoring the half- mile arm, together with the Shropshire Union Wharf area and its warehouses, as part of a wider regeneration scheme. A wide-ranging local consultation programme was undertaken by the Burslem Community Development Trust, and this gained considerable local support for the scheme.

In the West Country, Caradone District Council started to consider the future of the remains of the Liskard and Looe Union Canal. The Council's plans were aiming to clear up and interpret the 70 per cent of the canal line that remained intact. They also envisaged re-watering various features, such as locks, as a towpath trail amenity. Their scheme did not envisage full restoration for navigation.

The IWA Cambridge Branch felt unable to be as positive about the future of the Ivel Navigation, which they had first examined in the early 1990s. They tried to galvanise public and local business support for a restoration scheme, but no local support was forthcoming. After careful deliberations they indicated that whilst they were still keen on the project themselves, they were not prepared to undertake it on their own.

The South Lakeland Council and English Partnerships, were persuaded to look again at the longer-term potential of the Ulverston Canal. They jointly commissioned consultants, in April 1998, to review the options and opportunities, and to take local opinions on the best way forward. Nothing major subsequently emerged and the waterway slumbered on.

Towards the end of 1998 some positive progress was being made elsewhere. The order granting the transfer of Linton Lock to British Waterways was approved, subject to local consultation. This all took a long time. The deal arranging the transfer was finally concluded on 18 June 1999. In Oxford, enthusiasts were pursuing the idea of restoring the former Terminal Basin at Hythe Bridge, in Oxford, a provisional proposal for which had recently been recommended by a local consultation exercise. BW themselves were discussing the idea with Nuffield College, who owned the site. In Scotland, various solutions were being devised to overcome the various obstructions along the Lowland canals. This work all became possible after the riparian local authorities and BW agreed to bridge a funding gap that had arisen when promised EU funding failed to materialise. At much the same time BW in the North-West agreed to

support the River Weaver Navigation Society in their aim to restore the Frodsham Cut. The society, which was formed by members of the Chester Branch of the IWA, was undertaking a survey of the necessary work needed with a view to setting priorities.

On 19 February 1999 the Government produced its long-awaited statement on the waterways, entitled *Unlocking the Potential – a new future for British Waterways*. It did just that. It confirmed that "the Government is committed to ensuring that they are recognised as a valuable public asset, that their full potential is secured, and that as many people as possible, from all walks of life, can enjoy and benefit from what they have to offer. For far too long British Waterways has been starved of the resources to care for this national asset".

The report went on to note a huge backlog of outstanding maintenance, estimated at £260m, some £90m of which was for work that posed a serious public safety risk. "The Government considers this backlog of safety-related maintenance is unacceptable." To assist in overcoming the problem, the Government agreed to a progressive write-off of the accumulated debt and relaxed rules for the carry-over of funds from one year to the next, plus far greater commercial freedom for BW to enter into commercial partnerships and to use any profits to support their ongoing work rather than surrendering them to the Treasury. The report also suggested that BW start consultations on the concept of a public membership scheme, which was allied to a charitable trust to preserve and restore the canal heritage and to take care of the various historical artefacts and archives connected with the waterways. British Waterways quickly followed up this proposal, and issued a consultation document in June 1999 under the title "Partnership with the People". This discussion paper pointed up the value that had already been achieved by the "recently created waterways Trust" which had taken over responsibility from BW for the waterway museums, as well as organising various fund-raising appeals, such as those for the Forth and Clyde and Union Canals and the Anderton Boat Lift. By having a trust operate the National Waterways Museums, an immediate benefit was gained for the museums by giving them access to direct funding from the Museums and Galleries Commission.

On a local level, two significant projects on the Herefordshire and Gloucestershire Canal were proceeding on a tight timetable. The Herefordshire and Gloucestershire Canal Trust had reached an agreement with Swan Homes to reconstruct Over Basin as part of their housing development. This facilitated the former river lock site and interchange basin area, to be fully restored over a nine-month period. It also provided the trust with the facility to have rebuilt for them the

Wharf House as a potential new Canal Centre. This whole project became the number one priority for the Waterway Recovery Group for the following nine months. The second major project was the creation of the Ribble Link, where the Babtie Group were able to complete the final designs to allow the project to get underway in the spring of 1999.

As with many things in the world, all was not being kept simple on the national waterways scene. The EA had issued a consultation document, "Waterway Restoration and Environmental Assessments". The IWA felt this was completely unsatisfactory. The IWA responded with a strong critique of the proposals, indicating that the procedures proposed were far too demanding for small volunteer restoration bodies to even contemplate. They suggested EA should be working with such groups rather than creating obstacles for them.

The Waterways Trust, which had been created earlier in the year, was able to come to the aid of the Rochdale Canal restoration, where legal constraints on ownership and lack of collateral created cash flow problems that looked likely to stall progress. This difficulty was overcome when the Waterways Trust took over the freehold ownership of the canal from British Waterways, who retained a contract for restoration and maintenance. The Trust was thus able to take out various commercial loans, using the canal freehold as the security.

The disputes on the Grantham Canal were also resolved when a new Grantham Canal Partnership, comprising the two former societies, IWA, BW and the six local authorities along the route, joined together to coordinate the restoration works. This enabled BW to produce a draft business plan that identified a way of taking the project forward.

The long-slumbering Stover Canal was awakened when a group of local enthusiasts from the IWA West Country Branch and the Newton Abbot Fishing Association made proposals to the local Teignbridge District Council that they might open negotiations with Railtrack to facilitate the restoration of at least part of the waterway. They also started to formulate plans to create a local canal society to take these plans forward.

Earlier in the year, DEFRA (the Department for the Environment, Food and Rural Affairs) had made some positive suggestions towards the interface between waterways under restoration and new highway schemes. However, the Minister was at first very unwilling to assist the Lichfield and Hatherton Canal Society in their quest to avoid the new Birmingham Northern Relief Road construction from taking away their canal's through route. After extensive negotiations it seemed a compromise solution could be reached. This, however, rested on the society paying for the two crossings. David

Suchet subsequently agreed to lead their appeal for funds to get an aqueduct purchased and put in place before the toll road opened.

The IWA held its National Festival at Worcester in August 1999. This event provided the opportunity for the Upper Severn Navigation Restoration Trust to display models of the inflatable weirs that they proposed should be installed to return the river levels back to those that existed a century before. The major advantage these weirs offered was that in times of flood they could quickly be modified to facilitate optimum dispersal of the flood waters.

Restoration of the Elsecar Top Lock, by the Barnsley Canal Group, took a major step forward in May 1999 when new lock-gates were installed. The group managed to obtain a grant from the Yorkshire European Community Trust to finance the work. The group indicated that its next project was the restoration of Cobar Bridge.

An innovative project that was first identified at this time came from a partnership between Daventry District Council and BW to promote the potential of the canals within the area. The scheme was able to make grants available "for those who wished to enhance or promote these waterways". When the Grand Junction Canal was originally was built, there was a plan authorised in the Canal Act for a Daventry Canal Arm. In the end this was not built, but the Daventry Reservoir and canal feeder were constructed on the outskirts of the town. Daventry District Council were persuaded that to construct the arm now, almost 200 years after it was proposed, might offer a completely new focus for the town centre of Daventry. Thus the scheme was included in the Daventry Town Centre Vision for 2021.

The Environment Agency planned a far shorter timetable for their new link lock into the Flood Relief Channel at Denver. The scheme offered two major benefits: a safe route for craft to the outskirts of King's Lynn and, in the longer term, access to the Ouse, via a proposed Nar Link and a new marina, into the tidal river near the town centre. Designs for the new 97ft long and 15ft wide Denver lock were competed in October 1999 and the contract for construction had a start date of February 2000.

Everything did not happen so easily elsewhere. The Chesterfield Canal Trust had been for some time looking at options for completing the link between the newly restored eastern end and the partly restored western end of the canal. The key issue was to overcome the derelict mine workings that earlier had led to the loss of Norwood Tunnel through subsidence. One suggestion was the creation of a waterway link, with a marina, in a scheme to reclaim the former Kiveton Colliery site.

Forth & Clyde & Union Link,
Falkirk Wheel

Unfortunately these plans were refused permission by the local council. The trust noted the Planning Officer's comments and went back to the drawing board to prepare a scheme which might prove to be more acceptable.

In much the same way, a desk-top study of a scheme to connect the Upper Avon to the Grand Union Canal gained support from AINA. However, the plan was opposed by a conservation group, Campaign for the Lean and Avon Rivers (CLEAR), on the grounds that the scheme would be harmful to local wildlife. To counter this attack, the Upper Avon Navigation Trust commissioned an "environmental impact" assessment to provide the evidence that the navigation plan would not be detrimental to the local habitats.

On a more positive note were plans launched by the Fenlands Tourism Group. These included a package of funding measures to develop a series of projects in the Fenlands area. Included in these was a feasibility study to identify a potential route for a proposed Earith to Ramsey water link, along with other schemes to link the River Witham to the River Nene.

At this time, the IWA published the first of two restoration handbooks, which had been supported by DEFRA grants. The first was the *Technical Restoration Handbook*, with the second, the *Practical Restoration Handbook*, due out a little later. Both offered key guidance for those developing new schemes or completing current restoration projects.

The year 1999 ended on a positive note. A Heritage Lottery Fund grant of £295,000 was made towards installing back pumping on the Woodham flight of locks on the Basingstoke Canal. The SHCS then prepared plans for similar schemes on the St John's and Brookwood flights of locks. Similarly, final plans for the Falkirk Wheel, to link the Union Canal to the Forth and Clyde Canal, were unveiled on 13 December 1999. Work on the Wheel was set to start in the spring of 2000 and it was expected to take a year to complete.

On the Huddersfield Narrow Canal, considerable progress had been made in resolving the major obstructions to the restoration at Bates, Sellers and Slaithwaite town centre. Prospects for final completion augured well for the first year of the New Millennium. It was in that same spirit of positively looking forward that the Macclesfield Canal Society agreed to investigate the construction of a navigable link from the top of Bosley Locks, through to Rudyard Lake and to Leek following existing water channels whereever possible. It was suggested that four or five new locks would be required for the eleven-mile route, but that nine miles of it would follow existing feeder channels.

In an effort to enhance its case for the full restoration of the Sankey Canal, the local Society revised its eight towpath guides under the group title *The Sankey Canal Trail*. Likewise, the IWA Lincolnshire Branch stepped up its fund-raising and publicity for the restoration of Harlem Hill Lock, as the final stage of the River Ancholme Initiative. A similar fund-raising exercise on the Bude Canal paid dividends when it received a £222,000 EU grant to refurbished the sea lock, including renovating the gates.

A grant from the European Regional Development Fund Programme facilitated the restoration of a further 2½ miles of the Montgomery Canal, from Maesbury to Redwith. Further south, WRG itself sought out new restoration opportunities for development. The Sussex River Ouse, in the area of Sheffield Park, was identified as an opportunity for early restoration work. Although there was no formal restoration society in existence, a local enthusiast, Michael Walker of Lewis, offered to co-ordinate those interested in forming one.

The Waterways Trust actively began to expand its operations in the year 2000, with the development of two new partnerships. One was in respect of the Cotswold Canals, where it joined forces with BW and the local trust to investigate possible funding streams for a more comprehensive restoration programme. The other was with the Droitwich Canals Trust, the local authorities and BW. Here the local authorities had earmarked £2 million for restoration work. Both these developments laid positive foundations for the future of these two schemes.

In much the same way a letter in *Waterways World*, in May 2000, from Keith Rogers pointed up the opportunities offered by restoring the Hollinwood Branch of the Ashton Canal, since it could offer a valuable cross-country link to the Rochdale Canal. He suggested a local initiative ought to be mounted to take this forward. Subsequently, this led to the formation of the Hollinwood Canal Society to undertake that role.

British Waterways themselves were seeking funding opportunities to take forward the proposed restoration of the Northern Reaches of the Lancaster Canal. They had earlier commissioned a feasibility study which gave a positive steer to a possible way forward, indicating the prospect of creating 2,000 new jobs and bringing over a million visitors a year into the area.

Two other schemes also got a cash boost in mid-2000, when the IWA announced it had received two major legacies of over £100,000 each. The Wilkinson legacy went to assist with the Wendover Arm Project, whilst that from Neil Pitts went to the Droitwich Junction Canal project that was being undertaken by WRG. This project hosted some of the Work Camps that year. Other WRG Camps were based on the Wilts and Berks Canal, Sleaford Navigation, Wey and Arun Canal, Derby Canal,

Drotwich Barge Canal, "Big Dig", Clearing Lock 3

Uttoxeter Canal, first lock reopening

Herefordshire and Gloucestershire Canal, Barnsley, Deane and Dove canals, plus the Montgomery and Basingstoke canals. At the same time, the Caldon Canal Society were discussing holding a possible work camp to restore the first lock and lower Basin at Froghall on the Uttoxeter Canal.

In June 2000, DETR published its most positive proposals to date for the future of Inland Waterways, titled *Waterways for Tomorrow*, with the foreword by the Deputy Prime Minister, John Prescott MP. The paper built on the earlier document, *Unlocking the Potential*. This new report indicated that the Government recognised that "the waterways are a major national asset which must be conserved and developed in a substantial way for future generations to use and enjoy". It endorsed the role of the Waterways Trust; it asked BW and EA to work closely together to provide a more integrated service for the users of their waterways and identified the major contribution the waterways made to urban and rural regeneration. And, in particular, it indicated that the Government wanted to increase the economic and social benefits offered by the waterways, by encouraging their improvement, development and restoration, wherever possible in partnership with the public, private and voluntary sectors. It also stated that they would issue guidance in the Design Manual for roads and bridges to deal with new road proposals which affected waterway restoration projects.

To take these initiatives forward, the Government indicated it planned to organise a National Conference to discuss the document, to "bring together all those with an interest in the waterways, so as to maximise the opportunities waterways offer".

This positive message was reiterated in the BW Annual General Meeting, at the end of July 2000, when the Chief Executive, Dave Fletcher, was able to cite "a record spend of over £1m a week on restoration". He pointed out that "waterways were being restored at a greater rate than when they were built, in the great canal age 200 years ago".

The Waterways Trust, in its extended role, took over the responsibility for the Ribble Link Project. It was identified as the owner of the finished waterway, with BW contracted to operate it when the works were completed. A minor hiccup, over the length of the locks, was resolved after negotiations, and IWA agreed to contribute to the additional costs involved in providing full-length, 72ft by 14ft locks.

Elsewhere positive results were emerging on other restoration projects. The two locks at Cotgrave Colliery site were reopened within a country park, funded by a local restoration grant. On the Derby Canal, the local trust were supported by the council in their £3.2m bid

to the Heritage Lottery Fund to finance the Derby Canal Heritage Corridor Project. This was aimed at restoring the length of canal between Sandiacre and Spondon as a linear park.

At the end of July 2000, BW announced its commitment to the plan to build the new waterway link between Bedford and Milton Keynes. It was sad to record that the originator of the original concept, Brian Young of IWA Cambridge Branch, died on 31 July 2000, just as it seemed his dream was about to become a reality. Unfortunately, various funding cuts subsequently caused BW to backtrack on its earlier commitment. It was then left to the trust that Brian founded in 1994 to again take forward his dream, without direct official BW assistance.

Perhaps one of the most notable achievements of the Waterway Recovery Group occurred on 24 August 2000. After 18 months of sustained volunteer input, the Over Basin project, on the Herefordshire and Gloucestershire Canal, was completed, just four days ahead of the grand opening ceremony. The task had been priced by contractors at £500,000, but volunteers delivered it for £50,000.

New schemes were regularly coming forward. In July 2000 the Local Users Forum on the Gloucester and Sharpness Canal published the results of their preliminary feasibility study for the restoration of a side arm to Cambridge Village. The scheme offered the prospect of new moorings and access to the village itself. There were two potential obstacles to be overcome. The most difficult was a low-level road crossing, which needed to be raised. The other was the low-level pedestrian over-bridge at the entry to the arm. Both were not insurmountable if the funding could be raised.

The Monmouthshire Canal benefited from a BW bid to the European Regional Development Fund, which gained an award of £206,000. This enabled them to plan the refurbishment of Gwasted, Bettra and Drapers locks, as well as three miles of new towpath, during the following year.

After many years of lobbying by the Thames and Medway Canal Society, the Gravesend Borough Council finally published their proposals for the regeneration of the whole site to the east of the Canal Basin. As a centrepiece the outline plan indicated the reopening of the infilled section of the Thames and Medway Canal, which went through the site.

During the summer of 2000, the IWA West Country Branch carried out an initial appraisal of the entry lock and canal basin of the Rolle Canal, at its junction with the River Torridge. They concluded that, whilst the majority of the remainder of the canal had been infilled, apart from the stone aqueduct designed by James Green, it would be uneconomic to seek to restore the whole waterway. However, they confirmed the lock and basin should be saved and recommended the site as a venue for a future summer WRG work camp.

In October 2000, restorers noted their major concerns when new procedures for the Transport and Works Act came into force. These changes were implemented primarily to meet European requirements on Environmental Impact Assessments. Both the IWA and NABO sought assurances that they would be informed if any subsequent submissions under the Act were likely to affect Rights of Navigation.

It was heartening to see considerable progress on the two major schemes in the Lowlands of Scotland towards the end of 2000. Perhaps the most significant was the building of a new sea lock at Grangemouth and the completion of a diversion canal to link into the old line of the Forth and Clyde Canal. But equally pleasing was the completion of some of the key components for the new Falkirk Wheel being constructed by the Butterley Iron Company. At the same time, on the Union Canal in Edinburgh, a major redevelopment scheme was agreed for Lochrin Basin. The other step forward was the installation of new gates on Coates Lock on the Pocklington Canal. These were funded by the PCAS as the result of an appeal launched in 1995. Even though the lock was now restored, the limit of navigation still remained at Melbourne, 2½ miles downstream, while discussions were progressed with English Nature about the impact of boat movements on the SSSI.

Major flooding in November 2000 caused considerable damage to inland waterways in the Severn, Trent and Ouse valleys. This resulted in an added burden of repair costs where funding was already overstretched.

The year closed with BW announcing that it planned to create a new Liverpool Link Canal. This concept was developed to provide a connection between the Stanley Dock and linking locks from the Leeds and Liverpool Canal with the Albert Dock which BW were about to take over from English Partnerships. The scheme offered a new focus for the end of the "remainder" section of the Leeds and Liverpool Canal and the opportunity for it to receive more regular traffic. This announcement coincided with the launch of a Government White Paper on Urban Regeneration' BW, in turn, launched its own internal Regeneration Task Force, to focus on improving urban corridors. As a case study, it cited the improvement work being undertaken on the Ashton Canal to facilitate access to the Commonwealth Games to be held in Manchester in 2002.

At the same time, a new Shrewsbury and Newport Canals Trust was formed. This resulted from the work of a small sub-committee of the Shropshire Union Canal Society. It was perhaps ironic to note that some 35 years earlier, the then Shrewsbury and Newport Canal Association had been reformed into the Shropshire Union Canal Society. Sadly, later internal disputes within this new Trust, due to differences of opinion on varying restoration strategies, were to retard its progress.

Ashby Canal, Moira, new lock opening

Anderton Lift, reopened

The year 2001 started on a positive note. All the funding was in place for the construction works on the new Ribble Link waterway. These funds came from a variety of sources, including a £2.7m Millennium Commission grant, Landfill Tax rebates, a Single Regeneration Budget grant plus other donations from local councils and funds raised by the trusts, and made a start on the £6 million scheme possible. The Lapal Tunnel Trust also sought to explore the opportunity of getting the first section of their canal created, at Selly Oak, when Sainsbury's put forward plans for a new supermarket on their site that cut across the former canal line. The trust hoped to negotiate for a protected corridor, within the development, which offered a full canal width.

On the Chesterfield Canal, progress was being made at the Chesterfield end. Here plans for two new road bridges, offering navigable height over the canal, were being developed together with a commitment from Staveley Council to restore a low-level bridleway bridge to allow navigation under it. On the Ashby Canal, at

Huddersfield Canal, Stalebridge, official opening

Moira, work was underway on the extension to the already restored section at Moira Furnace. This work included a new lock to compensate for the mining subsidence in the area and a new terminal basin. The scheme offered the prospect of an extended cruising ground for the Furnace Museum's trip boat and for the craft launched from the newly built slipway. Work was also proceeding apace on the restoration of the Anderton Boat Lift in readiness for its planned reopening on 26 September 2001. Likewise work was on schedule for the "unofficial" reopening of the Huddersfield Narrow Canal on 1 May 2001.

On the Lichfield and Hatherton Canal, the prospect of solving the new Birmingham Northern Relief Road crossing came a stage closer when the road builders accepted the Trust's request to provide foundations for the new aqueduct on the Lichfield Canal. However, they had no similar obligation to provide an enlarged culvert to facilitate retaining the route of the Hatherton line. Fortunately the trust was able to negotiate with the road builders, and agreed to pay the cost differential between what the contractors were required to offer under their contract, and the larger culvert suitable for subsequent navigation. It then fell to the trust to raise the necessary cash.

A political problem loomed on the Montgomery Canal, when the Countryside Council for Wales designated large lengths of the waterway in Powys as an SSSI. The Trust immediately opened negotiations with them to make sure this action would not prejudice the ultimate restoration of the canal.

The Foot and Mouth epidemic in England and Wales created major restrictions on the majority of waterways when it was confirmed in February 2001. Towing paths went alongside, or passed through, areas where cattle were grazing and the risk of cross-boundary transfers was considered quite high. The restrictions not only delayed the waterway maintenance programme, but also meant that on many rural canals volunteer work on restoration sites had to be halted. Fortunately, ways were found to enable some works to proceed, but the crisis had a major impact on the rural economy and on the number of hire boat bookings, as people were forced to take their leisure elsewhere. It also caused the cancellation of the IWA Trailboat Rally at Bodium on the Rother Navigation. The main impact of the outbreak was of course on the farmers, and those in the countryside suffered badly with many livelihoods lost. Fortunately, the restrictions on the waterways were lifted at the end of May 2001, and this enabled some parts of the summer hire trade to proceed.

As one restriction was lifted, it seemed that another longer-term control mechanism was being launched. This time it was the final version of the EC Water

Framework Directive, which was agreed in the European Parliament in July 2000. This required governments to start to put in place River Basin Management Plans. These had to be operational by 2009, with the full range of environmental objectives, including controls on water quality, completed by 2015.

On 1 May 2001 the Huddersfield Canal Society, founded in 1974, saw its dream finally come true, with the first boats negotiating the whole length of the canal. Their journal, the *Pennine Link*, was able to carry the headline: "The impossible has happened!" Then, over the weekend of 26 to 28 May 2001, another dream came true. Boats were again able to traverse the full length of the restored Forth and Clyde Canal. This Scottish Lowland waterway was officially opened by the Prince of Wales on 12 June 2001. The final link, with the Union Canal, was still incomplete due to the timescale needed for the construction of the Falkirk Wheel, but even there the end was in sight.

It was thus very timely that in June 2001 IWAAC produced its updated review of waterway restoration and development priorities, entitled *A Second Waterway Age*. Their report recorded "the spectacular recent progress, building on years of sustained voluntary effort, of the four Millennium Lottery Projects. The Millennium Link (Scottish Lowlands Canals) and the Huddersfield Narrow Canal are substantially open again, the Rochdale and the Ribble Link are both likely to open in 2002/3". It recorded that there had also been progress on key projects, such as the Anderton Boat Lift, but limited or no apparent progression on a long list of other schemes. The report also highlighted a number of lessons that had to be learnt. These included taking an overall professional view; the importance of broad-based relationships; the value of obtaining local authority support from the outset; the practical merit of progressing in discrete steps; and the need to maximise the project's appeal to a range of potential funding partners.

This time the IWAAC report analysed 104 projects, on some of which it subsequently did not have sufficient information to conclude the assessment. It divided them, by assessment of progress made to date, into four groups: Advanced (7), Substantial Progress (19), Intermediate (18) and At an Early Stage (46). The report also offered a variety of assessments of the schemes, including their heritage and conservation benefits, and whether they were of national or only regional importance. New sections were developed in respect of funding opportunities, and the legislative changes that had taken place since the preparation of the first report in 1998. The report concluded with a warning note about the potential funding gap that might arise with the ending of the Millennium Lottery Funding for the major capital costs of forthcoming restoration projects. It also went on

to highlight the importance of ensuring that the longer-term revenue funding necessary for future maintenance was secured as part of any overall project package.

The General Election in June 2001 returned New Labour with a commanding majority. The election also brought a change in the department responsible for inland waterways, with Lord Whitty taking over ministerial control. There was a greater commitment towards public consultation. This was exemplified by an exercise promoted by the Environment Agency, which sought to review the potential for Lydney Harbour and the associated canal. The results identified considerable local support for the development of a marina, visitor centre and interpretation facilities. As a result, a £1.9m bid was put forward by the local consortium, seeking Heritage Lottery Funds to finance the works needed.

At this time, the Waterways Trust formed a partnership with IWPS to secure a permanent repair to the long-standing problem of leaks in the entry channel of Bugsworth Basin. Their aim was to make a funding bid to finance all the remedial works and open the basin up as a tourist attraction.

On 17 July 2001 the new lock at Denver, to link the Great Ouse to the non-tidal Flood Relief Channel, was officially opened. This offered a safe inland navigation channel between Denver and Saddle Bow, two miles from King's Lynn. The longer-term project aim was to link into the River Nar, for more direct access to King's Lynn town centre.

At much the same time Caerphilly County Borough Council began to consider the future of the Rogerstone Section of the Crumlin Arm, at Risca. They had three options: completely restore the canal, at a cost of £5.1m; restore part and infill the middle section, at a cost of £2.6m; or completely infill the canal, at a cost of £1.1m. A local public meeting was called to hear people's views. Some 400 were present and at the end of the debate there was a majority call for full restoration to take place. At the meeting, it was suggested the Monmouthshire Canal Partnership should be involved. In the interim, the Council allocated half a million pounds for urgent essential repair work It also took forward a commitment to seek external funding for the longer project works.

In July 2001, the Transport Minister announced an agreement whereby the Highways Agency would be required to formally take waterway restoration initiatives into account when planning new roads or altering existing ones, and to provide navigable culverts, where appropriate, where such proposed roads crossed the line of a waterway that was operational or under restoration. This seemed to offer all the assurances the restorers had earlier sought, but the details of the understanding did not prove as clear-cut as originally was thought to be the case. Even so, one of the first projects to benefit was the Manchester, Bolton and Bury Canal, where a new relief road was about to be constructed in Salford and where a navigable culvert was incorporated as an integral part of the road construction scheme.

A trail boat Rally in Bedford, and the IWA National Festival in Milton Keynes, at the end of August 2001, saw the launch of the Bedford and Milton Keynes Link public consultation exercise in respect of the choice of the preferred route. Nine options were on offer, the most difficult of which involved the selection of the corridors to be adopted to link into the Grand Union at Milton Keynes itself, and into the Great Ouse at Bedford.

At the BW AGM, in 2001, a map was distributed that indicated various restoration projects which BW itself had under consideration for help and assistance. Those identified included the Wey and Arun, Wilts and Berks, St Helens, Grantham, Ashby and Derby canals, plus the Crumlin Arm and the Higher Avon scheme. Mention was also made at the AGM of the £971,000 Heritage Lottery Fund grant to enable the complete restoration of the section of the Chesterfield Canal from Shireoaks to Norwood Tunnel.

The Heritage Lottery Fund subsequently also confirmed their support for the earlier EA proposals to restore the Lydney Canal, with the offer of an £873,000 grant. This project finance included new gates for the sea lock and the facilities for a new 50-berth marina with visitor centre. It was indicated that when the works were completed the whole complex would be managed by the Lydney Docks Partnership.

One of the main visitor attractions envisaged by earlier feasibility studies on the restored Huddersfield Narrow Canal was a tunnel trip. The new visitor centre and the trip-boat base were created in a converted warehouse beside Marsden tunnel mouth. HRH The Prince of Wales opened this complex, together with the restored canal, on 3 September 2001.

The year ended on a very positive note, with news that Lord Whitty had authorised a £345,000 funding package to make a navigable culvert under a new roundabout on the A5/A34 trunk roads where they crossed the new Birmingham Northern Relief Road. In much the same way, the Manchester, Bolton and Bury Canal Society were delighted when the £300,000 additional funding was finally authorised for the culvert under Manchester and Salford Inner Relief Road, which would allow the canal later to be reconnected to the River Irwell.

At about this time, the IWA itself took the view that there was a need for details of all societies involved in waterway restoration to be given a higher profile. To achieve this, it produced a *Waterway Societies Guide* that listed the details of 67 waterway groups and their

schemes. This gesture was a fitting close to a period when Millennium Funds had converted "impossible dreams" into reality. One must equally not underplay the steady role played behind the scenes by IWAAC in educating waterway ministers of the true value of canals as engines for regeneration. This sterling work provided the hidden asset that offered the solid foundation on which the waterway restoration movement could build upon in the new millennium.

During the period the following schemes emerged:

1. Burslem Arm, Trent and Mersey
2. Westbridge Arm, Northampton
3. Liskard and Looe Union Canal
4. Frodsham Cut, Weaver Navigation
5. Stover Canal
6. Daventry Arm, Grand Union Canal
7. Fenlands Links project
8. Macclesfield Canal to Caldon Canal Link
9. Sussex Ouse
10. Hollinwood Branch, Ashton Canal
11. Uttoxeter Canal
12. Cambridge Arm, Gloucester and Sharpness Canal
13. Lord Rolle's Canal
14. Liverpool Link Canal

XII 2002-2006:
A PERIOD OF CHANGE

Dave Fletcher, the BW Chief Executive, coined the phrase "post Millennium droop". He was worried that the raised optimism of the Millennium Heritage Projects might be difficult to sustain beyond 2003, when these became operational and further projects were added to the "shopping list". This was one of the reasons why BW launched its property regeneration company ISIS at this time. BW saw this joint venture company as adding value to its operational budget. It certainly did that as, by 2006, the Deputy Prime Minister was able to cite that some £6 billion had been invested in waterside regeneration and that this was a success story of the age.

The year 2002 was a time for new beginnings. The Chancellor, Gordon Brown, heralded the start of a major three-year public spending programme injecting £93.5 billion into the economy.

AINA (the Association of Inland Navigation Authorities) were first to seek to take advantage of this new period of optimism, when they released their report *Vision for Strategic Enhancement of Britain's Inland Navigation Network*. The report identified eleven high-priority projects, which included the Wey and Arun and the Cotswolds canals, the Bedford to Milton Keynes Link, the Nene to Witham Link, The Higher Avon and Grand Union Canal link, the extension of the Slough Arm to the Thames, the improvement of the Leicester Line between Foxton and Norton Junction and some minor improvements to a few commercial waterways.

This theme of looking ahead was mirrored by British Waterways when they sponsored a special conference, on 19 March 2002, entitled "Unlocked and Unlimited". This conference had three aims: to celebrate the completion of the first phase of major restoration projects, to introduce nine new projects and to share ideas about future possibilities. In introducing the presentation, Dave Fletcher sounded a rallying call. "This is a day I dreamed about six years ago… by the end of this year, 220 miles of new and restored waterway will be open… we must exploit today's successes and use them as a springboard for the future." The projects spotlighted at the conference were:

Completed Projects: Anderton Boat Lift (£7m); Chesterfield Canal (Worksop to Norwood (£19m); Huddersfield Narrow Canal (£32m); Kennet and Avon Canal (£29m); Scottish Lowlands Canals and Falkirk Wheel (£84m); Ribble Link (£6m); Rochdale Canal (£25m).

New projects: B&MK Link (£80–£150m); Bow Back Rivers (£17m); Cotswold Canals (£82m); Droitwich Canals (£9.5m); Foxton Inclined Plane (£9m); Liverpool Link (£15m); Manchester, Bolton and Bury (£32m); Montgomery Canal (£35m); Lancaster Canal, Northern Reaches (£30m).

Most attendees left the conference feeling that real progress was being made. Others were worried about if and when the balloon of euphoria might burst.

This did not stop promoters of those schemes not listed by Dave Fletcher from moving forward in the best way they could, In South Wales, W.S. Atkins were appointed to provide a feasibility study of disused opportunities to reopen 35 miles of disused canals. These results were due out in the spring of 2002. In the South-West, the Midford Ford Aqueduct, on the Somerset Coal Canal, was cleaned and restored using a Heritage Lottery Fund grant. In the North-West, British Waterways and local councils reviewed the opportunities for reopening sections of the Manchester, Bolton and Bury Canal and the likely prospects of getting EU funding and other financial support for the project.

A public meeting at Ironville was held on 13 March 2002 to discuss the state of the local derelict section of the Cromford Canal. As a result a new group, Friends of the Cromford Canal, was formed. That meeting was promoted by ECPDA, with the aim of formulating plans for the restoration of the derelict section of the Cromford Canal north of their own restoration site at Great Northern Basin. In a similar vein, a public meeting was called for 11 May 2002 to consider the formation of a Leominster Canal Action Group. Whilst only 18 miles of the canal were completed, this included two aqueducts, tunnels and bridges, all of which the group hoped to preserve.

This flurry of activity, in promoting new projects, was mirrored by a series of reopenings in early 2002. These were:

Anderton Boat Lift	26 March 2002
Falkirk Wheel	24 May 2002
Rochdale Canal	1 July 2002
Ribble Link	12 July 2002

This was mirrored by progress on the Pocklington Canal, where new bottom gates were installed on the Top Lock of the waterways, with BW also dredging the pound between the lock and the head of navigation. Following successful negotiations with English Nature, PCAS were

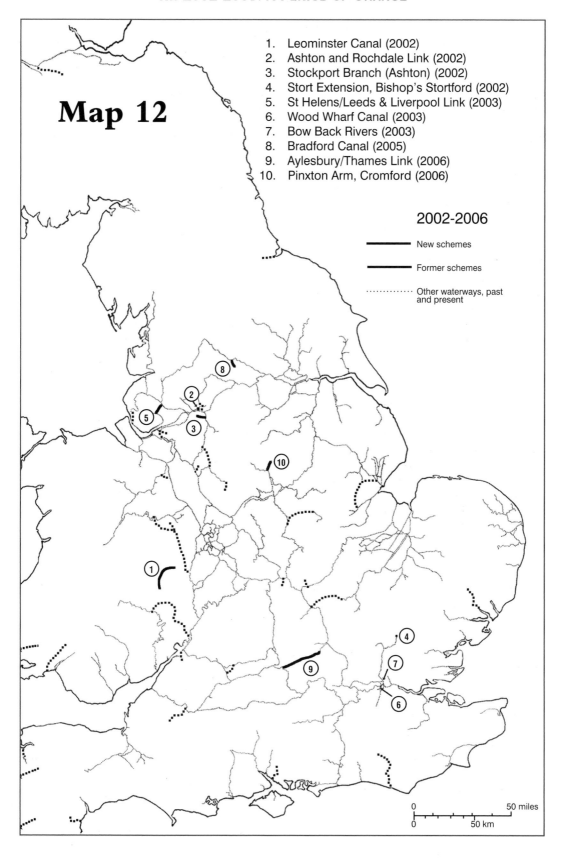

Map 12

1. Leominster Canal (2002)
2. Ashton and Rochdale Link (2002)
3. Stockport Branch (Ashton) (2002)
4. Stort Extension, Bishop's Stortford (2002)
5. St Helens/Leeds & Liverpool Link (2003)
6. Wood Wharf Canal (2003)
7. Bow Back Rivers (2003)
8. Bradford Canal (2005)
9. Aylesbury/Thames Link (2006)
10. Pinxton Arm, Cromford (2006)

2002-2006

New schemes

Former schemes

Other waterways, past and present

Ribble Link, official opening

also clear to prepare a bid to HLF to fund the remaining restoration works. It was interesting that research by their ecologists had shown that full restoration of the canal, and reopening the navigation to boats, was likely to be beneficial to both wildlife and biodiversity.

A public consultation exercise held in Liverpool indicated that there was wide public support for the Liverpool Link Canal project, especially for an inland route at the Pier Head, past the "Three Graces". Elsewhere, on the Wey and Arun Canal, a major new engineering project was underway. This was the construction of a new aqueduct at Drungewick, over the Loxwood stream. On this occasion the Wey & Arun Canal Trust decided to employ a contractor to undertake the bulk of the work.

In the North-West, BW was in discussion with a developer regarding a scheme, at concept stage, for a new linking canal between the Ashton and Rochdale canals. This envisaged reopening the former Ancoats Hospital Arm, between locks 2 and 3 of the Ashton Canal, and creating a new marina mid-way along the proposed link route. BW was also holding preliminary discussions regarding the feasibility of restoring the Stockport Branch of the Ashton Canal. On the Driffield Navigation, in the North-East, further progress was made with the replacement of Brigham Bridge.

On the Cotswold Canals, fairly rapid progress was being made on the restoration works. The Cotswold Canals Trust had raised £100,000, in cash and promises, towards the restoration work and this was placed with the Waterways Trust to be used as leverage to gain appropriate matched funding. A full-time Regeneration Programme Manager, Andy Stumpf, was appointed for the project, to promote a major bid to the Heritage Lottery Fund for finance to undertake the works. Local resident the Prince of Wales subsequently visited the canal as Patron of the Waterways Trust to learn more about their plans.

The whole nation was saddened when they heard of the death of the Queen Mother on 30 March 2002. She was especially remembered by restoration workers for officially opening the Southern Stratford Canal in 1964, and the Upper Avon Navigation in 1972. These projects were masterminded by David Hutchings and inspired others to follow his lead. These two events really brought waterway restoration into the mainstream. It was poignant that her daughter, Queen Elizabeth. II, followed her lead and officially opened the new Falkirk Wheel on 24 May 2002. This was the fourth key stage in the process of national recognition for the waterways restoration movement, the third having been the reopening of the Kennet and Avon Canal by the Queen in 1990.

At the Caldon Canal's Bicentenary Rally, in 2002, the Caldon Canal Society revived their previously stalled plan to extend the Leek Arm to a new terminus nearer to the town. The Macclesfield Canal Society also took the opportunity to explain their ideas to link the arm, via Rudyard Lake and a Macclesfield Canal feeder, to the top of Bosley Locks. These plans gained a good local hearing, but it looked as if lack of finances would lead them again to be put onto the "back burner".

As part of its aim to gain financial stability, the Herefordshire and Gloucestershire Canal Society became a charity in mid-2002. It was renamed the Hereford and Gloucester Canal Trust. They announced that their next project was to be the fitting out of the Wharf House, at Over Basin, as both a Trust HQ and a visitor facility.

The first boats to traverse the newly created Ribble Link undertook the passage on 10 July 2002. An informal opening took place on 12 and 13 July, with the official opening going ahead on 20 September 2002. The Ribble Link Trust members present felt that, at long last, their 20-year campaign to get the link built had been worth while.

The August 2002 *Waterways World* carried a letter from Keith Taylor of Stafford, indicating that he had uncovered the remains of the former lock which led from the Staffs and Worcs Canal into the infilled Sow Arm. He suggested that the "remains of the Sow Arm could be explored… as the former towpath is a recognised route leading to the centre of Stafford". His initial letter led to others undertaking further research in the area, and getting together to form a new group, the Stafford Riverway Link, to take forward the proposed restoration scheme. The group subsequently produced a leaflet setting out their aims and objectives, and used it to cultivate local authority and wider support for the restoration scheme.

The Waterways Trust launched the Foxton Fund-Raising Campaign in August 2002. Its aim was to raise the first £800,000 towards the £9 million needed to restore the Foxton Inclined Plane. This was the first stage of a partnership between the local society and the trust to develop the necessary studies needed to gain the full funding package for the project.

St Helens Metropolitan Borough Council gained a grant from the Single Regeneration Budget Fund to pay for a feasibility study into restoring the whole section of the Sankey Canal within St Helens as part of a plan to regenerate the eastern area of the town centre. Halton Canal, at the Mersey end of the canal, published their "Widnes Waterfront" plan, which developed their ideas

Upper Avon Opening, John Betjamin reads "R. Avon" to HRH the Queen Mother

Chesterfield Canal, restored Turnerwood Locks

for rejuvenating that section of the canal. The Sankey Canal Restoration Society themselves were proposing to replace a swing bridge at Spike Island to solve two problems: firstly to give permanent access to the Halton Show Ground and secondly to remove another obstruction to full navigation.

The Manchester, Bolton and Bury Canal Society and British Waterways produced a leaflet extolling the value of the restored canal. This was the precursor to the BW-led restoration scheme for the waterway, which was launched at The Lowry, Salford Quays, on 28 May 2002. Later in the year, details of a major redevelopment project, covering the first 500m of the canal at the Salford end, were unveiled.

The Lapal Canal Trust had good news later in 2002, when Birmingham City Council planners identified the route for the canal through the new Sainsbury's Development at the Selly Oak end of the canal. This included a road bridge of navigable height over the canal line. This complemented work by the Lapal Canal Trust volunteers, clearing a length of the canal beyond Hawne Basin, towards the southern tunnel mouth.

Volunteers in Melton Mowbray held a major clean-up of the River Eye in the town in 2002, also along the canalised section of the navigation, using funds from a Lottery Awards for All grant of £4,858 to purchase the equipment necessary to undertake the project.

The IWA, Lee and Stort Branch formulated a local campaign in Bishop's Stortford to seek an extension of the head of navigation into the park above Hockerhill Street Bridge. They suggested that this would have the dual advantages of creating improved facilities for boaters visiting the town, and would extend the water holding area of the top pound. Their scheme found support from British Waterways, who agreed to explore the engineering issues involved.

Three breakthroughs came towards the end of 2002. The first boat for over 70 years negotiated the restored Turnerswood Flight of locks on the Chesterfield Canal on 18 November. At much the same time the North West Development Agency made a grant of £150,000 to fund a full site investigation along twelve miles of the Manchester, Bolton and Bury Canal. This followed up an earlier local consultation exercise that showed overwhelming public support for the restoration scheme. Thirdly, the IWA provided a major grant towards a £60,000 Heritage Survey of the route of the Cotswolds Canals, which formed part of the necessary documentation required before a Lottery grant could be made. This was in addition to the Community Development Plan (£10,000) and the Visitor Management Strategy (£20,000) studies that also were required. In the East, on the Sleaford Navigation, the local council agreed to fund the restoration of the historic Canal Head Seed Warehouse and also the Navigation House, the Navigation Company's former offices which had fallen into dereliction. Additionally, Lincolnshire County Council agreed to fund a further study of the water resources that would be required to operate the canal. The year ended with the Waterway Recovery Group launching "The Right Tool for the Right Job" appeal, under which they hoped to raise £75,000 to procure the necessary equipment for volunteers in an ever more safety-conscious world.

One of the philosophical issues that restorers have to confront is that of "conservation" versus "rebuilding". This became an issue at Bugsworth Basin, a scheduled Ancient Monument, where English Heritage approval was needed to use modern waterproofing materials to solve the permanent leaks that caused longstanding problems in the entrance channel. Another similar issue was in respect of the extent to which past inappropriate repairs should be removed with a commitment to reconstruct the structure in its original form. BW gained funds for a two-year conservation project, costing £1m, on the Dundas Aqueduct on the Kennet and Avon Canal. This proved to be a case in point, as earlier repairs to the stone structure had been made in brick. Similarly, on the Huddersfield Narrow Canal, the process of upgrading old structures, so as to meet the needs of both modern

and historic craft, was a very important aspect of the restoration.

Two small projects were being undertaken at this time. One was the excavation of a short length of the Cromford Canal at Langley Mill by ECPDA, to offer extra moorings and more especially to identify the canal line. This project was financed through Groundwork by the East Midlands Development Agency (£35,000) with ECPDA providing matched funding through work by volunteers. Another project was that of undertaking repairs to Cefn Lock, on the Fourteen Locks section of the Monmouthshire Canal, Crumlin Arm. This project was especially important locally as it offered a prospective route for a local trip-boat operation. Another project that also got underway in early 2003 was "Restoration Froghall". This £800,000 scheme received funding from Rural Regeneration Funds in North-East Staffordshire and was part of a wider plan to improve facilities at Froghall, including excavating the first lock on the Uttoxeter Canal for access to a new, and much needed, mooring basin.

On 20 March 2003, an "Options Appraisal" feasibility report on the Lancaster Canal, Northern Reaches, was launched at a Public Meeting in Kendal. This included

Lichfield Canal, Tamworth Road site, 5th August 2006

innovative solutions to re-route the canal so as to avoid two motorway crossings by means of an inclined plane. The overall cost was estimated at £55m, with diversions adding between £2m and £7m. The estimated "payback" to be generated by the finished project was £24m per annum. This would come from increased visitor spending in the area, and from the 800 new jobs it was anticipated the finished project could create. At much the same time, the North West Development Agency awarded BW a £393,000 grant to study the feasibility of creating the proposed Liverpool Canal Link.

The issues of value for money, leverage from investment and the extent of job creation were much on the minds of all grant funding agencies. These themes were embraced by a new, good practice guide, *Demonstrating the value of waterways* , which was published by AINA in March 2003. This set out to identify the methods for the appraisal of restoration and regeneration projects. AINA chairman, Dr Dave Fletcher, in the foreword, made the point that "deciding whether a project is 'worth doing' requires more than just calculating the financial rate of return. It requires the tools which are capable of analysing and presenting the great wealth of environmental, social and economic benefit that waterways deliver – whilst also assisting in the proper management of the inevitable losses (beyond the simple costs in pounds and pence) which any project must incur." He

concluded that "projects which can show what benefits they deliver will be those most likely to win backing, secure finding and enjoy support." British Waterways themselves took heed of this report when, a year later, in 2004, they produced a study entitled *Waterways 2025 – Our vision for the shape of the Waterways Network*. Quite controversially, this identified 18 restoration schemes that BW believed might be completed within the 20-year horizon identified in their report. It also indicated they would be willing to support them. In addition the report identified three schemes – the Slough–Windsor link, Higher Avon Extension and Wey and Arun Canal – which they considered would contribute significantly to the national waterways system. Of the group of 18, eleven projects were chosen as priority Category One: Ashby Canal (to Measham), Bedford and Milton Keynes Waterway, Bow Back Rivers, Cotswold Canals (Phase 1), Droitwich Canals, Fens Waterways Links, Liverpool Link, Manchester, Bolton and Bury Canal, Montgomery Canal, Northern Reaches, Lancaster Canal and River Carron Navigation. Priority Category Two included the Ashby Canal (to Moira), Cotswold Canal (Phase 2), Grantham Canal, Lichfield Canal, Monmouthshire and Brecon Canal, River Leven, St Helens (Sankey) Canal, Wendover Arm and the Wiltshire and Berkshire Canal.

In putting the list forward, they made three fundamental points: the projects would only be delivered

Montgomery Canal. official opening, Aston Locks, 3 April 2003

in partnership with others; circumstances could change (e.g. they noted a growing interest in funding for the Bradford and the Grantham Canals); and some projects may be dropped as pressures on scarce resources required reassessment of priorities. Whilst the document was welcomed by those listed in it, others who were not felt it seriously undermined their case and their opportunity to raise funds for their local scheme. Many groups sought assurances from BW that such detriment to their schemes would not be allowed to happen. With hindsight, it was interesting to see that, two years later, BW carefully dropped the "2025" document as a statement of their formal priorities.

One of the benefits of devolution was the raising of the profile of Scotland's canals. This led to the production of a vision statement: *Scotland's Canals: An assessment for the future.* In it, the Minister for Enterprise, Transport and Lifelong Learning, Ian Gray MSP, set out the Scottish Executive's strategy for increasing awareness and appreciation of their canal network and indicated recognition of the role canals play in delivering wider public policy objectives. BW itself took the initiative of launching a similar document for Wales, in the spring of 2003, entitled *Waterways for Wales: Improved quality of life through the sustainable development of the Waterways of Wales.* This document was actively supported by the Welsh

Assembly, who similarly recognised the value of their canals in stimulating economic regeneration and acting as a catalyst for rural recovery. The document provided a valuable overview of current projects, but especially laid the foundations for new funded schemes that were likely to emerge, mentioning the £37m project for reopening the Monmouthshire and Brecon Canal, £50m for completing the Montgomery restoration and £55m to reopen the 38 miles of the Swansea, Neath and Tennant Canals.

New schemes were not being forgotten elsewhere. In the spring of 2003, the St Helens Steering Group discussed a longer-term project to link the St Helens (Sankey) Canal to the Leeds and Liverpool Canal, at Melling, following a possible route along Main Ford Brook. This was very much a conjectural scheme, but it had some local appeal.

The year 2003 had its share of reopenings, the most significant of which was at Aston Locks on the Montgomery Canal on 4 April 2003. Although the locks had been restored in 1997, they could not be opened for use by boats until the new off-line nature reserves, alongside them, had been completed. This innovation of providing off-line facilities for delicate ecological habitats set a useful precedent for the resolution of conflicts between numbers of boat movements and the

Wey & Arum Brewhurst Lock, 21st October 2006

protection from degradation required by SSSIs. A second important opening in 2003 was the Woodham Back Pumping Scheme, which secured a more reliable water supply to the Woking pound of the Basingstoke Canal, while a third was the opening of the new visitor centre at the Anderton Boat Lift, by HRH The Prince of Wales, on 28 April 2003. Yet another was the formal opening of the new Drungewick Aqueduct on the Wey and Arun Canal, on 3 May 2003. This was followed just over a month later by the reopening of the Thorpe Flight on the Chesterfield Canal on 26 June 2003.

Restorers had high hopes that when the Highways Agency and BW signed a Memorandum of Agreement, to ensure the two organisations worked together on the integration of road improvements with waterway development plans, it might offer a panacea to avoid future potential conflicts in such respects. However, the problem was that the agreement only covered schemes organised by the Highways Agency, and thus omitted local road improvement plans. Even so, all parties were pleased when the new Lichfield and Hatherton Aqueduct trough, paid for by donations, was lifted into place over the M6 Toll Road, on 16 August 2005, almost ten years after the Public Enquiry into the road scheme had taken place.

The Chesterfield Canal's longer-term future prospects were similarly assured, after a series of public protests at the Kiverton Colliery site caused the site developers to amend their plans so as to provide a 150ft-wide corridor for the canal through it, and also offered a potential resolution of summit water conservation measures to be achieved by the construction of a possible marina site. With this agreement in place, it was simply a matter of a lack of funding that was going to hold up the scheme from going forward rapidly. In much the same way, the Droitwich Canals restoration route was secured, when Supplementary Planning Guidance was issued to secure seven key sites and protect the line of the canal.

A problem of a different sort had arisen on the River Stour, where the local trust were growing increasingly concerned that restrictive byelaws, limiting the river to those craft on it in the 1980s or for sail or manually propelled craft only was not an acceptable solution for the longer term sustainable future development of the river.

In London, British Waterways had received some land and all the former dock water space as a legacy from the closure of the London Docklands Development Corporation. Spurred on by the success of Canary Wharf and other tower developments nearby, in the summer of 2003 it published its own multi-million

Lichfield & Hatherton Canals, Lichfield Aqueduct Lift, 16th August 2002

pound development plans for the last remaining large site in the area, at Wood Wharf. The plan included the provision of a new canal link, between Poplar Dock and South Dock, which avoided existing low lifting bridges, where growing road traffic volumes caused major operational difficulties. The proposed new canal had the added advantage of providing access to the development site, so that all the building supplies and waste could be moved by water.

The lesser-known Driffield Navigation also received a boost at this time when a report by W.S. Atkins, the consultants, indicated that the Navigation should be restored to the river head at Driffield. Whilst the cost was estimated at £6.4m, this would provide benefits to the rural area of over £310,000 p.a. Similar benefits derived from waterway restoration were extolled by the Prince of Wales when he hosted the launch of the Waterways Trust "Cotswolds Canals Appeal" at Highgrove in the spring of 2003. He indicated that the project would be a catalyst for both urban and rural regeneration in the area, bring in 1.7 million new day visitors and, each year, generating £6.8m for the local economy, as well as creating some 200 new jobs in tourism alone.

Plans for restoring the Runcorn Flight of locks had been raised at various times over the earlier decades. These plans were being reactivated once again, as local proposals were made to replace the Runcorn to Widnes bridge across the Mersey to resolve traffic congestion. The New Bridge approach roads would require a substantial realignment, and this would enable the removal of the existing road obstruction at the top of the locks. The Chester Branch of the IWA started pressing for the restoration plans to proceed and set out to form a Runcorn Locks Restoration Society, to drive the project forward. This group was officially constituted on 28 May 2004, and immediately planned a campaigning rally at Runcorn between 25 and 27 June 2004, to press home the value of their scheme.

The Sleaford Navigation Trust took the opportunity to purchase the bed of the River Slea, between Bone Mill and Carre Street, Sleaford, including Cogglesford Lock and the lock island, to facilitate their plans for the restoration of the upper end of the navigation. At about the same time, the ownership of the Old Liverpool Docks was transferred from English Partnerships to British Waterways. This donation, combined with a grant of £393,000 to complete the final studies into the line of the proposed Liverpool Link Canal, offered the ideal opportunity to promote this £15m project.

Plans for the Fens Waterway Link project were coming together well, with the launch of an "Implementation Strategy" to construct the missing links. Once completed, these links would facilitate the opening of a further 87km of broad waterways. It was envisaged that European Regional Development Funding, together with support from local councils, would offer the prospect of an early start to this longer-term project.

The earlier ideas for reviving the Stockport Branch of the Ashton Canal took a step forward in December 2003, when a Public Meeting was held to discuss the options. This led to a proposal to form a Stockport Canal Society, with an inaugural meeting planned for 3 February 2004. David Sumner, of the Huddersfield Canal Society, was one of the speakers who advocated the plans. After the meeting, Stockport Council gave a £1,000 grant to enable Hallamshire University students to prepare a pre-feasibility study of the restoration prospects.

Discussions were similarly developing locally on BW plans to restore the Bow Back Rivers, including the possibility of a new lock to facilitate access to the proposed 2012 Olympic site. These consultations were subsequently held over while the UK Olympic Bid was progressed.

The Chichester Canal Trust had for some time hoped a flood relief scheme for the town might incorporate the canal line, and so promote its chances of full restoration. When that did not materialise, the trust took the initiative and opened up discussions with the local council in an effort to further their aims. In consequence a Central Committee was formed to develop a "Chichester Ship Canal Master Plan". This was to identify how the various obstructions could be overcome and then to set out a strategy for achieving the restoration.

Soon after the Stockport Branch Restoration Society was created, other local enthusiasts promoted the formation of the Hollinwood Canal Society. Its first public meeting was held, in February 2004, at the Daisy Nook Country Park Visitor Centre. The Society set its first aim as restoring the Hollinwood and Fairbottom branches within the park area, with the second phase of the project to link those works back to the Ashton Canal and, in the longer term, create a new link through to the Rochdale Canal.

In mid-2003, the Derby and Sandiacre Canal Trust launched a major fund-raising and development strategy, covering the 12½ miles of the Derby Canal. By then, they had managed to secure the whole route of the canal in the local authority structure plans. This assurance gave them confidence that they could raise the £34m required for the complete restoration project, over a ten-year period, given the appropriate public support. At much the same time as the Derby plans were secured, Warwickshire County Council were canvassing the extent of public support for the Higher Avon Navigation Project. This had floundered in the past due to the objections from the major landowners en route. The County Council, however, viewed the project as a useful economic regeneration catalyst for the area, so felt it important that wider public feeling should be gauged again about the prospects of taking it forward. After receiving the outcome of the consultation results, together with objections from local business interests, the County Council decided they could not support the plans. This provoked renewed commitment from the supporters of the scheme, who created the Stratford and Warwick Waterway Trust at an inaugural meeting in Stratford-upon-Avon on 9 October 2004. The new trust had as its primary aim the promotion of wider public access to the river corridor, as well as the creation of a waterway link.

Just as problems arose for the Higher Avon supporters, so those for the Cotswold Canals also had worrying news. The National Lottery was coming under serious financial pressure from other calls on its funds, and indicated that it would have to defer consideration of the Cotswold Canals bid. They asked BW to reconfigure the bid, so it could be submitted considerably reduced in size. In consequence a modified, Phase One, bid was made, solely to cover the section of canal from the A38/M5 crossing, through Stroud, to Brimscombe Port.

Far better news was heard by the Manchester, Bolton and Bury Canal Society, when developers announced a major 27-acre development project at Middlewood Locks, where the canal joined the River Irwell. The developers' preliminary designs showed the restoration of the locks, and the canal section, as the central focus for the whole site.

Good news was also heard on the Monmouthshire and Brecon Canal, where the trust announced that their partner, Newport City Council, had won funding to restore Bettwas Lane Bridge and install a permanent slipway there. The Council were concurrently seeking further funds to restore the five Alt-yr-yn Locks, which they hoped could be completed in the following two years.

Elsewhere, the Thames and Medway Canal Association was being supported through the Urban Thames Gateway Project, in undertaking an Economic and Employment Benefits Study into the restoration of the whole section of their canal, between Gravesend Basin and Higham. Likewise, the IWA granted £2,000 towards the production of the planned Sussex Ouse Restoration Trusts document, "The Sussex Ouse – A vision for the 21st Century". The trust believed the document would enable them to develop local awareness of their plans and also bring forward project partners. The IWA also awarded £5,000 to the Friends of the Cromford Canal, towards an Ecological Assessment Study between Langley Mill and Ironville. This would review the proposed

restoration route, identified by earlier report by Binnies and, by provision of the facts, provide the platform for further detailed funding bids.

The World Canals Conference was held in Edinburgh in September 2003. Two major projects were unveiled during the proceedings. The first was the restoration of the remaining section of the Glasgow Branch of the Forth and Clyde Canal, through to Port Dundas. Here BW and the City of Glasgow were in the process of finalising a funding agreement which would secure 50% of the £5.7m for the major regeneration project. The other was the prospect of linking the River Clyde and Loch Lomond, by creating a bypass lock to overcome the difference in levels on the river linking the two. However, as this was a salmon river, it was recognised there could be a range of local objections that would need to be overcome if the scheme were to get the go-ahead.

The year ended with some better news on the Cotswold Canal. The HLF indicated that it was giving Stage One approval for an £11.3m grant towards the restoration of the Stonehouse to Brimscombe Port section of the Stroudwater Canal. In addition, some £2.9m of funding had been gained from the European Inter-Regional resources, to take the project forward. At much the same time, BW were able to join in a partnership, with the Caldon and Uttoxeter Canals Trust, to formally launch the £800,000 scheme to restore the Froghall Basin and the Top Lock of the Uttoxeter Canal, with a target project completion date of March 2005.

Unfortunately, not all was proceeding so well with the Bedford to Milton Keynes Link. The first blow was when the local Plan Inspector would not recommend inclusion of the Link in the new Local Plan. As a result, Milton Keynes Council reluctantly concluded they could not include it either. The trust immediately appealed against the decision, helped by the fact that one of their members was an expert in Planning Law, as a result of which the Council's Scrutiny Panel recommended the situation be reconsidered. The route in Milton Keynes was finally protected by a decision of the Council in March 2005.

Good news, however, was presented to the Shrewsbury and Newport Canals Group, when W.S. Atkins gave them the results of their feasibility study. This concluded that there were no insurmountable barriers to restoration. However, the costs were likely to be high, with full restoration priced at £86m, of which £19m was required to restore the Newport Branch, from Norbury Junction to Wappenshall.

In their aim to restore the infilled section of the Ashby Canal, Leicester County Council took their first formal steps in applying for a Transport and Works Act Order in early 2004. A Public Enquiry took place at the end of November 2004. It was concluded far more quickly than expected, as most objections were withdrawn. The only major objection, from English Nature, was also deemed close to resolution, with the offer of the provision of some off-line reserves along the existing canal. This proposal was accepted, and cleared the path for progress on the restoration plans to be made.

Proposals to restore the Horncastle Canal had been proceeding behind the scenes, for some 15 years, led by HATCH (Horncastle and Tatteshall Coningsbury Canal Heritage}. The outline proposals they had developed were submitted to local residents at a public meeting on 18 November 2003. The plans found favour and there was general agreement at the meeting that fund-raising should proceed to finance a full feasibility study.

Unfortunately, the Northern Reaches Restoration Group on the Lancaster Canal did not get similar immediate support from the North West Development Agency when they submitted their full funding bid. The Agency suggested that it needed to be broken down into three more manageable projects. The group did this, and proposed that the first phase should embrace the infilled section at Kendal. This had an estimated cost of £13.5m, but it was suggested this could be the catalyst for significant regeneration around Kendal town centre. This more focussed bid received a more favourable response. BW, on behalf of the group, gained a £750,000 grant for the design and planning work for Phase One on 8 March 2005.

A similar positive response came from a public exhibition prepared by the Wey and Arun Canal Trust, at Bramley Village Hall, in October 2004. The trust created a comparative factual display of the various route options for restoring the canal through Bramley village, where the original line had been built over. Over 700 visitors attended the exhibition and some 66% of those who completed the questionnaire indicated that they favoured the "river" route. This gave the trust a very clear steer on how they ought to develop their longer-term plans for this section of their restoration project.

Similar positive results were provided to the restorers of the Droitwich Canals, when the Heritage Lottery Fund announced a £4.6m grant to facilitate the completion of their restoration scheme. Other matched funding was to come from Advantage West Midlands and local councils. To facilitate the start of the restoration work, the Canal Trust formally surrendered its lease on the canals to British Waterways, so they could take the lead on the actual restoration work. This project was one of those Priority One schemes that BW indicated it would actively support in its forward vision, *Waterways 2025*, published in June 2004. Although the Higher

Avon scheme was also mentioned in this "vision", as a Phase Three project, it was interesting to hear BW indicate to Warwick Council at a formal Consultation Meeting, in June 2004, that it did not wish to continue its involvement with that project until stronger local support was shown for it.

This was in contrast to the speed at which part of another project on the Bow Back Rivers, also listed in the "vision", came to fruition. Here British Waterways reached an agreement with Bellway Homes to partially finance the restoration of the derelict City Mill Lock, which was adjacent to their development site. Another project mentioned in the document was the Fens Waterway Link. This project was formally launched by the Environment Agency on 11 June 2004. They indicated that the first phase would involve reopening the "lost" link at Boston, perhaps through the use of a combination of a new tidal barrier in the Witham, and by reconstituting a former lock into the South Forty Foot River, at Black Sluice, which was closed in 1967, to facilitate the addition of an extension to the Black Sluice Pumping Station.

Perhaps the most interesting development in 2004 was the initiative taken by the Wey and Arun Canals Trust. Although they were listed in the *Waterways 2025* as a Priority Three Project, the trust itself launched an innovative £1.2m scheme to overcome a difficult culverted road crossing at Loxwood, West Sussex. This involved lowering the canal by 1.8m, over a 300m length, building a tunnel under the B2133 road and constructing a new lock on the western side of the road to regain the 1.8m height. The volunteers undertook the detailed planning work for the project in 2004, and started on building the new lock in 2005. They then planned to lower the canal bed, below the lock, and also lower Brewhurst Lock in 2006, aiming to complete the works by the end of 2007 ready for a grand opening in May 2008.

The waterways restoration movement's forward progress suffered two blows in April 2005. The first was a major breach on the restored Rochdale Canal, where an embankment by an aqueduct over the River Irk gave way. This closed the canal in April 2005. It looked as if it might be closed for some considerable period of time, as British Waterways did not have the £1¼m required to pay for the repair work. The second misfortune, on a more personal level, was when it was announced that David Hutchings MBE, the architect of various Midlands restoration projects, had died on 22 April 2005. This was a sad loss, especially to those in the Avon Valley, where he had been the driving force behind the Upper and Higher Avon projects for many years.

In June 2005, Whinall Lock on the Driffield Navigation was reopened. The IWA provided a grant towards the associated Whinall Bridge repairs and also towards new gates for Wansford lock. This was a major step forward. Likewise, the reopening of Harlem Hill Lock on the Ancholme was achieved after a 30-year campaign. At this time, Liverpool City Council gave planning permission for BW to build the Liverpool Link Canal, across the Pier Head Park site. With this final go-ahead, BW were able to assemble the last few elements of the funding package for the project to proceed. Nearby, hopes for restoring the Runcorn Flight of locks took a step forward, when New Persimmon Homes agreed to restore the bottom lock in the flight, and the adjacent pound, as part of their associated housing development scheme.

On the Grantham Canal, the new partnership was investigating options for linking the canal back into the River Trent. The IWA were able to offer a £6,000 grant to finance an "optimum route" feasibility study. In much the same way the Derby and Sandiacre Trust hoped that an initiative by Heartwood Homes, to develop a ten-acre site in Derby, to incorporate a realigned canal and create a Marina Village on the canal, would "kick-start" their wider proposals for the restoration of the canal route at Spondon.

The official opening of the Uttoxeter Top Lock, and the associated new mooring basin, took place on 23 July 2005. This gave new impetus to the local enthusiasts who had ideas regarding the restoration of further lengths of the Uttoxeter Canal. By then, it had been announced that London's Bid had won the opportunity to host the 2012 Olympic Games. This gave the prospects for the restoration of the Bow Back Rivers a further boost. British Waterways were to lead on a project to build a new lock, adjacent to the site of the former Prescott Sluice. The concept of a new Prescott Lock went down well with the Deputy Prime Minister, John Prescott, who was a keen advocate of waterways revival, even though it was not directly related to his support.

From time to time, local enthusiasts had sought to improve and restore sections of the Itchen Navigation, but these earlier proposals had achieved very little success. It was thus pleasing when a new partnership, the Itchen Navigation Trust, promoted jointly by EA and Hampshire Wildlife Trust, started taking an interest in protecting the waterway. They did not propose a full restoration, but were at least committed to ensuring it was maintained.

In September 2005, the Secretaries of State for both Environment and Transport jointly announced that the Transport and Works Act Order (Ashby de la Zouch and extensions) would be made. This paved the way for the full restoration of the infilled section of the canal to Moira and beyond. This was another of the projects mentioned in *Waterways 2025*.

At about this time, IWAAC announced it was planning to review the progress made on restoration projects since its 2001 report, *A Second Waterway Age*. This announcement occurred almost at the same time as the Government indicated that it proposed to widen the remit of IWAAC, by transforming it into the Inland Waterways Advisory Committee (IWAC), with the wider remit of advising Government on all matters concerning inland waterways. It proposed to legislate for this change, during 2006, through a clause in the proposed NERC Bill. The initiative was warmly welcomed by all those involved with the waterways, as it raised the opportunity of covering all mainland inland waterways, and not simply those of BW, which were the focus of the original IWAAC remit.

The opportunity for reviewing the prospects for the creation of a River Parrett Tidal Barrage arose again in 2005. To take this forward, the original partnership consisting of representatives of 25 local organisations, which was formed in 2000, was reconstituted into the Somerset Waterways Development Trust. Its aims were to campaign for and support the widest recreational use of Somerset's waterways network. The team started to look again at the prospects for reopening the Bridgwater & Taunton Canal entrance lock, renamed the Oakley Lock after the local waterways campaigner. The lock, if restored, would provide access to the River Parrett in Bridgwater, and by virtue of the canal route, would also offer the opportunity for access to the River Tone at Taunton, the navigable section of which could be extended.

The Wendover Arm Trust was able to celebrate the achievement of their first objective on 28 March 2005, when they re-watered the restored section of the arm between Tringford Stop Lock and the new winding hole, which they had constructed beyond the rebuilt Little Tring Bridge. The grand opening of this section was scheduled for later in the year. By then, the trust was already hard at work organising Phase Two of the project, which was to restore and re-water the dry section and to link it into the new navigable culvert under the A41 Aston Clinton Bypass. They set themselves a five-year timescale to undertake this work.

Buxworth (Bugsworth) Basin was finally fully opened on 26 March 2005, after a long series of false dawns due to the recurring major leakages which had led to many earlier closures. The IWPS then turned its attention to clearing the other archaeological features of the basin, with the support of English Heritage, to turn it into a new tourist destination.

A further breakthrough came in 2005 on the Montgomery Canal, with a formal agreement between BW, English Nature and the Countryside Council for Wales to facilitate the development of off-line conservation areas to protect SSSI flora and fauna, yet to allow the full restoration to navigation to proceed. This gave an added impetus to the first work party at Newhouse Lock, at the Newtown end of the waterway. It was also agreed to undertake a full hydraulic study to quantify the impact of the growth of boat traffic on the restored lengths.

The summer of 2005 saw the final component of the Rochdale Canal remedial works put into place. This was the installation of a floating towpath under the M62 culvert, to complete the walkway link. The IWA itself commenced its Diamond Jubilee Year on 13 April 2005, with a re-creation of the original Aickman and Rolt meeting at Tardebigge. This came at a time when various other restoration and building projects were receiving the go-ahead. These included the Liverpool Link project, where all the funding was finally in place. At Boston, the South Forty Foot River link scheme received its outline planning permission. This included the £29m project for the Haven Barrage, which was seen as part of the first stage of the overall Fens Waterway Link. Work also began at Middlewood Locks, the major £4.2m regeneration project in Salford, within which the first 500m of the Manchester, Bolton and Bury Canal, with its entry lock from the River Irwell, was included as the central focus of the development.

The IWA itself offered a Jubilee Grant, of up to £100,000, for a restoration project that could be undertaken in the Jubilee Year. After a very strongly contested competition, the award was won by the Wilts and Berks Canal Trust, to enable them to create a new entry link for their canal into the Thames south of Abingdon. This project was opened, on schedule, at the end of August 2006. The Chelmer and Blackwater Navigation went into administration in 2004. To stop the waterway from being closed and parts sold, and so becoming yet another restoration scheme, the IWA took over the management of the navigation in November 2005, through a new subsidiary company, Essex Waterways Ltd. It then set out to develop a sustainable survival and maintenance plan for the waterway.

The IWA held its Jubilee Dinner at Stratford-upon-Avon on 6 May 2006. The newly created Stratford and Warwick Waterway Trust took the opportunity to capitalise on the IWA event by organising a major campaign cruise, on 7 May 2006, up to the then current head of navigation at Alveston. This event was a great public relations success, as well as a substantial fund-raiser.

Peak Forest Canal, Bugsworth Basin, first reopening, 3rd April 1999

Wilts & Berks Canal, Jubilee Junction, opening

In early 2006 a major planning application was submitted for the redevelopment of the town centre of Bradford. This envisaged plans, under the comprehensive £1.5 billion regeneration scheme, to restore the Terminus Basin of the Bradford Canal together with a short length of the canal leading to it, from locks 10 and 11. British Waterways worked with City of Bradford Centre Regeneration as a joint venture, being funded by the EU Community Initiative Programme, under the title "The Rebirth of Bradford Canal". As part of the scheme, BW also sought wider public support for the restoration of the whole Bradford Canal, which paralleled the local Bradford Beck.

Findings of the initial feasibility survey into the scheme, by Arup, suggested the total canal restoration project would cost £35m, including eleven locks, and should significantly boost the local economy and create a thousand new jobs.

The IWA provided the Wey and Arun Trust with a £4,000 grant to enable them to commission a "completion strategy". This project was led by a steering group and tasked with looking at all the issues likely to arise in the process of the full restoration of the Wey & Arun Canal. In much the same way, Yorkshire Forward made a £75,000 grant to the Chesterfield Canal Partnership, so that it could commission a design study on the section from Killamarsh to Kiveton Park. The aim of this was to offer the best engineering solution to resolving the problems created by the derelict and collapsed Norwood Tunnel.

In February 2006, the final and approved version of the Montgomery Conservation Management Plan was launched in the National Assembly for Wales, and, on the following day, in the House of Commons. This identified a "Stakeholder Group" within the project management structure, which it envisaged would co-ordinate the total restoration of the waterway. This enabled the release of a further tranche of Heritage Lottery funds, to both restore further lengths of canal and to pay for the creation of a nature reserve.

The Burslem Port Project, in Stoke-on-Trent, also took a significant step forward in early 2006, when the Joint Commissioning Committee accepted the Arup Feasibility Study on the project. The Arup report suggested that the likely total restoration cost would be £10.5m. This restoration expenditure would facilitate the "uplift" of the value of a variety of development sites adjacent to the arm by £65m. The problem the project manager faced was the facility to capture that "uplift" factor, in wider site values, to pay for the necessary works needed to restore the arm. It was envisaged that this equation might take some time to resolve.

Towards the close of 2005, the National Lottery announced two new award schemes, both of which had immediate relevance to waterway restoration. The key scheme was "Living Landmarks", with a "kitty" of £120m. It was anticipated this scheme would attract some 150 bids out of which six winners would be selected. Unsuccessful schemes would be eligible to apply for a second scheme, the "Changing Spaces" awards, with a prize fund of £260. These two new awards schemes were in addition to the standard Heritage Lottery scheme. The "Living Landmarks" scheme attracted bids from 29 restoration groups. By mid-2006, a shortlist was published of those groups who would receive development grants to add the technical details to their final submissions. The Somerset Waterlinks scheme was identified within the shortlist for large awards, whilst second-tier award development grants were offered to the Bedford and Milton Keynes Link, Cotswolds Canals, Forth and Clyde Canal, Lydney Docks, Monmouthshire Canal and the North Wilts Canal, amongst others. Much to their disappointment, the Derby and Sandiacre project, the Montgomery Canal and the Daventry Branch project failed to make this shortlist.

The development grants were provided to enable the necessary technical studies to be completed to advise and confirm information for the final project evaluation process. The B&MK Trust used this money to employ Halcrow to undertake the necessary consultancy work needed, to support their outline planning application, one of the key requirements of which was a full environmental assessment to examine how the proposed new canal channel would interact with the existing drainage scheme, particularly the adjacent Broughton Brook. All of this work, plus negotiations with Anglian Water, had to be completed in time for a planning application to be submitted in January 2007. This tight timetable was essential to clear all the necessary hurdles before the trust was required to submit its finalised lottery application in May 2007.

Elsewhere on the waterways network, other developer-funded restorations were pressing ahead. One of these was the New Islington Scheme at Ancoats, in Manchester. The ultimate plan was to create a new canal link between the Rochdale and Ashton Canals, using, for the most part, the lines of previously infilled arms. These included the reconstruction of the former Ancoats Hospital Arm, which it was envisaged would provide a new mooring basin. Final completion of the link was seen as part of a second phase, due to the problems of re-routing the services that went over the Old Mill Street Bridge. Work started on the various development sites in early 2006.

In the spring of 2006, the IWA held its Campaigning Rally at Brookwood on the Basingstoke Canal. This was very timely, as Surrey Council were threatening to withdraw their funding support for the restored waterway. The rally, together with a strong local campaign mounted by the Surrey and Hampshire Canal Society, persuaded the riparian county councils to undertake a thorough review of future funding options

for the Canal. The resultant report was considered by the Joint Management Committee on 20 October 2006. The committee concluded that more time was needed to determine the best longer-term solution, but in the interim current funding obligations should continue to be met.

During 2006, the Wendover Arm Trust's Phase Two project was well underway. This involved reopening the former dry section of the canal and installing a new waterproof membrane, at an estimated cost of £620,000. The Trust had to raise £420,000 for this work, which was in addition to a contribution of £200,000 from BW in lieu of their replacing a time-expired pipeline. In addition, separate fund-raising appeals were organised by the trust to provide two new footbridges where footpaths crossed the canal line.

In Oxford, the plans for restoring the former Hythe Bridge Terminus Basin appeared to be losing momentum. This encouraged local activists to form the Friends of Oxford Canal Basin at a public meeting they organised on 28 March 2006. The group were thus ready to fight their case with Oxford City Council, when the council produced a report, later in the year, which suggested that restoring the Basin was only an "alternative option". The Friends felt this statement was deliberately misleading and went into battle. They persuaded Oxford Council to retract their document and indicate it was "rethinking its opposition to reinstating the canal basin". Council officers admitted they now had a better appreciation of the value of the restoration scheme and indicated they planned to organise a public meeting to hear local views. Clearly the battle was not won, but at least a rematch had been granted.

The year 2006 presented the Shrewsbury and Newport Canal Society members with a dilemma. The feasibility study they had commissioned indicated two possible solutions for restoring the Norbury Junction to Wappenshall section of their canal. One proposal involved building an inclined plane, while the other suggested restoring the flight of five existing locks. These proposals split the group, but ultimately they were helped in making a decision through a consultation exercise with local residents, who firmly rejected the inclined plane idea, with two to one in favour of restoring the locks. In the interim, society volunteers were making progress in clearing the former junction area at Wappenshall.

Another positive development, in 2006 was the decision by Daventry District Council to start to plan to seek a Transport and Works Act Order to authorise the construction of their proposed new Daventry Canal. The project was expected to cost £11.7m, of which £9m could come from the West Northamptonshire Development Group. The driver for the project was the proposed redevelopment of their town centre, where a new terminal basin was proposed which they hoped to start early in 2007.

In the Autumn of 2006, the Peterborough Branch of the IWA managed to complete one of their long-term aims, the raising of a low bridge at Ramsey Hollow. For this they gained the help of the Royal Engineers, on a training exercise, but had to raise the £10,000 needed for the ancillary works. This opened up a range of new cruising routes on the Middle Level.

A similar venture was also developed by the Friends of Cromford Canal, in conjunction with Derbyshire County Council and UK Coal, in respect of the Pinxton Arm of the Cromford Canal. Here, a diversionary channel at the River Erewash was created to avoid an opencast coalmine Site. They planned to utilise that channel, as a diversionary route, to link the restored end of the Arm back to the main line of the Canal, above Ironville, with UK Coal contributing to the costs involved. Other societies, like the Buckingham Canal Society, were gaining funds from corporate sponsors, who were willing to fund supplies for their staff working on the canal on team building days.

The National Environment and Rural Communities Bill (NERC) received Royal Assent on 30 March 2006. Apart from bringing together the Countryside Agency and English Nature into Natural England, it provided the vehicle by which the role of IWAAC was enlarged to cover advising government on all waterways, by creating the Inland Waterways Advisory Council (IWAC). With this new wider remit, IWAC entered into discussions with the Heritage Lottery organisers to identify how best each organisation could assist the waterways. As a result the IWA linked with Heritage Lottery to organise a seminar for restoration societies to help them to be more effective in presenting future funding bids. At the same time, IWAC was conducting its third review of restoration projects, to identify the funding stage they had reached. This study examined a schedule of 118 projects, of which nine were Significant Projects that had been completed since their previous study in 2001. Of the remainder, IWAC determined 14 were at an advanced stage, needing immediate funding, 16 were substantially there and shortly would be ready for funding, 19 were in the Intermediate category, while 52 projects were at an early stage. Of the remaining eight, there either had been no response to the questionnaire, or the project had lapsed or had been subsumed into another project, for example the Fens Waterway Link.

The issue of future funding for the waterways became critical in mid-2006 when the Government, through DEFRA, announced substantial cuts to both BW and EA grants in aid. It seemed at first that BW was worst hit, losing grants to the tune of £7m. This immediately led to a £5.4m cutback in planned winter maintenance works and a potential staffing reduction of 180. This included the loss of the post of Regeneration Director. This decision by DEFRA and BW led to shockwaves within the restoration area, since many groups relied on BW for advice on overcoming practical problems. They saw that the lack of central funding for waterway maintenance and the decline in standards would erode confidence in waterway regeneration projects. It also meant that projects that had been supported by BW could no longer guarantee that help in future. A major campaign to persuade the government to reverse the cuts was undertaken under the banner "Save our Waterways". Just before Christmas 2006 it was learnt that tentative budgets for 2007/08 would remain at the lower base line, effectively taking £14m of potential grant in aid over two years out of the BW waterways funding. This led *Waterways World*, in an editorial, to quote from the memoirs of Sir Frank Price, the former BWB Chairman some 30 years before, who had said, "we should have known the Whitehall officials never give up. They should have realised, neither do we". The editorial continued: "The waterway movement has seen off many threats and, in this its sixtieth year of the IWA, is preparing to fight the battle again."

Just as there were threats to the system at the national level, so local groups had their own setbacks as well. Vandals destroyed a repaired footbridge over the Barnsley Canal at Haw Park, setting their restoration project back unnecessarily. However, elsewhere, sometimes a potential threat can turn out to be an advantage. This was the case on the Hatherton Canal, which was blocked by a motorway embankment. Here an upgrade to the M6 had initially been planned as an extra lane each side of the existing motorway. However, subsequent discussions with the Highways Agency gave the trust the firm impression that the works might easily provide a navigable culvert where the motorway widening encroached upon the canal line. At much the same time, work had started on the southern bypass for Lichfield. Here again, although at a cost of £490,000 to the trust, it was agreed that the canal route could be preserved by the provision of a navigable culvert.

Even with the best-laid plans and goodwill from all sides, sometimes a minor hitch can cause a problem at the eleventh hour. This was the case when the Port Dundas extension was opened on 29 September 2006. Sadly, the flotilla of boats could not go beyond the second lock, as there was a local land dispute on the strip of land that separated the lock from the original basin. Fortunately Glasgow City Council were dealing with this matter and hoped for an early resolution.

The year ended on some positive notes. The first was a £3.8m project to revive the lower section of the Bude Canal, with funding secured by the Bude Restoration Partnership. This restoration project was officially launched on 13 October 2006. A second was a clear indication that the funding package to reconstitute the entry lock into the South Forty Foot Drain at Boston was likely to proceed, Lincolnshire Waterways Partnership having gained the support of Lincolnshire County Council (£4m), East Midlands Development (£1.2m) and Lincolnshire Enterprise (£800,000) with an offer of the required matched funding for EU support to be approved. This lock creation project had to be completed by December 2008 to meet the various funding requirements, which meant it was likely to proceed in advance of the proposed Boston Haven Tidal Barrier. Whilst that would initially limit opening times for the new lock, it provided a clear start to the large Fens Waterways Link scheme.

The year end was also a time to hear of a strange quirk of fate. One of the major obstacles in restoring the Huddersfield Narrow Canal had been the problem of tunnelling under the Sellers Engineering site. At the time of restoration the firm was active and wished to retain its factory that had been built over the canal line. Restorers thus tunnelled under it. The firm had since closed down ands the site was available for redevelopment. Now the new developers' plans included reopening the tunnel, built only ten years before, to make the restored canal a central feature of the new development. Lastly, there was a welcome move by the Scottish Executive, who agreed a £2.445 million investment to fund further improvements on both the Highland and Lowlands Canals. This covered further dredging on the Forth & Clyde and Union Canals, plus embankment works and towpath upgrades at key destinations: a clear sign that the Scottish people valued their revived waterways.

Even at a time when there were apparent difficulties within Government in providing sufficient funds for the English waterways to keep the existing system open, new schemes for brand new waterways continue to surface. The latest is the revival of an eighteenth-century plan to link Aylesbury with the Thames, As originally planned, the Aylesbury Arm would have continued to join with the River Tame, meeting with the Thames below Abingdon. Although the route through Aylesbury town from the existing terminus has long since been built over, the Aylesbury Canal Society identified various alternative routes around the town, The society suggested that their proposed new line could provide a much needed marina, as well as creating a new cruising ring. They considered that by integrating the scheme into various planned new road schemes for the area, costs could be kept down. This

led the society to submit its proposal to Aylesbury Vale District Council, as part of the consultation on the new Local Development Framework documents.

During the period 2002 to 2006 the following schemes emerged:

2002

1. Leominster Canal
2. Ashton and Rochdale Canal link
3. Stockport Branch, Aston Canal
4. Stort Navigation Extension, Bishops Stortford

2003

5. St Helens and Leeds and Liverpool Canal Link
6. Wood Wharf Canal, London Docklands
7. Bow Back Rivers

2005

8. Bradford Canal

2006

9. Aylesbury Link
10. Pinxton Arm, Cromford Canal

At the end of 2006, the Waterway Recovery Group journal *Navvies* circulated an Archive CD, covering the all the issues of the past 40 years. This offered a tangible record of what the Waterway Recovery Group had achieved during that time. Also, *Navvies* No. 220, for December 2006, listed 29 active individual waterway restoration schemes around the country, where groups were organising their own regular work parties, plus the inputs from the various WRG units themselves. The WRG Summer Work Camps programme for 2007, circulated with *Navvies*, offered opportunities to work on ten very different waterway restoration schemes. These included the Chesterfield Canal, Cotswolds Canal, Grand Western Canal, Grantham Canal, Ipswich and Stowmarket Navigation, Lord Rolle's Canal, Monmouthshire Canal, Montgomery Canal, Sleaford Navigation and the Wilts and Berks Canal. This wide national range of volunteering opportunities offered a sure sign that even during a time when the Government seemed to be reining in on its financial support for the waterways, the waterway restorers still had a job to do, and were looking positively ahead at the many more miles of canal that would be restored during the twenty-first century.

XIII

SUCCESS OR FAILURE

The history of the waterways restoration movement can in many ways be defined by slightly modifying Churchill's famous words: "Never in the field of leisure provision was so much owed by so many to so few."

The flavour of this unique development was particularly well identified in *The Times* of 15 February 1977, when J. Chartres wrote:

"The restoration of canals and their redevelopment as playgrounds for those who like moving slowly for a change and who love boats of any shape, size or function, has become an important national pastime since commercial transport operators turned their backs on them ... for more than a quarter of a century canal enthusiasts ... have been spending weekends and holidays repairing lock gates, removing soggy mattresses, pram chassis and other objects to which canal water seems a magnetic disposal centre and forcing their way through abandoned stretches of famous waterways."

The vision of a new life for the decaying canal system was generated by the recollections of one man, Rolt, who recorded a nostalgic voyage through the canals of England in 1939 in his book *Narrow Boat*.

Even as he planned the voyage, section by section of the former canal network was apparently being lost forever. In the introduction to his book Rolt noted:

"There is something indescribably forlorn about these abandoned waterways. These waterways were gone, but how many more would fall to ruin before I got my boat."

After Rolt had completed his voyage, he had time to consider what he had seen before writing his book. He realised the gravity of what had already been lost and what also would be lost if something constructive were not done quickly. He identified in the waterways the symbol of man's creativity in a form that could be readily understood; yet at the same time they uniquely offered the pleasure of a good life for many if action were taken. He reviewed what action could be taken thus:

"The future of the English canals ... depends no less than that of the countryside on the order which we build after the war.... In a society framed to cherish our national heritage the canals can play their part not only as a means of transport and employment, but as a part of an efficient system of land drainage and a source of beauty and pleasure. But if the canals are left to the mercies of economists and scientific planners, before many years are

past the last of them will become a weedy, stagnant ditch, and the bright boats will rot at wharves, to live on only in old men's memories. It is because I fear that this may happen that I have made this record of them."

Rolt's book, *Narrow Boat*, provided the ideal medium through which to promote his own ideas about the reconstruction necessary to replace the devastation caused to both the country and people's lives by the ravages and disciplines of the Second World War years 1939–45. One person who had empathy for Rolt's ideals was R.F. Aickman. He noted that:

"There was, and is, the bad relationship between 'work' and 'recreation'. With every month that passes, a higher proportion of our population is committed to work that offers no direct satisfaction of any kind in doing."

He also saw that:

"On the waterways, it seemed to me that there should be less than the usual gap between work and pleasure: steering even a blackened coal boat is a vocation; and on the other hand, every pleasure boat that passes, helps the campaign to keep the waterway in being at all. On the waterways, unusually little seemed to be either compulsory or handed out; those being the apparently opposed, but, in fact, identical concepts, that at once restrict and mask the richer world around us."

Aickman and Rolt were able to combine their enthusiasm and philosophies through the Inland Waterways Association, which they and a few others formed in 1946. The earlier chapters have shown that the growth and development of the waterway restoration movement can be directly traced back to the inauguration of the IWA and the publication of its prospectus.

Aickman and Rolt used their skills as authors to provide readable records of both their actions and their ideals. They carefully cultivated the art of using the correspondence columns of the national and local press to enable individuals to personally identify with the IWA campaign. This subtle propaganda clearly defined the battle the IWA was waging with authority to retain and to use that which the authority seemingly wished to abolish and destroy.

Apart from using the media to promote the idea of a waterways revival, the IWA leaders actively pursued their campaign at the local level by going out and speaking to local groups, such as the founding of the Kennet and Avon Branch at Newbury, or by leading local protests. The best example of the latter was the protest cruise along the Northern Section of the Stratford Canal to seek the reopening of a fixed bridge at Lifford Lane, King's Norton.

The foundation of local IWA branches had a marked effect on the spread of the restoration movement. One of the first branches founded was in the Midlands. This both concentrated local efforts on the centre of the canal system and started to tap a potentially large enthusiast market. The creation of other branches in the North-West, at Manchester, and the North-East, at York, provided a means to gain practical support to reactivate decaying local waterways. The advances made at Linton Lock particularly identify this theme. The foundation of the Kennet and Avon Branch in Newbury provided a link with a waterway that in itself inspired a lasting local

commitment from those who saw its longer-term amenity value; whilst the foundation of the Fenlands Branch tapped the boating interests that inspired persistence in a campaign to get the Great Ouse Navigation restored to Bedford, which was finally achieved in 1978. In other areas, such as Scotland and East Anglia, the lack of local members and support initially greatly hindered the development of the restoration campaign.

The various IWA branches provided the local nucleus from which the idea of waterway restoration could be promoted at a local level through word-of-mouth and through the provincial press. In the same way, the general public's image of the potential of the inland waterways was similarly cultivated, both by the production of a number of articles on

Great Ouse, Little Ouse, new Brandon Lock

canal cruising in national magazines, and more particularly by a waterways exhibition first staged at Heal's in London in 1947, and later circulated to regional galleries in 1948 and 1949.

The early association of public personalities such as A.P. Herbert, Lord Methuen and Peter Scott similarly assisted in developing a greater public following for the campaign. The public understanding of IWA ideals was greatly advanced by a lecture tour through North-West England led by Aickman and Scott in 1948.

By 1949 the potential for further practical advances was becoming feasible. In the North-East, the closure of Linton Lock forced local enthusiasts to take action. In the same way John Gould, an IWA member in Newbury, was able to promote renewed commercial use of a section of the Kennet and Avon Canal, which later provided the basis of a legal battle to fight for its survival. It was, however, in the Lower Avon valley that the greatest potential for advance came, with the decay of the river locks. Public attitudes towards the revival of the navigation had been carefully cultivated over the previous years by the proprietor of the local paper, the *Evesham and Four Shires Journal*, run by the Gill-Smith family. The final catalyst to the promotion of the Lower Avon restoration scheme came from the willingness of a local industrialist and boat-owner, C.D. Barwell, to both invest money in the semi-derelict navigation and to commit his own energy and expertise towards its revival.

In much the same way, the sale of the Basingstoke Canal in 1949 provided a much-needed stimulus to the development of public interest in the canals. The IWA gained considerable publicity for its role in reviving the canal through the part that it played in promoting a canal purchasing committee.

The foundation of the Lower Avon Navigation Trust in 1950 provided the vehicle by which major tangible advances could be made. In the same way the foundation of the Bedford Boat Club and subsequently the Great Ouse Restoration Society offered the means of moving forward with the restoration of another defunct river navigation. The strengthening of public support for, and a more general appreciation of the amenity value of, the canals was undoubtedly developed by the extravaganza of the IWA Market Harborough festival, which did much to capture the public attention and at the same time highlight the leisure potential that the inland waterways had to offer. In that same year, public knowledge about the network of inland waterways was greatly enhanced by the production of a new range of waterway books. These included the historical *British Canals* by Hadfield, the realistic appreciation of their past grandeur in *The Inland Waterways of England* by Rolt, an artistic coverage

in *The Canals of England* by E. de Maré and popular coverage in *Know Your Waterways* by Aickman. Each in its own way developed a far wider understanding of the heritage that could be saved by the IWA campaign for the revival and restoration of the inland waterways.

This public perception was further developed at the Festival of Britain in 1951, where the IWA had both an exhibit and two narrow boats moored adjacent to the Festival site. In that same year, the now well-known *Jason* trip along the Regent's Canal was inaugurated by J. James. This has since provided many people with their first introduction to the special delights of the often concealed paths of the canals.

The change of government in 1951 paved the way for a reappraisal of official attitudes towards the inland waterways. In many ways the new approach, particularly under the British Transport Commission Board of Management, formed in October 1953, and the British Transport Waterways, formed on 1 January 1955, sharpened public resolve against the wholesale abandonment policy proposed in the report of a BTC Board of Survey, published in 1955.

During the period 1951–55 the slow but sure demise of the Kennet and Avon Canal, in contrast to the steady restoration of the Lower Avon Navigation and the Great Ouse, near Bedford, did much to rouse public feeling. The tale of woe depicted by the closure, section by section, of the Kennet and Avon, attracted considerable publicity, especially when the Caen Hill flight of locks was closed in July 1951; the Newbury to Reading Section in October 1952; the Bath Section in late 1953; and the Limpley Stoke Section in October 1954. By then public feeling had reached such a state of concern that when, in December 1954, the *Daily Telegraph* reported that BTC intended to abandon the complete canal between Reading and Bath, the county and local councils and many residents along the route were willing to actively fight for its retention and rejuvenation. This fight was developed in three ways: a High Court action, the foundation of a "Fighting Fund", and a petition to the Queen. The strength of public feeling was best identified by *The Times* of 2 December 1955 which noted: "It is certain that the proposals will be strenuously opposed in Parliament as well as outside." The final presentation of the petition in January 1956 sharply highlighted the divergence between official attitudes and public will. The growing public concern was recognised by the Government, and on 1 February 1956 it announced that an inquiry into the whole system of inland waterways would be made by an independent committee under the chairmanship of L. Bowes.

The late 1950s saw the steady spread of proposals for restoration schemes. These were boosted in 1957 when a local debate in Coventry, over the retention of the town's canal in relation to its potential use as the route of a new road, defined the decision that the public had to make. This local debate brought forth an individual, D. Hutchings, who had the latent skills and practical ability to carry forward the restoration movement to a more sophisticated level of development. The restoration of the completely derelict Wyken Arm in 1958 provided an insight into the way future schemes could evolve.

The same era also saw the slow but sure growth of the canal boat-hire industry, which for the first time provided many with the chance to sample the recreational facility that the canals could offer. The foundation of the Association of Pleasure Craft Operators on inland waterways, in 1954, and the move by L. Munk of Maidline Ltd, to invest large amounts of capital in new custom-built canal cruisers in the same year, greatly assisted this significant trend.

The publication of the Bowes Committee report in 1958 provided a justification for the earlier IWA campaign. It also proved to be the first sign of a turning point in official attitudes towards the future of the inland waterways by not only making positive proposals for the redevelopment of much of the inland waterways system, but also officially recognising for the first time the multiplicity of canal uses which added to the amenities of the countryside. As the result of the committee's findings, the Government created the Inland Waterways Redevelopment Advisory Committee to advise on the future of those waterways uneconomic for commercial use. The membership of the committee included Munk and Rolt, and through it they were able to promote the concept of multiple use.

This new climate provided the impetus for a further growth in the number of separate organisations concerned with waterway revival, with the foundation of the East Midlands-based Inland Waterways Protection Society, the East Anglian Waterways Association in 1958 and the Staffordshire and Worcestershire Canal Society in 1959. It also provided the means by which the IWA and the Stratford-upon-Avon Canal Society, formed in 1956, could interest the National Trust in the restoration of the southern section of the Stratford Canal.

The action of the National Trust, supported by a Government grant, in restoring the derelict narrow canal, provided the means by which the "take-off" of the restoration movement was achieved. The inspiration of the work of Hutchings, who converted the 13-mile canal from a dried-up ditch to an attractive rural waterway in three years, has guided the restoration movement since that time. Hutchings went about the country lecturing about the restoration scheme whilst the work was in hand and afterwards. He offered his practical knowledge as a means of spreading interest in the restoration of canals. In these lectures Hutchings often concluded: "Fortunately, we were none of us experts, or we should all have known it was impossible. Words that gave others the faith to try it for themselves.

The formation of the British Waterways Board in 1963 and the publication of their interim report, *The Future of the Waterways*, coupled with the reopening of the southern section of the Stratford Canal in 1964, provided further momentum to the growing public desire to reopen closed waterways. The experience gained from the Stratford Canal restoration equally gave a commitment for additional experiments to be tried. One of these was the restoration of the Stourbridge Canal, jointly by the BWB and the Staffordshire and Worcestershire Canal Society. The other was the complete rebuilding of the defunct Upper Avon Navigation, with the construction of new locks to replace the old locks which were beyond repair.

The recognition of the leisure and amenity potential that the waterways could offer rapidly gained a broader understanding in the mid-1960s and the network of restoration projects spread north, south, east and west, with many new schemes achieving local authority and public support. The public support for individual canals was further enhanced by the growing number of books detailing individual canal histories which appeared at this time. This trend in itself generated further public understanding and support.

Government support for the restoration and redevelopment of the inland waterways was finally expounded in the 1967 white paper, *British Waterways: Recreation and Amenity*. This was issued as a prelude to the 1968 Transport Act which formally established the Cruiseway network. It also identified a further group of waterways that could be rejuvenated if local support for them was forthcoming. To generate this support, various local canal societies were founded and the embryo Waterway Recovery Group began cutting its teeth.

To develop local authority support for the various restoration schemes proposed during this period, the IWA organised two important conferences that identified possible ways forward. These were the "Waterways in Planning" conference held in London in 1969, and the "Waterways in the Urban Scene" conference held in Manchester in 1970. Both were attended by many local authority representatives.

The late 1960s and early 1970s saw work developing on many restoration projects, all of which gained considerable local publicity. The success of one development was held up as the grounds for considering another, and success bred success.

In the prevalent climate of changed public attitudes in

the early 1970s, the spread in the number of waterway restoration schemes was further extended. Additional general interest and support was generated by the introduction of a specialist magazine, *Waterways World*, in 1972, which publicised developments. The Water Act 1973 equally provided the facility for the development of additional recreational water space, and this added further to the number of restoration schemes.

This support was additionally cultivated by a series of openings of restored waterways that took place in 1974. These included the Caldon Canal, the Cheshire Ring and the Upper Avon Navigation. The latter was opened by Queen Elizabeth the Queen Mother and provided a fitting culmination of the 25 years' work invested by volunteers in restoring the waterway links to Stratford-upon-Avon. It also identified the potential of further development for the restoration movement. This was a plan to build a new link to Stratford-upon-Avon from Warwick by converting the Higher Avon into a new navigation. The prospect of the development of this project and other similar schemes rested on the continuing growth in demand for additional water space.

In many ways the recent history of the waterways leading up to Stratford-upon-Avon define the five major stages in the development of the waterway restoration movement. The salient features are:

(1)   Keep open by the removal of illegal obstructions. (Lifford Lane Bridge, Northern Section, Stratford Canal)

(2)   Repair and reopen. (Lower Avon Navigation)

(3)   Revive from dereliction by rebuilding. (Southern Section, Stratford Canal)

(4)   Reopen a defunct navigation by constructing completely new works. (Upper Avon Navigation)

(5)   New construction to offer increased flexibility and additional water space. (Higher Avon Navigation)

Any future developments that emerge will necessarily relate to the continuing upsurge in demand for additional recreational water space. This feature has been perhaps placed in some doubt both by the changed financial and population growth estimates.

The way in which past developments were achieved can be directly related to public pressures on the politicians, and their willingness to meet the changing demands of a nation as it has developed socially. In many ways the waterway restoration movement has capitalised on the changes in society that have been evident over the past thirty years. One of the most prominent of these changes has been the growing amount of leisure time and willingness to devote this time to various recreational pursuits. This growth can be directly quantified by the increase in demand for water-orientated recreation and the growth of the boat-hire industry, which in turn can be related to the growth and spread in the number of restoration schemes, each of which is part of the wider theme known by many as the "Leisure Revolution."

One particular aspect clearly portrayed in the waterway restoration movement is that of the direct role of individuals in making it comes to pass. The IWA activists Aickman, Barwell, Edwards, Hadfield, Hutchings, Munk, Palmer and Rolt each in turn exemplify particular innovative actions and tangible achievements, all of which have played a vital role in the movement's overall development. By examining the roles of each of these individuals the composite structure of the elements of the restoration movement can be readily understood.

Aickman provided the drive, initiative and vision on which the IWA was able to build. Barwell offered the business acumen and entrepreneurship that enabled the Lower Avon Restoration scheme to get under way. Edwards revised the basic work of reference on the Inland Waterways, and Hadfield offered the facility to expand the range of canal books by founding a publishing house specialising in them and by writing many of the major works himself. Hutchings offered the flair for publicity and the organising ability that enabled both the southern Stratford Canal and the Upper Avon restoration schemes to develop and survive. Munk provided the leadership and negotiating skill that enabled the campaign-orientated IWA to respond to a rapidly changing political scene. Palmer provided the means by which co-ordinated volunteer efforts could be most effectively used to promote the restoration campaign. Rolt sowed the original seeds that made people realise that something had to be done if the inland waterways were not to disappear forever. Each in his own way has used the media, the abilities of others, and public goodwill, to enable the restoration movement to grow. All these things have combined to make development possible in a period of cultural and social change.

The growing public interest in industrial archaeology, since the term was first invented by M. Rix in 1955, has also led people to seek solace in the more leisurely and simple age that can so easily be recreated in the canals. Equally the tourist value of the canals, which has in part financed their revival, has also had considerable influence in the way in which wider public interest has been inspired. The attraction of the canals, offering equal rewards to all social classes, has similarly been a factor that has enabled people from different walks of life to become associated with restoration schemes, each

Llangollen Canal, Whitchurch Arm, reopened section

playing a part in carrying the project through and thus enabling them to participate in a "social adventure".

The growth and spread of the waterway restoration movement, shown by Map 1, can also be related to the original canal mania of the 1790s. At that time a variety of local schemes were promoted, some less viable than others, but all ultimately linking to provide a waterway network. The recent developments have, in a similar way, been composed of many separate schemes, some less likely to succeed than others, but all ultimately aimed at recreating a waterways network that will provide a valuable asset to the community. The "Leisure Revolution" has played a vital role in making this possible, in much the same way as the Industrial Revolution persuaded people to construct the original canals. The growth of the number of volunteer workers willing to devote time and effort to the provision of amenity facilities for the enjoyment of all members of society has been a significant factor in achieving the waterways revival.

The idea of the restoration of the waterways has, between 1946 and 1978, become a practical reality, in which a greater awareness of the value of the inland waterways, cultivated by the founders of the IWA, has played a vital role in creating a changed pattern of public opinion. This changed public attitude has in turn influenced the legislative processes, which have facilitated restoration schemes. It is a situation which is far removed from the attitudes of 1946 when the canals were in their death throes, with past neglect and lack of public interest speeding their decline. For this reason, the post-war waterway restoration movement must be deemed one of the success stories of our time.

Bricklaying Over Basin
April 2000

Postscript

When he wrote the foreword to the first edition of *Canals Revived* in 1972, IWA National Chairman, the late John Heap, made some prophetic observations:

1. "Restoration projects are still bedevilled by the unhelpful; restrictions on 'remainder' waterways incorporated in the Transport Act 1968. These oblige British Waterways to deal with them in the 'most economical manner', providing us with little protection." Since that time only four restored waterways have been officially upgraded to "cruiseway" status, amounting to some 67 miles – some 261 miles of restored waterway continue to be in the 'remainder' category, yet many are potential key new leisure routes.

2. "The greatest peril to restoration is the present power of the omnipresent Highways Authorities, who plan new roads or construct new bridges with insufficient headroom for navigation." Even today, when nominal agreements are supposed to be in place to cover the additional costs of upgrading works, these can place a punitive cost burden on canal societies and their supporters. The problems encountered by the restorers of the Lichfield & Hatherton Canals really highlight this concern.

3. "The mass of restrictive legislation passed during this decade is causing increasing difficulties in arranging voluntary work to commence." All of us are well aware today of the way in which EC Directives seem to be converted into reams of UK regulations, whereas other countries in Europe seem to manage with far less regulation.

4. "The readers of this book will soon be aware and appreciate that progress can only be made as the result of continuous pressure. The momentum must never be allowed to flag. Those in authority in all political parties have become aware that thousands of people are determined and willing to donate time, effort and money to the task of getting the waterways back in good order. The full potential of our waterways for multipurpose recreation has yet to be fully realised and it is not appreciated as yet that the country has a priceless asset. For the expenditure of very little money, in national terms, some 2,000 miles of waterway could give immense pleasure and benefit to us all. Modern technology will ensure that we all have much longer periods of leisure in the future." Surely, waterways are an admirable medium for realising the obvious and undoubted potential for outdoor leisure and recreation. One wonders, in this context, the extent of current Government thinking about their future. This mismatch was exemplified by cuts of some 7 per cent to the grant in aid imposed on BW in 2006/7, and a similar level of reduction within the 2007/8 budget baseline. Similar reductions were also imposed on EA navigation budgets. It seemed likely this reduction in direct Government Finance for the waterways might be compounded by the potential siphoning off of Lottery funds to pay for the increasing cost of the 2012 UK Olympics. Both of these losses of funding will potentially give waterway restorers in the future real cause for concern.

Dudley Canal, Park Head Locks derelict and restored

Wilts & Berks Canal Seven Locks, Lyneham, 14th April 2007

However, all is not gloom and doom. Over the thirty years since the first edition of the book *Canals Revived* was published, much of benefit has happened within the world of restored waterways. Since then, the long-term schemes, such as those for the Kennet and Avon and Basingstoke Canals, have been completed, with "Royal" reopenings.

A good indicator of the extent to which the restoration movement had evolved was a review conducted by the IWA during 1995. The IWA Restoration Committee sent out a total of 49 questionnaires to the voluntary waterway restoration societies known to be involved in active restoration projects; 41 replies were received. These were then collated into a report, the findings of which are outlined below.

"Of a total length of 652 miles of waterway then under restoration by these societies, some 139 miles, or 21% were by then restored. Interestingly, the number of locks restored, as a proportion of the total proposed for restoration, was also 21% (124 out of 589). The total length of towpath restored was 102 miles, or 25% of that which had been closed. Prominent amongst work still to be done were the 534 un-navigable road crossings which needed replacement. When completed, 75% of the restored waterway mileage will join the interconnected national system." The then estimated rate of completion, "of nearly 10 miles per year over the last 30 years, looked set to double over the following 30 years, with a spurt at the millennium."

The estimated cost of restoration, if undertaken by contractors, averages at £907,000 per mile (adjusted to 1997 prices). The value of restoration work funded in the three years up to 1995 was £8.1million. Of this, 75% came from Government, local authorities and Europe; 23% from voluntary contributions and labour, and the rest from commercial sources. Of the 22 schemes responding to the specific question, they estimated they would provide 27 new hire bases and 1,115 off-line moorings. Ten of the projects estimated that 2,793 "full-time equivalent" jobs would be generated by their restoration endeavours.

The total membership of societies in the survey (counting families as two members) was 17,398. The number of members in each society ranged from 100 to over 2,000, with the majority in the 100 to 500 range. The total annual subscription income of these societies was about £117,000 per year. Thirteen societies ran a total of twenty trip boats, on a regular basis, as both a publicity exercise and for fund-raising.

It was also reported that 76% of the riparian local councils support their local restoration schemes and over 73% of the total length of these canal projects was protected in local plans. Some 42% of councils had provided significant direct assistance (valued at over £10,000 in the previous three years) and 25% were members of a trust or similar body promoting the restoration.

The results from this survey give a good impression of the restoration scene in 1995. Since then, many "second phase" schemes, which started in the 1970s, have also sped ahead, mainly due to the wonderful generosity of the National Lottery and in particular the Millennium funds. Those "impossible dreams" of restoring and reopening the Forth and Clyde and Union Canals in Scotland, and the two trans-Pennine routes, the Huddersfield Narrow and the Rochdale Canals, have become a reality. Longer-term plans for new waterways, such as the Ribble Link, have been brought to fruition. Further schemes are now benefiting from the generosity of the National Lottery in its many forms. Lottery funding has replaced the Manpower Services Commission and Derelict Land funding grants of earlier years.

What do these restoration schemes deliver, apart from restored waterways? We are fortunate that recent research by ECOTEC has been able to pinpoint exactly what impact the restoration and reopening of the Kennet and Avon Canal has achieved. The Queen reopened the waterway in 1990. Since then more remedial work has been undertaken. The final phase of remedial work was completed in December 2002, with the formal opening in May 2003 for the summer cruising season.. Had that restoration not taken place it is likely two-thirds of the canal would have been closed for boating, with a cost of over 700 local jobs. Now it is fully restored, day visitors and those who travel by boat record 7.7 million visitor days on the canal each year. These visitors spend £26m in local economies a year, of which £5m comes from boating and £21m from towpath visits. Since 1995, £350m has been invested in 23 commercial developments alongside the canal. Eighteen of these have been on brownfield sites. The Kennet and Avon now supports around 1,000 tourism and leisure jobs. And 180 of these jobs have been created since 1995. The restoration has safeguarded over 700 tourism and leisure jobs, which would have been lost had the canal not been restored. The facts speak for themselves. Canal restoration is a catalyst for local economic growth. Nationally, over £6 billion has been derived from waterside regeneration projects. Over 300 million day visits are made to the waterways each year. Many see these as providing the life-blood to rural economies.

Thirty years ago, I concluded that "the post-war waterway restoration movement must be deemed one of the success stories of our time". Thirty years on, I suggest that statement still rings true today. I am sometimes asked, what are the factors that have led to the successful completion of recent key restoration schemes? The elements are various, but can best be identified as:

Local vision – people with ideas, who are willing to spread the message.

Local champion – individual local people who are willing to fight hard for the project.

Local Society – the public face of a project and a means of gaining support.

Avoiding internal disputes – warring factions can dissipate goodwill.

Get the Politics Right – the support of local politicians is a key to success.

Stakeholder interests – partners, each looking towards a common goal.

Inter-agency support – linking up the various funding bodies.

Positive feasibility study – a recognised tangible way to substantiate project benefits to potential funding agencies.

Persistence – it can take up to 25 years to get an idea accepted and gain the funding. The work itself also takes time.

Plural funding routes – matched funding is the only way forward today.

Resilience when things appear to fail – sometimes there is a need to bide your time, then start pushing forward again when the local climate of opinion changes.

Good publicity – tell the story of your success. People like to support "winners".

That is what waterway restoration is all about.

Roger Squires

(A) Books and Papers

AINA (Association of Inland Navigation Authorities) *'Demonstrating the value of the waterways: a good practice guide to the appraisal of restoration and regeneration projects'* AINA Watford. March 2003.

Aickman, R. *'The River Runs Uphill'* J M Pearson, Burton on Trent, 1986.

Anon *'Macclesfield Canal Conservation Area'* Macclesfield Borough Council, Macclesfield, 1975.

Anon *'The Rochdale: Then and Now'* Rochdale Canal Society, Rochdale, 1974.

Arnold, H. *'The Montgomery Canal and its restoration'* Tempus, Stroud, 2003.

Baldwin, M. Burton A. *'Canals a New Look'* Phillimore, Chichester, 1984.

Barr, J. *'Derelict Britain'* Pelican Books, Harmondsworth, 1970.

Bolton, D. *'Race Against Time; How Britain's Waterways were saved.'* Methuen, London, 1990.

Boughey, J. *'Charles Hadfield - Canal Man and More'* Sutton Publishing, Stroud, 1998.

Bracey, H.E. *'People and the Countryside'* Routledge & Kegan Paul, London, 1970.

Braithwaite, Lewis *'Canals in Towns'* A. & C. Black, London, 1976.

British Transport Commission *'Canals and Inland Waterways'* Report of the Board of Survey, BTC, London, 1955.

BTC *'British Transport Commission Report and Accounts for 1948'* London, 1949.

British Waterways London *'Olympic Class Waterways - Delivering a Green Legacy'* British Waterways, London, 2006.

British Waterways *'Public Benefits from Historic Waterways'* Annual Report and Accounts - 2005/06, British Waterways, Watford, 2006.

British Waterways *'Partnership with the People: A consultation document'* British Waterways, Watford, June 1999.

British Waterways *'Inland Marina Investment Guide'* British Waterways, Watford, March 2006.

British Waterways *'Unlocked and Unlimited: Waterways - A link to the future'* British Waterways, Watford, 19 March 2002.

British Waterways *'Waterways for Wales: Improved Quality of Life through sustainable development of the Waterways of Wales'* British Waterways, Watford, 2003.

British Waterways *'Waterways 2025: our vision of the shape of the Waterways network.'* British Waterways, Watford, June 2004.

British Waterways *'Water Ways: Inland Waterways and sustainable rural transport: a good practice guide'* British Waterways, Hatton, August 2004.

British Waterways Board *'Address Book: second edition'* BWB, London, 1973.

British Waterways Board *'The Facts about the Waterways'* HMSO, London, 1965.

BWB *'British Waterways Board Annual Report and Accounts'* 1963-5. HMSO, London.

British Waterways Board *'Waterways Users' Companion'* BWB, London, 1975 and 1976.

Burlingham, D. H. *'To Maintain and Improve: the history of the Lower Avon Navigation Trust'* Tempus, Stroud, 2000.

Burton, A. & Pratt, D. *'The Anatomy of Canals: Decline and Renewal'* Tempus, Stroud, 2003.

Burton, A. *'The Canal Builders'* Eyre Methuen, London, 1972.

– – and Pratt, D. *'Canal'* David & Charles, Newton Abbot, 1976.

Button, K.J. *'No. 6 The 1968 Transport Act and After'* University of Loughborough, Dept. of Economics, Loughborough, 1974.

Carden, D. *'The Anderton Boat Lift'* Black Dwarf Publications, Lydney, 2000.

Clew, K.R. *'The Kennet and Avon Canal'* David & Charles, Newton Abbot (second edition) 1973.

Cumberlidge J. *'Inland Waterways of Great Britain'* (seventh edition) Imray Laurie Norie & Wilson, St Ives, 1998.

Edwards, L.A. *'Inland Waterways of Great Britain'* Imray, Laurie, Norie & Wilson, St Ives, Huntington, 1972.

Farrington, J.H. *'Morphological Studies of English Canals'* Occasional Papers in Geography No. 20, University of Hull, Hull, 1972.

Fullerton, B. *'The Development of British Transport Networks'* Oxford University Press, Oxford, 1975.

Garner, E. *'The Seven Canals of Derbyshire'* Landmark Publishing, Ashbourne, 2003.

Gayford, Eily *'The Amateur Boatwoman'* David & Charles, Newton Abbot, 1973.

Gibson, K. *'Penine Dreams; the story of the Huddersfield Narrow Canal'* Tempus, Stroud, 2002.

Gibson, K. *'Pennine Pioneer; the story of the Rochdale Canal'* Tempus, Stroud, 2004.

Gladwin, D.D. *'The Canals of Britain'* Batsford, London, 1973.

– – *'The Waterways of Britain: A Social Panorama'* Batsford, London, 1976.

– – and White, J.M. *'English Canals: Part 1 A Concise History'* Oakwood Press, Lingfield, 1967.

Goss, K. *'Waterways World Annuals: 2004/2005/2006'* Waterways World, Burton on Trent.

Green, A. H. J. *'The History of Chichester's Canal'* Surrey Industrial Archaeology Society, Brighton, 2005.

Hadfield, C. & Boughey, J. *'Hadfield's British Canals'* (eighth edition), fully revised by Joephy Boughey, Allan Sutton, Stroud, 1994.

Hadfield, C. *'British Canals: An Illustrated History'* David & Charles, Newton Abbot (fifth edition) 1974.

– – *'The Canal Age'* David & Charles, Newton Abbot, 1968.

– – *'Introducing Canals: A guide to British Waterways Today'* E. Benn, London, 1955.

– – *'Introducing Inland Waterways'* David & Charles, Newton Abbot, 1968.

Hamer, M. *'Transport and Society'* Background Notes on Social Studies, No. SS 24. Workers Educational Association, London, 1975.

Haskell, T. *'By Waterway to Taunton'* Somerset Books, Tiverton, 1994.

Hopkins, W.G. *'An Outline Account of the Glamorganshire Canal: 1790-1974'* Cardiff Naturalists Society, Cardiff, 1974.

Hoskins, W.G. *'The Making of the English Landscape'* Pelican Books, Harmondsworth, 1970.

Hutton, G. *'Scotland's Millennium Canals; the survival and revival of the Forth & Clyde and Union Canals.'* Stenlake Publishing, Catrine, 2002.

Ives, W.L. *'The Problems of our Inland Waterways'* Paper to the Metropolitan Section, Chartered Institute of Transport London, 4 February 1959.

IWAAC *'Priorities for Action on the Waterways of British Waterways Board'* Inland Waterways Amenity Advisory Council, London, 1975.

IWA *'1980 Inland Waterways Guide'* Haymarket Publishing, London, 1980.

Jackson, T. *'Uses and Abuses of the Countryside'* Background Notes on Social Studies, No. SS 21-22. Workers Educational Association, London, 1975.

Jones, P. L. *'Restoring the Kennet & Avon Canal'* Tempus, Stroud, 2002.

Mackersey, I. *'Tom Rolt and the Cressy Years'* M&M Baldwin, London, 1985.

McKnight, Hugh *'The Shell Book of Inland Waterways'* David & Charles, Newton Abbot, 1975.

Owen, D.E. *'Water Rallies'* Dent, London, 1969.

Patmore, J. Allan *'Land and Leisure'* Pelican Books, Harmondsworth, 1972.

Potter, Hugh *'The Cromford Canal'* Tempus, Stroud, 2003.

Potter, H. *'Waterways World Annuals: 2000/2001/2002/2003'* Waterways World, Burton on Trent.

Pratt, D. *'Waterways past and present; A unique portrait of Britain's waterway heritage'* Adlard Coles Nautical, London, 2006.

Pratt, E.A. *'British Canals: Is their Resuscitation Practicable?'* John Murray, London, 1906.

Raistrick, A. *'Industrial Archaeology'* Eyre Methuen, London, 1972.

Ransom, P.J.G. *'Waterways Restored'* Faber, London, 1974.

Rolt, L.T.C. *'Landscape with Machines'* Longman, London, 1971.

– – *'Narrow Boat'* Eyre & Spottiswoode, London, 1944.

– – *'Navigable Waterways'* Arrow Books, London, 1973.

– – *'The Inland Waterways of England'* George Allen & Unwin, London, 1950.

Russel, R. *'Lost Canals of England and Wales'* David & Charles, Newton Abbot, 1971.

Salter, H. (Editor) *'The Broads Book'* Waterways Series, Link House Publications, Croydon, 1973.

– – (Editor) *'The Canals Book'* Waterways Series 1976 Edition, Link House Publications, Croydon, 1975.

Savage, C.I. *'An Economic History of Transport'* Hutchinson, London (second edition) 1966.

Squires, R. and Lovett Jones, G. *'Canal Walks'* Hutchinson, London, 1985.

Squires, R. W. *'The New Navvies: A history of the modern waterways restoration movement'* Phillimore Chichester, 1983.

Stevenson, D., and others *'Organisations and Youth: Fifty Million Volunteers'* HMSO, London, 1972.

Thomson, D. *'England in the Twentieth Century'* Pelican Books, Harmondsworth, 1965.

Toyne, P. *'Recreation and Environment'* Macmillan, London, 1974.

Vine, P. A. L. *'London's Lost Route to Basingstoke; the story of the Basingstoke Canal'* Expanded and Revised Edition, Sutton Publishing, 1994.

Vine, P. A. L. *'London's Lost Route to Basingstoke'* David & Charles, Newton Abbot, 1968.

– – *'London's Lost Route to the Sea'* David & Charles, Newton Abbot (third edition) 1973.

Wilson, Harold *'The Labour Government 1964-70'* Penguin Books, Harmondsworth, 1974.

(B) Magazines and Periodicals

'Canals and Rivers; Boating and Leisure' (monthly) A E Morgan Publications, Epsom.

'Canal Boat and Inland Waterways' (monthly). Archant Specialists, Saffron Walden.

'Waterways World' (monthly) Waterways World Magazine, Burton on Trent.

IWA, Head Office Bulletin (monthly) IWA Rickmansworth.

(C) Society and Trust Newsletters and Journals

'AEGRE' (occasional) Journal of the East Midlands Branch of the IWA.

'Anglian Cuttings' (occasional) Newsletter of the Ipswich Branch of the IWA.

'B & MK News' (occasional) Newsletter of Bedford and Milton Keynes Waterway Trust.

'B. W. monthly' Staff magazine of British Waterways. (Previously *'Waterways News'*)

'Basingstoke Canal News' (occasional) Journal of the Surrey and Hampshire Canal Society.

'The Bore' (occasional) Newsletter of the Gloucester and Hereford Branch of the IWA.

'Broadsheet' (occasional) Journal of the Staffs. monthly & Worcs. Canal Society.

'The Buckingham Navigator' (occasional) Newsletter of the Buckingham Canal Society.

'Bulletin' (occasional) Newsletter of the Railway & Canal Historical Society.

'Cargoes' (occasional) Newsletter of the Guildford & Reading, Oxfordshire and Solent and Arun Branches of the IWA.

'The Chester Packet' (occasional) Journal of the Chester and District Branch of the IWA.

'Chiltern Grapevine' (occasional) Newsletter of the Chiltern Branch of IWA.

'Cut-A-Way' (occasional) Newsletter of the Thames and Medway Canal Association.

'Cut Both Ways' (occasional) Magazine of the Litchfield and

Hatherton Canals Restoration Trust.

'Cuttings' (monthly) The Journal of the Shropshire Union Canal society.

'D N A A' (occasional) newsletter of Driffield Navigation Amenities Association.

'Dragonfly' (quarterly) Magazine of the Wilts & Berks Canal Trust.

'The Easterling' (occasional) Journal of the East Anglian Waterways Association.

'Erewash Outlook' (occasional) Journal of the Erewash Canal Preservation and Development Association.

'The Historic Narrowboat Owners Club: Newsletter' (occasional)

'Hereward' (occasional) Journal of the Peterborough Branch of the IWA.

'IWAKES News' (occasional) Journal of the Kent and East Sussex Branch of the IWA.

'East Yorkshire Branch; Newsletter' (occasional) IWA.

'JUNCtion Mail' (occasional) Journal of the Hertfordshire Branch of the IWA.

'Journal of the Railway and Canal Historical Society' (occasional)

'Knobsticks' (occasional) Newsletter of the Stoke on Trent Branch of the IWA.

'Mersey Flat' (occasional) Newsletter of Mersey Side and West Lancashire Branch of the IWA.

'Mile Post' (occasional) Magazine of the West Riding Branch of the IWA.

'Lock Lintel' (occasional) Journal of the River Stour Trust.

'Navvies' (Bimonthly) Journal of the Waterway Recovery Group.

'Navigation' (occasional) Newsletter of West Midlands Region of the IWA.

'Neath and Tennant Canals Trust' (quarterly) Newsletter.

'News from the Mill' (occasional) Newsletter of Chelmsford Branch of the Chelmsford Branch of the IWA.

'Newsletter' (occasional) Lincolnshire Waterways Partnership.

'The New Wych Magazine' (occasional) Journal of the Droitwich Canals Trust Ltd.

'Northumbria Branch Newsletter' (occasional) IWA .

'One Seven Four' (occasional) Newsletter of the Inland Waterways Protection Society Ltd.

'Ouse News' (occasional) Newsletter of the Cambridge Branch of the IWA.

'Pennine Link' (occasional) Magazine of the Huddersfield Canal Society.

'Plane Informer' (occasional) Journal of the Foxton Inclined Plane Trust.

'The Portal' (occasional) Journal of the Friends of the Cromford Canal.

'Rochdale Canal Society Newsletter' (occasional)

'S & N News' (occasional) Journal of the Shrewsbury and Newport Canals Trust.

'Shroppie Fly Paper' (occasional) Newsletter of the Shrewsbury District and North Wales Branch of the IWA.

'Sleaford Navigation Trust' (occasional) Newsletter of the

Sleaford Navigation Trust.

'Swansea Canal Society Newsletter' (occasional) Journal of the Swansea Canal Society.

'Towpath Telegraph' (occasional) Journal of the Milton Keynes Branch of the IWA.

'Towing Path Topics' (occasional) Newsletter of the North Lancs and Cumbria Branch of the IWA.

'The Trow' (occasional) Magazine of the Cotswold Canals Trust.

'Waterways' previously titled 'Bulletin' (occasional) The National Journal of the Inland Waterways Association.

'Waterwitch' (occasional) The magazine of the Lancaster Canal Trust.

'Wendover Arm News' (occasional) Newsletter of the Wendover Arm Trust.

'Wey South' (quarterly) Bulletin of the Wey and Arun Canal Trust.

'Winding Ways' (occasional) Journal of the Leicestershire Branch of the IWA.

(D) Government Publications

D.E.T.R. Environment, Transport, Regions 'Unlocking Potential – A new future for British Waterways' DETR London, February 1999.

D.E.T.R. Environment, Transport, Regions 'Waterways for Tomorrow - Integrated Transport' DETR London, June 2000.

IWAAC 'The benefits of sustainable waterways; British Waterways since 1996' IWAAC London, May 2003.

IWAAC 'Britain's Inland Waterways: An Undervalued Asset' IWAAC London, June 1997.

IWAAC 'Waterway Restoration Priorities' IWAAC London, June 1998.

IWAAC 'The inland Waterways - towards greater social integration' IWAAC London, April 2001.

IWAAC 'Inland Waterway restoration and development prospects in England, Wales and Scotland' 'Third Review Report' IWAAC London, December 2006.

IWAAC 'A Second WATERWAY Age; Review of waterway restoration and development priorities' IWAAC London, June 2001.

Scottish Executive 'Scotland's Canals: an asset for the future' T.S.O. Edinburgh, 2003.

Waterways Ireland 'Report on the Economic Contribution of Private Boat Owners' Dublin Institute of Technology, for Waterways Ireland, Dublin, June 2006.

(E) Leaflets and Manuscripts

'Boundary Post, Commemorative Edition, Titford Canal Restoration Rally' March 1974, BCNS, Birmingham, 1974.

'Co-operation '72' British Waterways Board, London, 1972.

IWAAC 'News Release' (various) Inland Waterways Amenity Advisory Council, London.

1. Kennet & Avon Canal (1946)
2. Northern Stratford Canal (1946)
3. River Stour (1946)
4. Linton Lock (1949)
5. Llangollen Canal (1949)
6. Lower Avon Navigation (1949)
7. Basingstoke Canal (1949)
8. Barnsley Canal (1950)
9. Derwent Navigation (1950)
10. Great Ouse Navigation (1950)
11. Brecon & Abergavenny Canal (1951)
12. Southern Stratford Canal (1952)
13. North Walsham & Dilham Canal (1953)
14. Ripon Canal (1954)
15. Bridgwater & Taunton Canal (1954)
16. Derby Canal (1956)
17. Coventry Canal (1956)
18. Wyken Arm (1958)
19. Dearne & Dove Canal (1958)
20. Driffield Navigation (1959)
21. Upper Cromford Canal (1959)
22. Chesterfield Canal (1959)
23. Ashton & Peak Forest Canals (1960)
24. Buxworth Basin (1960)
25. Caldon Canal (1960)
26. Buckingham Arm (1961)
27. Grand Western Canal (1962)
28. Stourbridge Canal (1963)
29. Droitwich Canals (1963)
30. Dudley No. 1 Canal (1963)
31. Grantham Canal (1963)
32. Well Creek (1963)
33. Welford Arm (1963)
34. Ports Creek (1963)
35. Upper Lancaster Canal (1963)
36. Upper Avon Navigation (1964)
37. Shrewsbury & Newport Canal (1964)
38. Forth & Clyde Canal (1965)
39. Union Canal (1965)
40. Rochdale Canal (1965)
41. Brayford Pool (1965)
42. Erewash Canal (1967)
43. Montgomery Canal (1967)
44. Wendover Arm (1967)
45. Slough Arm (1967)
46. Monmouthshire Canal (1967)
47. Glamorganshire Canal (1967)
48. Crumlin Arm (1968)
49. Wey & Arun Canal (1968)
50. Pocklington Canal (1968)
51. Shropshire Canal (1968)
52. Royal Military Canal (1968)
53. Leven Canal (1970)
54. Old Engine Arm (1970)
55. Prees Branch (1971)
56. Hazelstrine Arm (1971)
57. Titford Canal (1971)
58. Ivel Navigation (1971)
59. River Lark (1971)
60. River Little Ouse (1971)
61. Louth Canal (1971)
62. Carlisle Canal (1972)
63. St Helens Canal (1972)
64. Market Weighton Canal (1972)
65. Lower Cromford Canal (1972)
66. Slea Navigation (1972)

67. Bure Navigation (1972)
68. Waveney Navigation (1972)
69. Thames & Severn Canal (1972)
70. Westport Canal (1972)
71. Chichester & Arundel Canal (1973)
72. Thames & Medway Canal (1974)
73. Neath & Tennant Canals (1974)
74. Higher Avon Navigation (1974)
75. River Gipping (1974)
76. Upper Trent Navigation (1974)
77. Huddersfield Narrow Canal (1974)
78. Itchen Navigation (1975)
79. Saltisford Arm (1975)
80. Wyrley & Essington Canal (1975)
81. Stafford Arm (1975)
82. Hatherton Branch (1975)
83. Horncastle Canal (1975)
84. Witham Navigable Drains (1975)
85. Nottingham Canal (1976)
86. Coombeswood Basin (1976)
87. Hythe Bridge Arm (1976)
88. Wilts & Berks Canal (1977)
89. Rase-Amcholme Navigation (1978)
90. Manchester, Bolton & Bury Canal (1978)
91. Tamar Manure Navigation (1978)
92. Herefordshire & Gloucester Canal (1980)
93. Swansea Canal (1981)
94. Upper Great Ouse (1982)
95. Wreak Navigation (1982)
96. Somerset Coal Canal (1982)
97. Upper Severn Navigation (1983)
98. Whitchurch Arm (1983)
99. Coalport Canal (1986)
100. Higher Thames (1987)
101. Monkland Canal (1987)
102. Kidwelly Canal (1987)
103. Bude Canal (1987)
104. Ipswich & Stowmarket Navigation (1988)
105. Manchester & Salford Jcn Canal (1989)
106. Bedford & Milton Keynes Link (1993)
107. Titchfield Canal (1994)
108. Tees Barrage & Navigation (1994)
109. Burslem Arm (1998)
110. Westbridge Arm (Northampton) (1998)
111. Liskard & Looe Union Canal (1998)
112. Frodisham Cut, Weaver (1998)
113. Stover Canal (1999)
114. Daventry Arm (1999)
115. Fenlands Waterlink (1999)
116. Macclesfield/Caldon Canal Link (1999)
117. Sussex Ouse (2000)
118. Hollinwood Branch, Ashton (2000)
119. Uttoxeter Canal (2000)
120. Cambridge Arm (S & G Canal) (2000)
121. Lord Rolle's Canal (2000)
122. Liverpool Link Canal (2000)
123. Leominster Canal (2002)
124. Ashton and Rochdale Link (2002)
125. Stockport Branch (Ashton) (2002)
126. Stort Extension, Bishop's Stortford (2002)
127. St Helens/Leeds & Liverpool Link (2003)
128. Wood Wharf Canal (2003)
129. Bow Back Rivers (2003)
130. Bradford Canal (2005)
131. Aylesbury/Thames Link (2006)
132. Pinxton Arm, Cromford (2006)

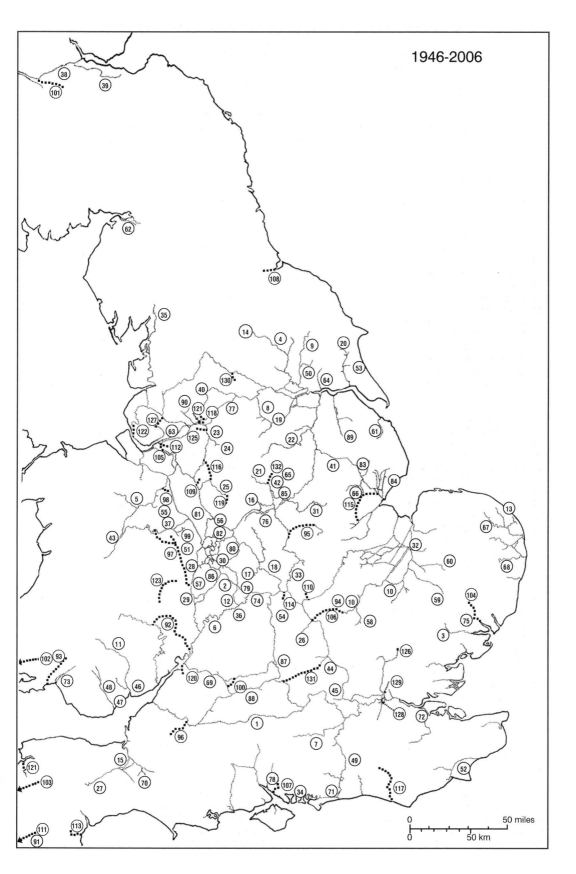

1946-2006

Y

Published in the UK by
Landmark Publishing Ltd,
Ashbourne Hall, Cokayne Ave, Ashbourne, Derbyshire, DE6 1EJ
☎ (01335) 347349 Fax: (01335) 347303 e-mail: landmark@clara.net
website: www.landmarkpublishing.co.uk

1st edition

ISBN 13: 978-1-84306-331-5
ISBN 10: 1-84306-331-X

British Library Cataloguing in Publication Data: a catalogue record for this book is
available from the British Library.

Print: Cromwell Press, Trowbridge
Design: Sarah Labuhn

Cover photographs (from top left to bottom right):
Cromford Canal, Great Northern Basin; Cromford Canal, Great Northern Basin, AWCC Rally;
Montgomery Canal, Official Opening, Aston Locks, April 2003;
Anderton Lift before restoration; Chesterfield Canal, restored Turnerwood Locks;
Dudley Canal, official reopening April 1973

Back cover photograph: Wilts & Berks Canal, Seven Locks,
Lyneham, 14th April 2007

DISCLAIMER

While every care has been taken to ensure that the information in this book is as accurate
as possible at the time of publication, the publishers and
author accept no responsibility for any loss, injury or inconvenience
sustained by anyone using this book.